OVERPACKING DISEASE, TELLING YOUR CHILD ABOUT NORDSTROM AND OTHER TRAUMAS OF ADULTHOOD

*More Humorous
KPBX Commentaries
by Doug Hurd*

Overpacking Disease, Telling Your Child About Nordstrom
and Other Traumas of Adulthood

Also by Doug Hurd:

Brain Rot, Shopping at Costco and Other Joys of Middle Age
ISBN 0-9658630-0-X

To Ed Bremer,
who first let me on KPBX.

INTRODUCTION

Sometime during 1987, Don Hamilton, a photographer and filmmaker who generally knows more about living well than I do, turned me on to KPBX FM, Spokane Public Radio. He literally walked me across his studio during a commercial shoot and made me listen. Then he made sure I knew how to find it on my car radio. It was the best thing on the air, he said. It would change my life.

As usual, he was right.

At the time, the station was still young as radio stations go, and the Program Director, Ed Bremer, felt the public should have the opportunity to be heard on public radio. If listeners wanted to contribute and be on the air, they could become what he called Community Producers. Looking back, I'm not sure if Community Producers were the outcome of an altruistic "peoples radio station" philosophy, or just a cheap way to fill up airtime.

It didn't matter to me. I had found a radio station I loved and I wanted to help it if I could. I wrote a cover letter and three samples what I would write if I were a Community Producer. "The observations of the aging baby-boomer," is how I described the material.

"Your stuff feels like Friday morning," Ed Bremer said, putting me into a 7:30 Friday morning time slot.

That was in November of 1988. Ronald Reagan was President and my daughter was a first grader who had a problem with the hot lunches at school. Now Bill Clinton is President, and my daughter is a junior in high school. She still has a problem with school hot lunches and I'm still doing Friday mornings. That's a lot of Friday mornings.

This book represents what I think are the best of those Friday mornings.

I hope you enjoy reading them. I certainly enjoy writing them.

Plus, they're a cheap way to fill up airtime.

Doug Hurd
October, 1997

ACKNOWLEGMENTS

Don't ever write a book.

It's *really* hard work. It is much harder than anything else I do (which, admittedly, isn't all that hard). I wouldn't even do it except that by writing radio commentaries once a week, there comes a point where you have enough material for a book, and all you really have to do is assemble it.

And I didn't even do most of that. So I must thank those who did.

I owe a large debt of thanks to Lynn West, David Palmer, Betsy Newman, Jonnie Hansen and Lea Weatherred. They functioned as a literary selection committee, separating the keepers from the losers. I trust their judgment completely. (Well, almost completely; I slipped in a couple of my own favorites.)

Betsy Newman and Jonnie Hansen also deserve additional thanks for proofing and helping me get these radio scripts ready for the printed page. This means they both read the entire book – word for word and comma for comma – *twice*. That's more of me than even I can stand.

WhiteRunkle Associates was named by Washington Magazine as one of the twenty best places in Washington to work. They got that right. One of the reasons is their support of employee community involvement – which includes the time I volunteer to KPBX and for projects like this. For their generosity and the help of everyone there, I am grateful.

Naturally, I must thank my wife, Jeannie, and daughter, Allyson for their love and support, and for allowing me to share so many of our family moments with what has become an extended KPBX family.

And finally, I must thank everyone at KPBX FM, Spokane Public Radio, and the KPBX listeners. You make it all worthwhile.

CONTENTS

TELLING YOUR CHILD ABOUT NORDSTROM AND
OTHER FACTS OF LIFE

Telling Your Child about Nordstrom 3

Nose Diamonds 6

Personal Dating Disclosure Forms 8

Watching the Game 11

The Longest Day 14

Don't Do Anything Stupid 16

Role Models 19

The Last Summer of Freedom 23

Sally Gray 25

The Werewolf and Other Scary Things in the Night 29

Going to Summer Camp 33

Big Weddings 36

THINGS MY FATHER COULD HAVE TOLD ME ABOUT BEING A MAN, BUT DIDN'T

Keeping Nature in Balance by Going Bald 41

Memory Black Holes 44

Surfing the Net 48

Snowblower Rules 51

Gadgets 53

Cool Roof Tacks 56

Global Warming 60

Asking Directions 63

Big Boys' Toys 66

Tipping 69

Certification 72

Love and Money 76

Old Husbands' Tales 79

FINDING TRUE LOVE IN THE WANT ADS AND OTHER THINGS I DON'T QUITE UNDERSTAND

Speaking in Code 83

Credit Card Fees 85

Eating Your Vegetables on Vacation 88

The Accident 90

Assault With a Deadly Strip of Bacon 97

Wedding Pictures in the Paper 99

SWM, Looking for True Love in the Want Ads 103

The Implausible Awards 106

Tanning Booths 109

Reading Divine Signs 112

Re-Naming Things 116

I Can; Therefore I do 119

JELLO ON THE CEILING AND OTHER PARENTING TRAUMAS

My Daughter, the Appaloosa 123

Jello on the Ceiling 126

The Rival 130

The First Homecoming Dance 133

The Removing of The Braces 137

Applying For That First Job 140

OVERPACKING DISEASE AND OTHER THINGS THAT WEREN'T COVERED IN YOUR WEDDING VOWS

How Not to Get Divorced 143

Overpacking Disease 146

Male PMS: Premenstrual Stupidity 149

Threshold Compatibility in Marriage 151

Wallpapering With Your Wife 154

Cross-Finishing Stories 158

Country Living 161

Checkbook Adjustments 164

Holding Garage Sales 167

Old Married Couples 171

Selective Deafness in Men 173

Wife School 176

9 TO 5: THE INVERSE LAW OF SIMPLE EXPLANATIONS AND OTHER WORK RULES

The Inverse Law of Simple Explanations 181

Casual Fridays 184

Soap Operas 187

Technology I Can Do Without 190

Getting Home from Vacation 194

How to Do Business Meetings 197

HOLIDAYS, HIGH AND LOW

My Zermatt Christmas 201

Mission Control Christmas '96 206

Valentine's Day 209

Christmas Giving 211

Taking Those Holiday Family Pictures 214

Post-Holiday Shoulda's 217

Mother's Day 219

Thanksgiving 222

Christmas Presents You Should Not Buy 225

Christmas Cards 227

Making New Year's Resolutions 230

xii

MAINTAINING A HOUSEHOLD BY HUNTING, GATHERING, AND BECOMING RAMBO OF THE NIGHT

Adopting Cats 235

Gardening 238

Gathering Wood 241

Cleaning the Garage 244

Rambo of the Night 248

Refrigerators 251

A Most Respectful Letter to the IRS 255

Doing the Wine Thing 258

Dealing with Life Insurance Agents 260

Finding the Right Housesitters 263

Why Saying Goodbye Takes So Long 266

Thatch Me 269

OVERPACKING DISEASE, TELLING YOUR CHILD ABOUT NORDSTROM AND OTHER TRAUMAS OF ADULTHOOD

More Humorous KPBX Commentaries by Doug Hurd

DOUG HURD

TELLING YOUR CHILD ABOUT NORDSTROM AND OTHER FACTS OF LIFE

Telling Your Child about Nordstrom

Like you, I try to be a good parent. But let's face it – it's harder to raise our kids than it was to raise us. The world is a different place, and we have a lot more critical choices to make for our children than our parents had to make with us.

For instance, there are lots of things we want to shield our children from until they are old enough and mature enough to handle them. Things that our parents just didn't have to contend with.

For instance, my daughter is in second grade; and the way kids talk, she is coming home asking some very difficult questions. It is clear that one of these days, we are going to have to sit her down and have "the talk" about ... Nordstrom.

Now, I am not looking forward to that.

I have asked other parents, and there seems to be no set rule about when a child is able to handle the concept of Nordstrom.

Some say it's five years after they understand K-Mart. Others say you have to ease them into it, you know, over a period of years, take them from K-Mart to Penney's to Lamonts. Then Nordstrom won't be such a shock to their little systems.

Personally, I think 23 is about the right age to introduce them to Nordstrom.

You'd have thought Doctor Spock would have had a chapter on this, but he doesn't.

One mother I know simply ignores the whole issue.

"I just pretend it doesn't exist," she told me. "They're only children once – why should they have to deal with something that even adults have trouble handling?"

"But, doesn't your child ever catch you and your husband in a compromising position?" I asked. "I mean, what do you do if she catches you opening a Nordstrom bag?"

"We lock the bedroom door," she said. "There are some things you just don't do in front of children." She seemed a little perturbed with me.

She said, "I don't care how open and permissive society gets, I still think there are some things that are private between a man and a woman, and sharing your Nordstrom treasures is one of them."

"Have you taken your daughter to Jay Jacobs?" I asked.

She just looked at me like I'd lost my mind.

Other parents have a completely different outlook.

One father said to me, "I told my son, 'you want to do it, you tell me; and we'll go to Nordstrom together'." There's some male bonding for you. It sounds like a trip to Wallace, Idaho, or maybe the Mustang Ranch. He said that he figures his boys are going to be going to Nordstrom for the rest of their lives, and he wants them to know it's normal and natural and nothing to be embarrassed about.

Yeah, well, that's great if you've got sons, I told him.

Of course when you have boys who are 12 or 13, you have to explain the facts of Nordstrom to them. If they're real mature and they can handle it, maybe you explain about The Squire Shop, too.

But I've got a daughter. It's different with girls.

"Send her to a convent," was his advice.

"Thanks a lot," I said.

He's right about one thing, though. You do want to let your children know that going to Nordstrom is a natural act.

I remember my first time in Nordstrom. I was already out of high school. Most guys have already done it by then. I was kind of embarrassed. It was obvious I didn't know what I was doing; I was awkward and very self-conscious. I think I blew my five bucks at the first checkstand.

The whole thing couldn't have taken more than about three minutes. But that's common; a lot of men suffer premature spending their first few times in Nordstrom.

Now, as an adult, I know that one should just enjoy the pleasures of the store; take your time in whatever departments feel best to you.

Then, when you can't stand it anymore, buy something.

Some couples say they always arrive at the checkstand together; but my wife and I just aren't that coordinated. I usually buy before she does.

But she buys more. And more often.

Some people spend a lot of time in the store and then don't actually buy anything; but we don't find that very satisfying. It's just all in what turns you on, I guess.

I read something somewhere that said that it used to be that girls had their first Nordstrom experience when they were juniors in high school. But in recent years, that age has been dropping. Now the average age is seventh grade, with some regularly active in Nordstrom as young as fourth grade.

So you can see my problem with a second grade girl. Kids talk, after all.

A friend of mine is a child psychologist who deals with a lot of troubling questions like this all the time. He told me, "Children are naturally curious. They'll tell you when it's time to tell them about Nordstrom. You just have to accept the fact that one day they're going to outgrow Toys R Us."

I guess he's right.   And he knows it's going to be worse for him. His daughter is only three years old. If the trend continues, she could be active in Nordstrom by the time she's five.

"After you've told them about Nordstrom," I said, "should you tell them about credit cards and all that?" I asked.

"I wouldn't go that far," he replied.

Nose Diamonds

I have always tried to be very cool, very sophisticated – even laid back – when I come face to face with a part of the popular culture I haven't seen before and I don't understand. I work very hard at keeping my outward, nonchalant look intact when faced with something like, say, a young woman with her hair dyed pink.

I try to keep my face and manner in a very urbane, non-judgmental mode when I see something like that; but, I must admit, I'm not very good at it.

That's because as I am trying to make my eyes say, "Hey, cool. You're doing your own thing," like any self-respecting child of the sixties should. Inside the parent in me is saying, "You've got to be brain-dead to do that to yourself."

Of course, that's what our parents said about us when we let our hair grow, tie-dyed every perfectly good J. C. Penney tee-shirt we owned, and took to wearing bib overalls.

To our own weddings.

"The bride was resplendent in her overalls – a gift from an uncle who used to be a Milkman. Or a railroad engineer. The groom, who wore daisies in his shoulder-length hair, sat in the full lotus position and played "White Rabbit" on the flute while they pledged their oneness to each other."

Well, I admit, the '60s was a weird time. And I'm only now beginning to understand what it must have done to our parents.

This came home to me the other day when I chanced upon a young woman with a diamond in her nose.

For some things, I can still be cool. Like when the pizza delivery boy wears dangly earrings, I don't say anything. I don't eat the pizza, but I don't say anything. And Mohawk haircuts I hardly notice.

But a diamond in the nose puts me over the top of my self-control, and I'm afraid my surprise showed.

Now understand, this was not an Indian or Pakistani woman where her diamond might have been seen as a normal part of her culture once removed; this was a pudgy little garden variety American girl in dirty hair, dirty tee-shirt and jeans.

In an instant, I was so dumbstruck by the sight of it that I almost forgot to say "excuse me" when I bumped into her.

What I should have said was, "I get it. You're engaged to an Eskimo." But I didn't, of course.

I looked up from that little diamond to her eyes, and there was no hiding it; she caught me looking at her nose. And it was clear from her expression that I didn't quite get my non-judgmental face on in time.

And then, against all my parents' advice about not staring at people who are mentally defective, and even against all my own will power not to make a big deal of it, I looked from her eyes back to her nose, which, yep, had that diamond stuck to the side of it.

As my eyes must have bulged with surprise, my brain went into overdrive.

Does it go all the way through, I wondered. I wanted to ask her if it's stuck on there with superglue or is there a little lug nut on the other side? What happens if she gets a head cold? Does the Afrin nasal spray get hung up on it? If she sneezes, does she blow it out, putting people to her right at risk? At night, does she take it out and clean it? (Oooo, yuck!) And when she sleeps, does air whistle in and out of it, keeping all the dogs in the neighborhood awake?

Does she have trouble finding a job? "Your qualifications are excellent, Miss Jones. Plus, I'm sure the diamond in your nostril will reassure all our clients that you can be trusted with important decisions about their money."

Well. All this has taken about a tenth of a second. Then I noticed behind her another woman – clearly nosewoman's mother.

Ooops again.

The best I can do with my face is a sort of half smile to the mom. It says, "It's not your fault," but she and I both know better. Because of all the indignities a child can heap on a parent, being weird is the worst.

Being weird is worse than being criminal. If you're a criminal, a parent can always say, "He got in with a bad crowd in high school."

But when your child is just plain weird, it's, well, genetic. You didn't just fail as a parent, you failed as half a gene-pool donor. You failed in the grand, cosmic mating game of life.

So there it was. Twenty years ago, it was long hair and bibs.

Today it's diamonds in the nose, and it's not hard to appreciate how our parents must have felt.

But there was something else in this chance meeting. In nosewoman's mother's eyes, I saw the clear message: Just wait, your child will do this to you some day.

And if it's diamonds in the nose today, what in heaven's name will it be in ten years when my time comes?

I can hardly wait.

Personal Dating Disclosure Forms

Every once in a while, you come across an idea that is so simple, so obvious and so elegant in its clarity that it makes you wonder why you never thought of it before.

Like sticky notes. Or refrigerator magnets.

Things that make you think, "Why didn't I think of that?"

At the home of a friend recently, I stumbled upon another: Personal Dating Disclosure Forms.

You know how when you buy a house these days, you have to fill out a disclosure form and disclose all of its warts? You know how you have to tell prospective buyers that the foundation is cracked and the dishwasher periodically explodes and the R-value in the walls is minus 15 and the whole house, while it looks good, isn't structurally sound? And you do all that on what they call a home disclosure form so the new buyer can know what isn't readily obvious?

Well, we parents need something like that for teenagers. Especially if you have a teenage daughter.

"You want to go out with Billy? No problem. Just have him fill out a Personal Dating Disclosure Form and submit it to the parental approval committee – that's me – two weeks in advance."

This is not as far-fetched as it sounds. I have come to learn that teenage boys are a lot like houses. You just can't tell by looking which ones are okay and which ones are hiding some serious defects in workmanship. (It may just be me, but it seems to me that the most common defect among teenage boys is that a lot of them are simply wired up wrong. Every once in a while their brains just sort of short circuit. "Gee dad, I don't know why I skipped school with Ryan and knocked down all the neighbor's mail boxes. It seemed like a good idea at the time.")

So how are we to know who is okay and who is out of plumb, so to speak?

The Personal Dating Disclosure Form. I see it as a sort of cross between a job application, a college entrance form and an IRS Tax Form.

Naturally, it would have the normal stuff like name, address, phone number, date of birth, height, weight, IQ, merit badges, major addictions, traffic citations, time off for good behavior, that sort of thing.

Then it could be multiple choice:

Do you live with your parents? Yes. No. Sometimes. You mean right now?

If yes, does that mean one male and one female parent? If "no" please explain.

Do your parents always claim you? Yes. No. Sometimes. You mean, right now?

How many years do you expect it to take you to complete four years of high school: A. four years or less. B. more than four years. C. Not sure. D. High school?

Do you drive a car? If yes, has it ever been upside down while you've been driving it? If yes, stop and turn in your form.

A speed limit sign is: A. A suggestion. B. A safe speed for old people. C. The speed you go when a cop is around. D. Speed limits?

Do you have a beeper? If yes, and understanding that anything you say can and will be used against you in a court of law, why?

In the phrase, "Don't be home late," What does the word "Home" mean? A. In the same area code. B. In the same zip code. C. At the closest McDonalds. D. In the driveway making out. E. My home or your home? If E, stop and turn in your form.

In the phrase, "Don't be home late," what does the word "late" mean? A. Midnight. B. 1 a.m. C. Sometime tomorrow. D. Before Wednesday.

Do you have any tattoos? If yes, please explain any tattoos other than those that say, "Mother."

Please list all parts of your body that are pierced, with what, and how they got that way. Use the back of the form if you need more space. If you need more space, stop and turn in your form.

See how nice this would be? A few standard questions and we could all know who is okay and who has a leaky basement or drafty attic, so to speak.

You could get an idea about their future prospects by asking a few simple questions, like, "Which do you think would be a great place to work?" A. A bank. B. A factory. C. A brewery. D. A methanphedamine lab. E. Work?

Now, I realize that I have focused on what a Personal Dating Disclosure Form for boys would say, because I have a daughter. But if you have sons, you can imagine that it wouldn't be too hard to come up with a list of questions for girls.

The thing is, as we all know from our own experience, you never know which of the dates who float into and out of your children's lives is going to be the one who sticks and with whom you're going to have to endure years of Christmas Holidays.

There is one problem with this form, however.

And that is having your daughter ask, "If you had had to fill out this form as a teenager, Dad, what would your answers have looked like?"

Watching the Game

Tonight, the high school football season begins.

And if you are the parent of a first-year high school student, you are no doubt wondering if you should go out to wherever the teams play and watch the game or not.

This is assuming, of course, that your child is not on the football team. If he is, you have to go – you don't have a choice. (Unless you want to be forever branded as a non-attending, derelict parent and be whispered about by attending parents in terms generally reserved for lepers and city council members, that is. If that's the case, well, never mind.)

As the parent of a high school-aged daughter, allow me to offer one word of advice. Go.

You want to watch the game.

Now, I know what you're thinking. You're thinking that you know you should support your child's high school teams and show some school spirit, but the stadium is a long ways out there, and it's cold and wet out there. And really, isn't your attending on a par with, say, attending a PTG meeting where you have no intention of getting involved? And besides, when it comes right down to it, you just don't like football all that much.

To which I reply, who said anything about watching football? I said, "You want to watch the game."

The GAME. Not what's happening on the field. We're talking about the game that's happening in the stands. And if your son or daughter is there, they're in it. For all you know, he or she may be a first-string player.

Now that's a scary thought.

Another bit of advice: If your daughter sort of scrunches up her face like she's turning ninety right before your eyes and says, "You're not going to the game tonight, are you?" – trying her hardest to communicate that you are such a humiliating example of humanity that if you show up anywhere near the bleachers, she'll just die – you <u>really</u> have to go to that game.

Now, if you're still thinking, "Gee, I don't know ... " allow me a personal anecdote.

It was at my first high school game when I first laid eyes on the lovely and beguiling Eloise. As deeply in love as a hormonally out of control fifteen-year-old can instantly get, I had no greater goal that night than to keep deviously rearranging who I was sitting next to until I got next to her (a total stranger to me at that moment, you understand) so in the frenzied emotion of a touchdown, we could hug. It took me until half-time to get there, but that was okay. Our team always scored all of our touchdowns in the fourth quarter, anyway.

And when they did, I would be in place and ready.

Now, like any teenage boy with too much testosterone (which is all of them), I thought my movements through the crowd were so subtle as to be invisible, when in fact, to the parents observing from above, mine included (duh!), it was probably pretty obvious what I was doing.

And that's why you want to be there. Because I don't think teenage boys have changed much since then.

Granted, this puts you into roughly the same category as Margaret Mead observing the natives of Borneo or Jane Goodall watching the behavior of mountain gorillas, but what the heck.

When you get to the game, you don't want to sit alone. It will take too long to identify all the players in the game, their relative positions, and make sense out of the apparent random chaos of the student section. What you need is battlefield intelligence; and for that, you will need to find the parents who know the kids. This will be a group of moms who look like a bunch of FBI agents on stake-out.

It has been my observation that parents at a high school football game can appear to be every bit as cliquish as their children when it comes to sitting next to their friends. This may give you a flashback to your own high school days where the seating arrangements were dictated by whether or not you were one of the cool kids, uncool kids or wretched reject kids. But don't let that appearance deter you. In fact, you'll find the parents much more inclusive. This is because everybody is willing to share intelligence. So just sit close to the FBI Moms, introduce yourself, offer up a few tidbits about your child for their files, and you'll be in.

There is always one FBI mom who has an encyclopedic memory of all the kids, all their relationships, their parents, and the current pecking order. This is the person you want to sit near.

"Who's that talking to Heather?"

"That's Brent. Great skier. Nice kid. Parents go to Our Redeemer. Has an older brother who's trouble, but he's cool. He's going with Rachel, but she's in the Tri-Cities tonight with the volleyball team. They're just friends."

The FBI Moms tend to see things you won't until your observation skills get sharpened.

"Uh, oh."

"What?"

"Brian's not with Erin. He sent her flowers last week, but now he's talking with that cute blonde. Who is she?"

"That's my daughter. Are we seeing a bad thing?"

"Based on the body language, I'd say that depends upon whether you're Erin or not. We'll know more if they hug after the next touchdown."

What the kids are doing is what kids have always done, which for lack of a better term, is a mating dance. And it hasn't changed much since you were in high school.

Which ought to give you additional guidance when after the football game, your child scrunches up her face and says, "You're not going to chaperone the dance after the game, are you?"

The Longest Day

If you ask anybody who took part in World War II what The Longest Day was, they will tell you June 6, 1944: The day the Allies invaded Europe.

If you ask anyone younger than that, especially anyone with high school age children, they may have quite another response. They will tell you The Longest Day is the day the varsity coaches decide who makes – and doesn't make – the team.

For volleyball players, the last two days have been The Longest Days.

In junior high, the guiding paradigm at the schools is a modified, "everybody plays" philosophy. There are 12 varsity players and 372 junior varsity players. Players are divided up, but nobody really gets cut.

When I went to high school, that was the prevailing philosophy for football turnouts. If you wanted to show up and practice in the rain and the muck and stand around on the sidelines on freezing October Saturday nights, they gave you a uniform.

Nobody ever said you would play, you understand, but you made the team. Everybody made the team.

So you self-cut. You asked yourself, do I really want to do this? Your parents, meanwhile, were earnestly praying you would realize that your future was not in a football uniform, so they would not have to show up and freeze to death watching football games you probably weren't going to play in. It wasn't that they weren't supportive, they just didn't want a severe case of hypothermia.

For all I know, football is still that way.

But volleyball, like basketball, cheerleading, some musical ensembles, trying out for a part in the school play and any number of other activities, is competitive.

And limited. You make it or you don't.

For three or four days, the kids play their little hearts out. And then one day, they go home, and wait.

I don't know how it is at other schools, but at my daughter's high school, they like posting the final roster. They tell the kids to come back at 7:00 p.m. and a list of who made the team will be posted on the gym door.

And the hour from the end of the last practice to the time they post takes about three days to pass.

When your child comes home from that last practice, your job as a parent is to be non-existent. Your child may be home, but you are in the land of Wrong. As in anything you do or say will be Wrong.

"So how were tryouts today?"

"I hate you! Get out of my life."

"What would you like for dinner?"

"I hate you! Get out of my life."

I heard one parent comment that during The Longest Day, she doesn't talk at all to her daughter because no matter what she says, her daughter will bite her head off. "And I treasure my head," she said.

Some kids just get quiet. Deathly quiet.

"How was practice today?

Silence.

"That good, Huh? Well, uh, since you don't want to talk, I'll just go upstairs."

The problem is that all your parental instincts want to get you involved, to gather information, to nurture, to reassure, even to prepare them for the worst. And that's exactly wrong. (Especially if you feel compelled to explain to your child what they should have done. "I told you you should have practiced harder!")

This isn't about you and your needs. It is about them. It is about their ability to meet a standard set by someone else, and measured impersonally (and in some cases, even unfairly). It is about their ability to demonstrate a given skill and have that compared to everyone else's.

Your job is not to get in front of them and protect them from the answer to that, but to get behind them and support them, whatever the answer turns out to be.

And that's hard.

Personally, I think it's pretty good training for real life, where competition is the norm.

(Of course, in real life, you're not always in such open competition. I mean, can you imagine if surgeons had to make the "Varsity Surgical Team?" "Okay, people, let's go! Let's get those tonsils out! Go! Go! Go! Last one done has to do a ruptured appendix and give me thirty pushups!")

Ultimately, of course, they'll live through it. And they'll be stronger for it.

The question is, will we parents?

I'll know the answer to that when The Longest Day is over.

Don't Do Anything Stupid

It's that time again for me. Time to change the out-the-door advice I give my daughter.

Out-the-door advice changing time is when you realize that the advice that you have been giving your child as he or she is heading out the door is no longer apropos; no longer germane.

It may be good advice, it just no longer fits.

For instance, if you have toddlers, the standard out the door advice may be, "Stay in the yard." Or, if you have a boy, "Don't go in the street." Later that becomes, "Don't throw rocks at the neighbor's windows." (I should say here, if that's the advice you're giving a toddler, you have a <u>very</u> long parenting journey in front of you.)

One day you realize that this advice no longer makes a lot of sense, and you change it, update it, if you will, to your child's new reality. "Don't go in the street" changes to "Look both ways before crossing the street." And you add others, like "Never talk to strangers," and "Stay out of the juvenile court system." Things like that.

As your children grow older, the out-the-door advice may shift from issues of safety and security to issues of manners and etiquette. For instance, if you have pre-teens, you may send your children off with a final reminder to always say please and thank you.

It may not keep them alive, but at least they'll die being polite.

None of this, of course, presupposes that your child has ever paid the slightest bit of attention to what you said in the first place, or for that matter, ever will.

Witness the "drive carefully" advice your parents still give you when you leave their house. I mean, have you ever been driving along, doing 25 over the speed limit and said to yourself, "Gee, Mom said to drive carefully, so I'd better slow down for this hairpin curve up ahead," and then slowed down? Of course not. (That is why in our family, we send people off with a hearty, "Drive like a fool." I mean, if they are not going to pay attention anyway ...)

Still, before the age of sixteen, there is a single constant in the out-the-door advice giving thing; and that is, at some point, you are going to go retrieve your child from somewhere and be in a position to find out if, in fact, your child did what you told her to do.

At 16, all that changes. Overnight.

All of a sudden, there is no easy way to check to see if she said please or thank you or drove carefully or, for that matter, even went where she said she was going and did what she said she was going to do, much less what you told her to do.

Not only that, but the number of danger areas a sixteen-year-old in a car can get into expands exponentially from those of a non-driving fifteen-year-old.

This is partly because once they drive, you, the parent are no longer in the loop, and partly because of the convergence of opportunity for trouble, out-of-control hormones, increased social obligations, the disinclination to listen to anyone adult and the invincible feeling that naturally flows from the certain knowledge all teenagers have that bad things only happen to other people.

Consequently, simply saying "drive carefully" as your child drives off doesn't pack it. In fact, drive carefully doesn't begin to cover the dangers lurking out there. It is simply way too narrow and too specific.

Hence, the need for an out-the-door advice update.

For a while, I thought about something like, "Anytime a man says the words 'love' and 'respect' in the same sentence, he's lying." But that's kind of a mouthful when your kid is going out the door, it makes the neighbors wonder, and again, while true, it is pretty narrow in focus.

I thought about saying, "Don't do anything I wouldn't do," a trusty 1960s send-off, but that sounds pretty dated even to me; plus my daughter probably knows more about my personal history than she should to make that good advice.

(This an aside, but isn't it strange how, now that we baby boomers are parents, that almost all of what we did in the '60s is precisely what we do not want our children to do in the '90s?)

It was during this struggle to find just the right words to send my daughter out the door with that a friend passed along the out-the-door advice he has used successfully with his three kids.

"Don't do anything stupid."

Yes!

I knew in an instant I had found the perfect out the door advice. "Don't do anything stupid." General enough to be of use behind the wheel, alone with a date, with a group at a party or in the presence of a vice principal; specific enough to relate to everything from danger to matters of personal judgment. It's perfect.

Now, I realize that it could be argued that "Don't do anything stupid," is both a condescending instruction and an unattainable goal for a teenager, given the teenage proclivity – even God-given talent – teenagers have for doing stupid things.

And it was passed along with solemn instructions to first hold the Calling-Home- With-Immunity-From-Prosecution, No-Questions-Asked if you do do something stupid, family talk, which I also like in theory, but I'm not altogether sure I could live up to under combat conditions.

Still, "don't do anything stupid" is better than anything else I have come up with, so I am going to try it.

I just hope my daughter doesn't say, "Define 'stupid'."

To which I'd probably have to answer, "Just drive carefully, okay?"

Role Models

I've been thinking a lot about role models lately. Partly because my daughter has a new role model: Marilyn Monroe.

Not exactly my first choice out of all the people in the world, living or dead.

The other reason is because I happened upon a magazine with a picture of Frank Voogd the other day.

Frank was my pee-wee football coach. Thirty years ago, he was a young twenty-something who agreed to take on 26 sixth-grade boys and fifty-two parents who couldn't be pleased and teach them all to endure football in the rain.

It was weird to see Frank's picture at this particular time. I hadn't seen him since I was in eighth grade, although I had thought about him from time to time.

What was weird was I saw Frank's picture the day I agreed to help coach a volleyball team of seventh-grade girls.

Have you ever been around a group of 12- and 13-year-old girls? I have a renewed respect for anybody in the teaching profession, I can tell you that.

First of all, I have to confess, I'm not sure what I'm doing coaching. Mostly, I'm helping the real coach, who is a real teacher and seems to know how to get these girls to function.

I play volleyball, but I have learned that playing it and coaching it, especially to 13-year-olds, are altogether different skills.

And then, there was that picture of Frank.

You see, Frank taught me a lot about football. Skills like tackling and blocking and reading which way a play would go. And he taught me about teamwork. And against all his best efforts, we learned about losing. He taught us about trying, about keeping at it until the game ends. We even learned a little something about winning.

I learned that in sports, the U.S. Constitution not withstanding, we are not all created equal.

I learned that lesson from the bench.

At the start of the game, I always wanted to play. ("Put me in, coach!") Around the middle, I wasn't so sure anymore. Toward the end, when it looked like we were either going to a) win or b) lose and my participation wouldn't make a bit of difference either way, I began to appreciate the fact that my uniform was dry and comfortable and that, with any luck, I wouldn't be substituted in and have to get out into the mud and be run over and get stomped into a puddle and risk death by drowning, hypothermia, or a sucking chest wound from the cleats of some big kid whose pituitary was out of control. But Frank always played all of us, however briefly. And I always came home muddy and cold without much game time to show for it.

But I learned something else from Frank that was more subtle and, over the long haul, infinitely more important. Frank was one of those people who showed me what it was to be a decent adult male.

I don't mean he was a great molder of men or anything. I don't think he saved any of us middle-class Scandinavian kids from a life of crime or anything. He was just a super nice guy, with enough passion for football (or for kids) to make him stand out in the rain four days a week with a bunch of boys, none of whom he was related to.

And <u>that</u> made an impression, although it would be thirty years before I would fully realize the real impact Frank made on my life.

Now, to be fair, I had a lot of good people for role models as I grew up, starting with my parents and the parents of all my friends, because they were all good people. All great role models. But that's your job when you're a parent. You're supposed to set an example.

Or at least say "King's X" when you're not.

The thing is, it wasn't Frank's job to be a role model. He could have been a jerk and made us hate him, and if we'd won more than half, most of us would have felt we got a fair deal. After all, whoever said that coaches are supposed to be nice guys and good role models?

Winning is what it's all about, isn't it?

Well, now that I'm a coach, and with Frank looking at me from out of the past, I'm not so sure it is.

At least, not at this age. Not at the age he had me and I have these girls.

It's about growing and learning and skills and sportsmanship. And it's also about fun. Because, if you can't have fun, through the winning and the losing, then none of it's worth it. And running through it all, down deep where it can't be seen and it can't be measured but it is happening just the same, it's about being an adult.

So under all the volleyball I'm trying to teach, there is this thought that what I'm doing out there is more than passing on athletic skills; that I am probably passing along my vision of how an adult should act and behave.

Oh, please, God, don't let me screw this up. It's way too important.

And then I come home, and my daughter wants to be Marilyn Monroe. Marilyn Monroe! Well, she wants to be gorgeous and sexy and built. And, when you think about it, who among us doesn't?

It could be worse, I suppose. She might want to be Madonna. Besides, she does a deadly imitation of Marilyn in a tight slinky dress singing happy birthday to JFK.

Still, it makes me wonder what kind of role model I am. As a coach. And father.

Just about when all these thoughts combine to induce total inertia in me, I remember that most of us are who we are not because of one person we've encountered, but because of all of them. We're probably all making impressions, for better or for worse, all the time, on everybody we meet.

So I figure, what the heck. And I go back to the volleyball court and concentrate on teaching these kids something about passing and blocking and setting and serving. And if they learn a lesson about my idea of being an adult along the way, so be it.

I hope it'll be as positive as Frank's was on me.

Perhaps in thirty years I'll find out.

As for my daughter, when she was little, we used to ask her, "What are you going to be when you grow up?" And we taught her the right answer was, "Anything I want to be."

And I guess right now, that includes the possibility of being Marilyn Monroe.

The Last Summer of Freedom

I have a question for those of you who have already raised your kids: When they were 15, did your kids sleep enough to make the cat envious?

Did you periodically wonder if you should be calling either your family doctor – "Doctor, I'm telling you, she's got a case of encephalitis lethargica," or the circus – "You could bill her as the amazing sleeping teenager"?

Just wondering.

I am concerned that my daughter is sleeping away this summer.

Now, I admit that most of this concern probably stems from my being a morning person and her not. At least I don't think she's a morning person. One can't be completely sure – she hasn't seen a morning since school got out.

I went in to wake her the other morning (about 10:30, mind you) and watching her sleep, two quotes came to mind. The first was the one about youth being such a wonderful thing, it's a shame it's wasted on the young.

The second was from my mother.

It was summer. I was fifteen. My parents were trying to instill in me some sort of work ethic that I was resisting with good success. I was lying about in the sun one day, looking like a human walrus-in-training, and my mother, no doubt feeling the same sort of frustration I feel when I look at my daughter sleeping her life away, said, "Well, I hope you're enjoying it because this is your last summer of freedom. Next summer, you work."

The last summer of freedom.

The words had a ring to them; a truth that spoke vaguely of a world I would be moving into from another I would be losing forever.

Do you remember your last summer of freedom? For some, it was the summer they were 14; for others 16 or 17, but that had to be pushing it. (I know: right now there is someone who is newly divorced and shouting "Hey, this is my summer of freedom and I'm 34!" – but that's not what we're talking about here.)

Mine was the summer I turned 15.

Your last summer of freedom was the last time when someone said, "Why don't you get a job," you could turn to them and say, "I can't; I'm too young." That was a lie, of course. Everyone had friends who worked and held real jobs who were 15. You simply got a permit of some sort. But who wanted to do that?

And you weren't really free, of course. Since you didn't drive, you were limited by how far you could go on foot. Or bike. And because you didn't have a job, you also didn't have much money, so any activity that cost money tended to be out of the question.

And it wasn't like you had no responsibilities. There were some household duties. Mowing the lawn and babysitting, for instance.

It was that summer that my parents gave me one job. Paint the house. Today, I would simply point to the OSHA laws and tell them to talk to Child Protective Services and then have their people call my people; but in those days I didn't know any better, so I just did it. What a chore that turned out to be. If I whined about taking out the garbage, you can imagine how I felt about painting the house.

It was my first exposure to the summer work paradox: when it rains, you can't really do any summer work; and when it is sunny, you don't want to waste a nice day working.

I must confess, I still haven't quite figured that one out.

Mostly during that summer, I hung out with my friends, Jim and Mark and Greg. And our activities revolved mostly around finding something to do with Boo and Linda and Kay. Preferably something where they would have to be in swimsuits. (You have to remember that our 15-year-old male hormones were driving a lot of our thought processes that summer.)

It was a time before renting videos; and even though we had TV, I can't remember spending any time watching it. Instead, we would gather and then wander from one friend's house to another or down to Carkeek Park or Golden Gardens. It was like doing Huckleberry Finn in cutoff Levi's with Buddy Holly music playing.

It was a magical time. And mom was right. It was a time of freedom.

Though we never discussed it, I think we each knew that never again would we be without the tyranny of a job schedule or of a real need for money. We knew that at the end of this summer, we would cross some invisible boundary where the simplicity of this existence ends and something else begins.

And with it would go a freedom we would never again experience.

Knowing this, and knowing that this is my daughter's last summer of freedom, I don't want her to sleep through it.

"Time to get up," I say to her. "You've got very important work to do."

"Like what?" she mumbles.

I'm tempted to say, "I was thinking you should paint the house," but I don't.

Instead I just say, "Everything. You've got everything to do."

Sally Gray

One day recently my third-grade daughter referred to one of her friends as a spastic.

I kind of winced at it. "You know, it's not really nice to call people that," I said.

"Why?" she asked.

"Because some people are spastics," I said.

"Oh," she said. "What's a spastic?"

So I told her about Sally.

Sally was the girl who taught me not to use the term spastic to describe someone. You see, Sally was spastic.

Sally joined our class in sixth grade.

She was 14 on this try through the sixth grade. That alone made her different enough for most of us to regard her as a freak. But Sally had this extra thing: she twitched.

And she didn't just twitch a little. Her whole body twitched. Her arms and head and shoulders were in constant motion, all of it fast and none of it fluid.

I'd never seen anything like it in my life.

Sally was rail thin and had hair that was chopped more than cut. It was short, really short. And it stuck out in patches that didn't seem to know where to go. Sally's family didn't have much money to begin with, and what money they had was probably eaten up by tutors and the special care Sally needed. Haircuts were probably a long ways down on the priority list.

Sally may have had other learning disabilities that today we have names for. She might have been hyperactive. She might have had attention deficit syndrome.

Or maybe not.

Maybe all her difficulties in learning stemmed from her inability to hold a book still or keep her head in one place long enough to focus on a group of words. All I know is she had a tough time sitting still in class.

And she was years behind.

Being older than all of us, she thought we were twerps, which wasn't too far off the mark, probably. School had been tough for Sally, both educationally and socially. As such, she had a defiance about her, a defensiveness that kept most of us away.

She also had, as I recall, a foul mouth for a sixth-grader, something we attributed to her age and regarded with some wonder.

Before she joined the class, our teacher explained about Sally and told us since being a spastic wasn't something that could be helped, we were not to tease her about it; and I don't think anyone did.

But if we didn't tease her, neither did we offer much in the way of friendship, either. School must have been a lonely place for Sally.

She did have some friends, though. Mark Jorstad was one. Mark was a high-energy kid, big for his age, who always seemed to function at the far edge of the rules. He had a raw edge about him that made him hard to control or predict. In a lot of ways, Mark was socially what Sally was physically.

He and Sally hit it off immediately.

They would chase each other around the school yard at recess like two puppies. Sally would run with arms and legs flailing around, and Mark would dodge in and out of her grasp. Mark would laugh at her, but it was laughter with no malice in it. Mark laughed at everything, including himself; and somehow, that made them equals. Mark treated her like she was just another one of the guys, and she could take it or leave it.

It was the closest thing to a friend she had, I think, and she took it.

Sally may have had learning difficulties, but she wasn't without a sense of humor. She had a way of being self-deprecating, of making jokes about herself when she made mistakes that could be very funny.

One day, Sally was asked to read aloud to the class. On this day, when she stumbled in her reading, she made a wisecrack. Mark made a wisecrack back; and in a few moments, it was like a stand-up comedy routine and the whole class was laughing hysterically.

She really broke us up.

And then, all of a sudden, it wasn't funny anymore.

Suddenly Sally was crying; and screaming that she couldn't do it, that it wasn't fair. And in her frustration, she tried to throw her book; but Sally couldn't throw anything, much less a book. And she banged her hand on her desk in the attempt, which also made us laugh but wasn't funny, if you know what I mean. And she screamed at us to shut up, to just shut up, which we did. All 32 of us.

Then she bolted from the room.

Our teacher, Mrs. Stavney, went out after her. We all hoped Sally wouldn't run far because Mrs. Stavney was about 75, plus she had a knee that didn't bend, so she was probably the one person in the whole school who couldn't outrun Sally.

But no one had more sympathy or understanding or gentleness than Mrs. Stavney; and Sally, apparently, didn't want to run from that.

Meanwhile, inside the teacherless classroom, everybody was wondering what happened.

"I didn't know she was upset."

"I thought she was joking."

"Did you laugh?"

"I wasn't laughing."

We all agreed it was Mark's fault. What the hell. He always got blamed for everything anyway.

In a few minutes, Mrs. Stavney came back into the room.

"Sally feels she owes you an apology," said Mrs. Stavney. "And she would like to do something for you." With that, she went to the door, and with her hands on Sally's twitching shoulders, ushered her back into the room.

Then, standing in front of the class, head and shoulders moving in that constant twitching motion we had come to know so well, Sally sang, a cappella, The Lord's Prayer.

So when I hear my daughter refer to someone as a spastic, what I see is a gawky young girl named Sally, in front of a sixth grade class, asking, in perhaps the most eloquent language I have ever heard, for a little human understanding. For a little acceptance of what she couldn't control. For us to see past a problem that has a name: spastic.

So I ask my daughter to find another word to describe her uncoordinated friend.

Just do it for me, I tell her.

And do it for Sally. Wherever she may be today.

The Werewolf and Other Scary Things in the Night

The other night, my daughter went to a scary movie with friends.

Not scary scary, like <u>Friday the 13th</u> or <u>Nightmare on Elm Street</u>, just a little scary, like <u>Gremlins</u>, or even <u>The Wizard of Oz</u>, which scared the beegeebers out of us both a generation apart, but which we both came to like anyway.

At about 10:30, she came into our room, clutching everything to her that bolstered her security – a blanket and selected stuffed animals. She leaned way over until her head was next to mine.

"I'm scared," she whispered. "I can't sleep."

Taking care of demons in the dark is my job.

"Was it the movie?" I asked.

She nodded her head. She wanted to stay.

In our house, we have a parental policy that covers this sort of thing, which is, we try not to cave in right away. So I reached out into the darkness and gave her a strong reassuring hug and told her to go back to her room and try to sleep; that there was nothing to be afraid of.

She hesitated there a second, then padded off.

In about a minute she was back, this time with extra blankets, and a pillow. Saying nothing, she quietly laid down the blankets, making a soft place on the floor next to our bed, and then arranged her animals, and then crawled in between the blankets, and promptly fell asleep.

Had her motivation to sleep in our room been anything but a scary movie, I might have been tougher. As a rule, I think kids sleeping with parents is a mistake for all concerned. But on this night, I knew I had to make an exception, because I knew just what she was going through.

I knew because of an enduring and deeply moving personal relationship I had with The Werewolf.

When I was about her age, my brother and I went down to the Ballard Theater in Seattle to see a Saturday afternoon double feature of Earth Versus the Flying Saucers and The Werewolf.

I got through Earth Versus the Flying Saucers without any major trauma. There was one scary part where the aliens separated the brains from the bodies of their captive earthlings, but even I knew that was mostly cheap Hollywood trick photography (as we called special effects in those days). And in the end, the good guys won and everything was okay.

Then came The Werewolf.

As I recall, this was not your classic werewolf tale with full moons and all that. It was more like The Hulk, with this werewolf guy making his big change when he got riled up, which was about every twelve minutes.

The first time he changed from ordinary guy to werewolf, I freaked.

There I was in a totally black theater, watching a guy with a twenty-foot face grow enormous teeth, a wolf-like face, and paws. My pulse went from about 85 to 190, my blood pressure to 320 over 240, and my ocular pressure made my eyes bulge out so bad I would look like Betty Davis's illegitimate child for about the next two weeks.

I became mildly catatonic, unable to scream and unable not to look.

I was beginning to think going to the movie wasn't such a hot idea.

(I didn't know it at the time, but I wouldn't react to a change in hairstyle like that again until 1964, when on the night of my senior prom, I saw what the hairdresser had done to my prom date. But that's another story.)

As the movie progressed and this guy changed back and forth, sending me in and out of hysteria, a couple of snippets of dialogue lodged in my brain. The first was when one character explained that the werewolf guy had received three drops of wolf blood in a perverted scientific experiment, to which the other replied, "I went to school; I know what that means: he's a were-wolf."

My little third-grade brain went into hyperdrive, with the left side screaming at the right side, "You mean to tell me this is common knowledge? This can happen? You learn about this in school, like an aberration in the multiplication tables? Two times two is four, two times three is six, three drops of wolf blood and you're a werewolf, three times three is nine ... ?!!" It was getting to be more than I could handle.

It didn't help any that my brother, who had been charged with getting me home alive, wouldn't let me bolt from the theater like I wanted to. He <u>liked</u> this stuff and was going to stay, so he made me stay, too.

The other bit of dialogue that took root was when they were hunting down the werewolf, and someone said, "If I were a wolf, I'd be hiding ... there."

Well, that particular line would have me looking for were-wolf hiding places for the next ten years of my life. Especially when I had to walk someplace at night. Alone. Past werewolf hiding places.

And it didn't take a rocket scientist to know that the most obvious place a werewolf would hide was under my bed.

This fact was aggravated by my older brother, who, for months would say, just as I was about to fall asleep, "Hey, Dougie, I think there's a werewolf under your bed. Oh, God, HE'S CHANGING!"

Older brothers can be soooo funny.

So, and this is the point of all this, for three nights after the movie, I slept with my parents. There were just way too many hiding places for a werewolf in the attic next to my bedroom, especially since my brother seemed to be the werewolf's buddy.

And I didn't just sleep with my parents. I slept between them.

That's how much security I needed. I might be a fraidy cat, but I wasn't a fool. If there was a werewolf in the closet, he was darn well going to get one of my parents first.

In a few months, the outward manifestations of my terror subsided, my brother found making me hysterical less amusing and stopped, and I somehow came to terms with the werewolf.

I learned how to simply, and quite literally, push him out of my mind.

And even though I never, ever saw another werewolf movie, (not even the one with Michael Landon in the teenage werewolf title role – not even in re-runs) the werewolf and I both knew he was never very far away. Walking home at night from, say, a Boy Scout meeting, I was never sure that he wasn't lurking in the dark bushes of the vacant lots I had to pass or in the shadows behind the hedges.

So when my daughter comes in and makes her bed next to mine because she's seen a scary movie, I know that adult intellectual explanations aren't going to help. I know the security that the presence of a parent can give. I'm glad my parents were there for me, and I'm glad I can be there for her. So I let her stay.

Just as long as she doesn't tell me there's a werewolf under the bed.

Going to Summer Camp

It was the check-in line for camp. Even though I was surrounded by kids with their parents, I began to feel terribly alone.

What was next, I wondered? Where would I go?

I could see the swimming area off to the right.

The camp counselors were conducting the dreaded swimming test.

New arrivals were climbing down the ladders into the lake like cattle being dipped for hoof and mouth disease. No one made so much as a whimper of protest. Then they began swimming the perimeter of the swimming area – an impossibly long distance.

How did they get there? I wondered. Did someone tell them what to do? Where to go? This camp thing was beginning to seem like maybe it wasn't such a hot idea.

We had already passed a great hall that had the look of a place where great numbers of grumpy kids were served great amounts of mush.

Mush. Yuck.

It all seemed so bewildering. There wasn't a lot of talk in the line between the other kids and their parents. "You've got to do this," I told myself. It's part of growing up.

Some of the kids were obviously returnees. They were greeting camp counselors like long-lost friends. That made me feel a little better. At least some people enjoyed this experience when it was all over. But watching other people connect somehow made me feel more isolated, more alone.

My mind raced ahead. I began to think of what it would be like tonight at bedtime.

I wanted to cry for the fear of it all. "I don't like camp," was what I was thinking.

I turned to the lady next to me. "I'm getting homesick," I said.

There was a pause, and then my wife said, "Why are you getting homesick?"

My daughter, who was next in line to check in, said, "Yeah. I'm the one going to camp."

"Are you getting homesick?" I asked, somewhat plaintively.

"No," she said.

"Hmmmm." I replied.

They say that everything that has ever happened to you is stored away somewhere in your brain, and with the right stimulus, just about any experience can be recalled.

It's true. Checking my daughter into YMCA camp was dredging up memories of when I went to YMCA when I was about her age. Memories that had lain undisturbed for 35 years.

"We got on a bus," I said.

"Huh?" came my daughter's distracted reply. She was looking for her friends.

"We got on a bus in downtown Seattle and they took us to Anacortes, where we got on a Ferry for Orcas Island. It was like being sent to Alcatraz."

My daughter, who was taking this imminent family separation thing much better than I was at the moment, couldn't have been less interested. In the first place, she didn't know where Orcas Island was; and in the second, she had never heard of Alcatraz.

Well, this camp might turn out to be a lot of things, but one of them certainly wasn't Alcatraz.

All the counselors at camp have special names, like fighter jocks. Except the camp counselors tended to have outdoor woodsy sorts of names.

We were told to go find Bambi. I was looking forward to this until this guy who looked like he could play center for the Seahawks came up and said, "Hi, I'm Bambi." Right. Well, Bambi was a male after all, wasn't' he? I decided to forego the Bambi jokes.

We lugged all her gear to her cabin, where we met her junior counselors, who looked younger than some of the campers we had seen. In fact, some of the junior counselors go straight from being guests to employees. Not a bad deal.

By this time, I was getting over being homesick once removed, as it were.

But one peek into that cabin, and it all came back – the squeaky bunkbeds, the sleeping bags staking out a claim to a bunk, and the smell of the cabin.

Most of all the smell. The aroma left behind by a thousand kids with wet hair and sneakers who've slept in those bunks before you. In all camps in all places, I'm sure the cabins all smell the same.

It's the smell of going to sleep lonely your first night at camp.

My daughter changed and dragged me out of there. She knows when I'm not doing so hot. "Come on," she said. "I've got to take the swim test."

We took a swim test on Orcas Island, I remember. We took it in the waters of the San Juan Islands in water that had recently been a glacier. The big challenge was being in the water long enough to prove we could swim but not long enough to induce hypothermia. Just the memory of that cold water and some of my body parts headed north for warmth.

She passed her test with flying colors. She held up the colored string bracelet which cleared her to swim in all areas.

Her first badge of achievement at camp.

By this time, some of the friends from school were anxious to show her where their cabin was and to do some exploring before orientation.

At that moment, parents were suddenly excess baggage. So my wife and I got those hugs that would have to last for a week and made the long walk back to the car.

As we walked, I was thinking that camp was a good thing, a growing experience, a fun time.

And it was good that she wasn't as wimpy as I had been when I went to camp. Maybe it showed that she was stronger than I was at the same age. I hoped so.

Because I was clearly homesick enough for both of us.

Big Weddings

Does sleep-teaching work?

You know, where you put on a tape when you go to bed and it plays to your subconscious while you sleep? Periodically over the years, you read about these systems that purport to make you whatever you're not – outgoing, confident, aggressive, a good golfer, whatever.

Well, I need to know if they work; because if they do, I'm going to have to start a new nighttime routine. I'm going to have to start sneaking into my daughter's bedroom at night after she's gone to sleep and play a tape that whispers in her ear, "You want a small wedding. A small intimate wedding. And no reception at all."

I've just come back from a big wedding.

Not BIG big, just medium big. Actually, it was probably small big by today's standards depending upon how you measure these things.

Do you measure a wedding's size by the number of people who show up to watch, or by how many people are up there with the bride and groom? Or by how much it cost? I don't know for sure. In this case, the guest list was reasonably small; but the wedding party was huge. The size of this wedding wasn't really the bride's fault; she had four sisters of her own, plus she was gaining two sisters-in-law. She only had one non-family brides-maid, and it was still the biggest thing the wedding planner had ever seen.

This being the case, the groom got to ask everyone he ever knew to be in his wedding. "Remember me? We were in seventh grade together. Want to be in my wedding?"

Small weddings. Small intimate weddings.

Now, before I go further, I should tell you that when I got married, the hot trend was to get together in a park somewhere, or up on a mountaintop, and commune with nature and 100 or so of your hippy friends and whomever happened to be in the neighborhood, sing some Joan Baez folk songs, and declare yourself in oneness with each other and nature, make the peace sign and declare yourselves married. Some people actually signed legal papers and everything.

It was, I think, an attempt to get to the meaning of the event.

Well, I'm here to tell you, those days are gone.

Big weddings are back.

And the thing about big weddings that is so blindingly obvious that it's pretty easy to miss is somebody has to pay for all of it. And that somebody is traditionally the father of the bride.

(It's worth noting that this tradition can be shifted to the step-father in most cases.)

Now, I ask all parents: In all of your financial planning for your children's future and your retirement, did anybody ever even mention the fact that one day you would need to write a check for about 25 grand *for a wedding*? For each child? Not that I recall.

Sitting with the father of the bride at this wedding, I mentioned that for the cost of the wedding, the photographer, the flowers and the reception, you could just about send a child through law school.

"Law school's a little less, actually," he said.

You would think this would force a choice: You can go to college for four years or you can have a big wedding, but you can't have both. But it doesn't.

All of this is not to say that the big wedding, with its lovely bride and handsome groom and beautiful bridesmaids with their big hair and groomsmen in their tuxes and squirmy candlelighters and ring-bearing children, all delivered with a huge party afterwards, is not a wonderful and magnificent thing to behold.

It is. (I would prefer that people not have the bad manners to schedule them in the summer when church temperatures are apt to hit 110, and fainting and bashing your brains out on the pew in front of you becomes a real health hazard; but that's a minor quibble.)

I like big weddings. Especially if I don't have to pay for them.

For me, the best moment of the wedding is during pictures when the groom first sees his bride in her wedding dress. To me, that's the most genuine moment of the entire event. This used to be a moment shared by everybody at the wedding, but now it is seen only by those in the wedding party since a good set of wedding pictures takes at least four hours of diligent effort, and thus must precede the wedding instead of follow it.

And, all things considered, it's a good thing that traditional weddings have generally been a female-driven thing, even though that makes most men at most weddings absolutely superfluous.

It is arguable that weddings could really be spectacular if you could just find a way to get rid of the men altogether.

At the wedding I attended, the men concluded that if men were in charge, weddings would probably be held en masse at half-time of some larger, more significant male-oriented social event, like the UW - WSU football game or the Indy 500 or something.

We decided that if men had been steering the ship for 100 years, there would be no flowers, no one would sing "The

Wedding Song" ever again, and the wedding march would probably sound a lot more like the theme to the "Rocky" movies.

All in all, we decided it's probably for the better that women are in charge.

I wondered out loud if the couple would have preferred the cash to the event.

"No dice," said the father of the bride.

"You offered?" I asked.

"Yep," he said.

Of course, nobody would care how much a wedding cost if there was a correlation between how much you spent on a wedding and ensuing marital bliss. Unfortunately, there's not. A marriage can crash and burn regardless of the cost of the launch.

So to my daughter I say, "Small weddings. Small intimate weddings."

There is one problem with all this. And that is I already know that if my daughter wants to stand up there with a dozen bridesmaids and feed everyone she knows champagne and shrimp afterwards, and it means selling the house to pay for it all, I probably won't be the one to say no.

Actually, I doubt sleep-teaching will do any good. I think big weddings are in your genes or they're not, and no amount of social re-programming is going to change that.

I'll let you know in ten years.

In the meantime, where can I find out about sleep-teaching?

THINGS MY FATHER COULD HAVE TOLD ME ABOUT BEING A MAN, BUT DIDN'T

Keeping Nature in Balance by Going Bald

If you've ever gone to a company picnic at the lake, you can't help but notice that all the women wear shorts over their bathing suits. This is after they have arrived, spread out their blankets, introduced their hubby to everyone, sent the children off to spill pop on everybody, and are starting conversations which always begin with the phrase, "What a cute top! Where did you get that?"

The reason they are wearing shorts, I am told, is that they are paranoid about their thighs, hips and tummies bulging out all over, whether they actually do or not. Apparently, while women may share their inner most thoughts with the people they work with, they're not about to share their outermost cellulite.

We men have no such paranoia, even when we should. We just don't care, even when nature and common sense cries out for us to keep our overflowing selves covered up.

Men peel off their T-shirts without a second thought about who might sit in judgment about the state of their sagging pectorals or fleshy paunch. Then we compound the problem by either lying about like like a bunch of beached walruses with a taste for beer or by playing touch football – as if we just finished high school (albeit high school for pale, tubby, wheezing geezers).

Either way, it's not a pretty sight.

Why don't men care about how their bodies look, the way women do?

I think I know. I think it's one of those little tricks of nature that keeps everything in balance. I think it's because while women must face hips and thighs that have a mind and metabolism of their own, men must face something far worse. It is the loneliest, scariest, least spoken of and most humiliating thing that can happen to a man.

Bad knees? Not hardly.

Sexual dysfunction? Nope. Something infinitely worse and embarrassingly more public.

It's almost as if some divine force with a perverse sense of humor said, "Let's give women fat thighs and a standard of thinness they can't possibly live up to; and just to keep it even, let's have men lose their hair! And let's make it take years! Won't that be fun to watch?"

So there. I've said it. I have spoken of that which is not spoken of.

Going bald.

Not being bald, which isn't so bad, but going bald, which is the pits, and of which no man, ever, speaks.

Oh yes, there are the jokes about the growing shiny spot on the back of the head, seen during the family videotape replay, or the growing forehead or the receding hairline. These hilarious jokes are about as well received by us men as you women receive the observation that the lady down the street, who's just a little older than you, sure has a great little figure and how does she do that?

No. The situation I am speaking of is that of true balding, as measured from the time a man consciously combs his hair in a way designed to camouflage it, which, everyone knows, doesn't work.

From that moment on, a man is on a solitary, lonely path. This is a road he must go down alone.

For once a man calls attention to his balding by trying to hide it, he cuts himself off from all further discussion of his hair. I have never known one man to ask another, "What do you think? Should I part my hair back here about where my brain stem ends and bring it all forward and cover all this empty space between my eyebrows and the back of my skull?"

It just doesn't happen. We men just don't share personal stuff like that.

Sex? Yeah.

What a ditz your ex-wife is and how much you hate her lawyer? Easy. One beer and that conversation flows like water. But balding and what you do about it? Never. We do not speak of it.

First of all, you just don't want to put a friend on the spot with the question, "Do I look stupid combing these last few hairs from earlobe to earlobe and gluing them down with petroleum jelly?"

And does anyone want to just volunteer the observation that someone's hair looks a lot like a weather satellite picture of a hurricane?

So balding is something a man must endure in solitude. It is the look of age that he must face in the mirror every morning. Judging from the number of married men with a few lonely strands gooped together and arcing across some vast empty cerebral cortex cover, we can safely assume most men don't even talk to their wives about it.

We don't even talk about it when it's impossible to ignore.

I was riding in a car with a friend who parted his hair just above the ear and carefully combed it up, forward, over, back and down to the other ear. It was like all the hair on his head was hinged at the part. Suddenly, the window opened and it sort of flopped over on the hinge and hung there next to his ear like a robin's nest made of industrial grade steel wool.

He just flipped it back in place like it was a hat while everybody else concentrated on passing traffic. No one said a word.

And what about wigs? Does anybody look at Burt Reynolds anymore without staring at his hairline?

Who wants that? And if you have a wig, when do you put it on? At what point in a dating relationship does one take it off? "Excuse me, but because you might mess up my hair in the heat of passion, I'll just take it off and set it over here."

The odd thing, of course, is that most men wear hair pieces or try to cover up their balding pates because they think being bald makes them less attractive. But that may not be true.

On a talk show recently, the actor who played Guido the Pimp in "Risky Business" – a hard working actor, if ever there was one – and a bald actor – asked the women in the audience if they liked bald men. The audience of women applauded wildly, so he took off his hair.

What a great moment. And what he demonstrated was that it doesn't matter. Trying to look like we have more hair doesn't make us look better, anymore than wearing shorts to cover up fat thighs makes women look thinner. We are who we are, aging, paunchy, balding, fat thighs and all.

And I suspect we'd all be a lot happier if we just could accept the way we look; especially if there isn't anything we can do about it anyway.

Which is all well and good until you look at all that hair in the brush each morning and decide maybe today isn't the day you unhinge your carefully shaped, sprayed down hair, and show the world the real top of your head. Not as long as there's any hair left.

Because being bald may not be so bad, but going bald is the pits.

Memory Black Holes

Astronomers and astrophysicists are still debating whether or not black holes exist. You know: where theoretically, at least, a star collapses in on itself until its gravity is so strong that nothing, not even light can escape.

What a dumb question.

Of course there are black holes.

I've got several in my brain alone. One has a sign in front of it that says "Names."

It's blacker and deeper than the one named, "Short-Term Memory."

It's pretty clear to me that the wrong scientists are looking for black holes in the wrong place.

This is a job for a psychologists and neurosurgeons. Find out where the names of people you've just been introduced to go, and you'll probably be able to pinpoint the location of a black hole.

I really admire people who have a knack for remembering names. There are certain tricks to it, and I've been told what they are, but they usually don't work for me. More often than not, I am saying to myself, "Now try to remember this person's name," at the moment I am introduced; and since I can't listen to myself think and someone else talk at the same time, their name slides into the black hole. Goodbye!

The other problem with memory tricks is I forget them. This may not be entirely my fault. It may be genetic. My father once forgot a book he had been reading on the bus. The name of the book was, "How to Develop a Super Power Memory." That's a true story.

So maybe this is just a family thing.

But I don't think so.

I don't think I'm alone in forgetting people's names.

Most names I forget immediately. I mean, right now.

Two seconds after hearing a name, it can be spiraling into the black hole, and gone forever. This normally is not a big problem because, in all likelihood, the person I have just met has forgotten my name, too. So when we part, we use name avoidance phrases like, "It was nice meeting you," as opposed to, "It was nice meeting you, Ron."

This name avoidance technique falls apart like so much Bayer Aspirin in water, however, if you happen to have the misfortune to still be talking to the person you've just met when a friend of yours walks up. Because social custom dictates that you must introduce them.

Under the pressure of these situations, I have been known to forget the names of everyone concerned.

This is a very awkward situation for everybody, and one in which I often seem to find myself. The new person doesn't get introduced and is standing in social limboland, beginning to wonder if maybe they've stumbled into a conversation that they are specifically not intended to hear, like say, whether or not next Friday is going to be their last day at work, so they don't know if they should exit, which is awkward, or stay and chance hearing bad news.

The person you just met probably doesn't know if you know this person, so they don't know if they should say anything. And you, who can't remember either of their names just wish they would both go away so you could go talk to your wife, who undoubtedly has a better head for names than you do and could tell you who all these people are. Again.

The thing to do, of course, is try to get both parties to introduce themselves to each other; but sometimes that can be tricky.

What I do is begin with a long winded apology about how I thought they both knew each other and how I've been rude all my life; and I figure if I keep going like that for a while, they'll both jump in with their names and get me off the hook.

It usually works.

My wife has learned to recognize the signs that I am falling, body and soul, into my own memory black hole, and she will pull me out by introducing herself to the person whose name I forget. When that happens, I am extremely grateful.

The Black Hole for Names must be hard to find because it floats around in your brain. Either that or names that we know float around and occasionally drop into it.

There's nothing quite so disconcerting as seeing someone come walking up to you whom you know – maybe quite well – and suddenly realize that his or her name has momentarily evaporated from the memory banks.

You never know what to do in those times, do you? Especially if you know them well enough that you shouldn't be forgetting their name.

When I think that is happening to someone with my name, I try to work my name or my wife's name into the conversation real quick.

This may sound artificial, but trust me, to the person who is looking at you and nodding, and right behind his eyes his brain is screaming, "What is this guy's name!?" they'll never notice the artifice.

To prevent black hole doom, my wife and I try to review the names of people we are apt to forget on our way to company picnics, Christmas parties and such.

"Dave is married to Becky, and Ed's wife is Debbie."

Usually that is enough to get us through the evening. Plus, we now have a standing policy to mention each other's names in the presence of people who might not have reviewed our names on their way to wherever we are.

The really odd thing about a memory black hole is that certain names that should go into it don't. This is why you inexplicably remember the name of someone's husband you met ten years ago and haven't seen since.

Scientists tell us that the gravity in a black hole is so great that not even light can escape from it. But occasionally, apparently, a name does.

One year during the Bloomsday run, I ran past a couple who live on the course and were having a race party. I met them once, fifteen years before, through a friend who had to stop by their house (that house) to pick something up. Against all odds, both of their names popped into my head as I ran along.

As I passed, I couldn't resist yelling at them, "Hey Melvie, hey Robert, how're you doing?" as if I were their best friend.

They waved back at me with those big, there-goes-a-friend-of-ours- waves you give to runners, and then their smiles became frozen and perplexed, and I saw them turn to each other and ask in unison, "Who the heck is that?"

It was just me.

A face from the black hole of their memory; the one with the sign in front of it that says, "Names."

Surfing the Net

I have some bad news. My wife is about to become a widow.

Again.

She was a widow once before. A volleyball referee widow. For about 12 weeks each year, I would be gone just about every night calling a volleyball match somewhere.

"See you for Thanksgiving?" she would ask plaintively at the end of August. "Sure you will, honey," I would say. "If the NCAA doesn't call."

Now, there are lots of different types of widows out there. NFL widows. Ski patrol widows. Street rod widows. ("I'll be out in the garage for a bit, okay, Hon?" "Yeah, fine. See you next Wednesday.")

Some activities just eat up a lot of time.

And I have discovered the new grand champion of all time eaters.

Something that takes more time than building a street rod?

Yes. Surfing the Internet.

I have surfed the Internet. And I'm here to tell you guys, it's cool. How cool? This is a marriage-wrecker, that's how cool. (I can almost hear you guys responding: Whoa! That's really cool.)

Now, I don't mean to imply that I'm the Big Kahuna of Internet surfing or anything; I'm not. I'm not even the Little Kahuna of Internet surfing. Figuratively speaking, I've only just gotten my feet wet, but I can tell you, it's cool. Even for a techno-idiot like me.

Or maybe more appropriately, <u>especially</u> for a techno-idiot like me.

For instance, I now have an e-mail address.

I don't know what it is or how to use it, but I have one.

And I can send e-mail. You know how on Morning Edition they say, "e-mail us at something, something, something dot something, at NPR dot org dot something?" Well, I can do that now!

Of course, there is one problem: There is no phone book for e-mail and no "Information" as near as I can tell.

There is some logic to the addresses; but logic has never been one of my strong points, so that doesn't help me much. Plus your e-mail address has to do with what service gets you on the net; so without that information, you're pretty well stuck. My nephew has been on the Internet for years, but I don't know what his e-mail address is, so I can't e-mail him to ask him how to do e-mail.

Hence, the paradox: Before you e-mail someone something through the phone lines, you have to call them to get their e-mail address.

But that's neither here nor there.

The point is, now I can do e-mail. At least, I could if I knew how.

Now, I know that some of you wife-types are probably asking the practical question, "Can't you just pick up the phone and call him?"

Well, yeah, you can, but how cool is that?

Plus you know all those Internet web site addresses that you are starting to see at the bottom of advertising? That WWW-slash slash slash stuff? I can go there and see those.

I realize that it is advertising that's giving me directions to where I go to get more advertising. But hey, I'm in advertising. For us, this is a dream come true. Besides, who ever said any of this would make sense?

There are a few things you should know getting on the net.

The first is: to do it, you have to buy a big, fast, expensive computer. And it doesn't matter if you already have a big fast computer because of the first law of cyberspace: "Whatever you've got isn't big enough or fast enough to do whatever it is you want to do next."

Next, you have to think of your computer as a $2500 telephone.

Which means you have to get a new phone line, which the nice folks at the phone company will be delighted to put in for a modest installation charge and a monthly fee.

Then, you need to join some sort of service that connects you and your computer to the Internet.

You also have to be emotionally prepared for the possibility that you'll have to take remedial Internet lessons from some kid who looks like he's skipping junior high school and who is apt to have little patience for adults he considers to be computer-challenged.

But you do all that, and one day, you're in. And what you're in is a whole new world. And one that is growing and changing daily. Hourly.

And that eats more time than any computer game ever thought about eating.

You go up to do a little exploring, and the next thing you know, it's midnight, everybody's gone to bed, and you're not close to wanting to stop.

The classic widow-maker. An Internet widow.

But can't my wife surf the Internet too?

Well, yeah, but if she did that, what would I do?

Snowblower Rules

Yesterday, Thursday, December 5th, was a day of Male One-ness.

A time when all men in the northwest rose from their beds, looked outside at the snow, calculated the days left until the middle of April, and shared one common thought. "I need a bigger snowblower."

The kind of snowblower you have says a lot about what kind of man you are. Or aren't.

On the one extreme, there are the anti-snowblower types.

Anti-snowblowers tend to be gamblers or macho types. Sometimes both at the same time.

The gambler simply plays the odds and figures that in seven out of ten winters, you don't really need a snowblower for more than a few days, and that anyone can get through a few days. These are the same people who don't get their air conditioning fixed in the summer on the principle that you only really need it a few days out of the summer and so why spend the money?

The other anti-snowblower type is the guy who likes shoveling.

These are the people that face whatever nature throws at them with disdain, secure in the knowledge that there is no drift that they can't shovel through, drive over or just ignore until it goes away.

On the other end of the spectrum are the snowslingers. Guys who know that real snow takes a real machine to clear away. They know the big snow is coming. It's just a matter of time. But when it comes, they are going to be ready.

So they buy a big machine. Electric start, reverse, chains, headlights – something that will throw snow not just off your driveway, but clear across the street onto your neighbor's driveway. We're talking something that will grind up and spit out everything from ice and snow to small trees and unfortunate game animals, if you can get close enough.

The true snowslinger buys his machine in August. And then he waits. (Part of the anticipation is knowing The Rule of the Dominant Snowblower: He with the largest snowblower clears everybody's driveway in the whole neighborhood. Contrary to what it seems, this is a <u>good</u> rule.)

Now overlaying the male self-image part of the equation is the issue of how much snow do you have to throw? Some people only have a sidewalk to clear, and anything mechanical seems like overkill.

This is where the law of expanding concrete comes in. This law states that every new house you buy will have more flat concrete in driveways, walkways, patios and decks than the house before.

About the third move, even an anti-snowblower has a little epiphany – a little moment where somehow, all the reasons why shoveling snow has hitherto before been such a noble cause, fall away – and he is struck with the overwhelmingly simple thought that shoveling snow, when you could have a machine do it, is really stupid.

The exact words that often occur to men in this situation are, "This is stupid."

Sometimes, the agent of change is marriage and having a wife.

Women have an entirely different idea of how much snow on a driveway is acceptable to walk through than men. This is because not very many men wear high heels. Or pumps. Or skirts. Or dresses.

And for reasons that I suspect have to do with testosterone levels as well as the physio-mechanics of the female body versus the male body, women just don't bond with snow shovels like men do and don't have nearly the same level of satisfaction at seeing a driveway that has been cleared by hand.

In fact, they don't have much satisfaction in seeing a driveway cleared by using a snowblower, either. They just want it cleared.

So what used to be an ignorable amount of snow in a pre-married state suddenly becomes something that has to be dealt with post-marriage. And before long, the idea of owning a snowblower begins to look pretty good.

So you buy a snowblower. And unless you are making the transition from shoveler directly to neighborhood snowslinger, you buy just enough snowblower to get by.

And then one day it snows. And snows. And snows. And it's not even December yet. And you're thinking about pushing all that snow around with your just-big-enough snowblower before work, after work, on Saturdays, in the middle of the night, and you think those magic words that will get you into a real snow-blower: "This is stupid."

And it is then we have the moment of male one-ness, and we all simultaneously think the same thought: "I need a bigger snowblower."

So am I going to get a bigger snowblower?

Well, I was, but then it warmed up a bit, and now I'm think-ing, "How bad can it get?"

Gadgets

I'm a real sucker for a gadget.

My wife won't let me go to the fair alone anymore because the last time I went, I came home with a multi-bladed cutting device that slices, dices, chops, peels, makes French fries, gar-nishes, and turns potatoes, tomatoes, apples and onions into the most impressive shapes imaginable.

"But it was only $29.95. And look what it will do!" I said.

Then she hit me with a real low blow. "Show me," she said.

Naturally, I can't ever make it do all those neat things the guy at the fair made it do. Besides, the only thing I ever do with a potato is bake it.

(This point, however, never comes up, because it is consid-ered an irrelevant argument and not allowed in the discussion, the theory being that of course I don't do anything but bake potatoes – I've never had one of these gadgets to help me do anything else. I mean, we wouldn't want to preclude any self-improvement, would we?)

But I forget my culinary limitations under gadget-sales combat conditions. In the frenzy of the demonstration, all I think is, "Wow! I've gotta have one of those!"

One year I almost came back with a gyrocopter. The main reason I didn't, as I recall, was because it was over my credit card limit. Shucks.

I'm not sure what it is about gadgets that is so fascinating. Maybe it's the novelty of the way they work, or the promise of greater convenience, or money saved, or both. I'm not sure. I just know it works.

I can remember going to the Puyallup Fair as a kid and watching my dad watch a demonstration of a new device that whipped just about anything into a marvelously healthy drink. It was called a blender.

And it was marvelous. A gleaming stainless steel canister sitting on top of a powerful little motor that twirled razor sharp blades that turned anything into liquid.

I remember the guy at the fair making juice with carrots, eggs (shells and all!), oranges, tomatoes, liver, wheat germ, and all kinds of stuff I didn't think you could drink, and explaining how, because all the peels, rinds and shells were still in the mix, it was so healthy for you. Mix in a little ice cream and milk, and presto – a health food breakfast that tastes like a milk shake.

My dad saw eternal health.

I saw an endless stream of milk shakes. We both agreed we needed a blender.

So we bought one. Ours had two banks of buttons. It did about twenty things: chop, puree, blend, whip, liquefy. You name it – it had a button for it.

As near as I could tell, though, all it did was go around real fast.

For a while, my dad treated us to the most bizarre milk shakes anybody had to endure. Very healthy, we thought. Raw eggs, milk, wheat bran, powdered liver, ice cream, a little Hershey's Chocolate, whew! Of course, in those days, we didn't know about eggs and salmonella and cholesterol and fats and all that stuff.

But it didn't matter much, because soon it was making basic milk shakes (which is all I wanted it for all along, anyway) and not long after that, even that stopped, and pretty soon it went beneath the counter and was forgotten.

Which is the down side to gadgets that we always forget. That to get used, we have to make changes in our life-style. And that, for most of us, is real hard to do.

For instance, during the CB radio craze, I just had to have one. I felt so left out, with everybody getting Smokey reports and saying "10-4, Good Buddy," and everything.

Every time I drove past a State Patrol car, I cursed myself for not having one. "I'd have known he was there, if I'd only had a CB," I'd say to myself. I'd think of all the conversations I was missing, all of the risk I was taking being out on the road with no way to call for help, should my car break down.

Well, it was just not a tolerable situation. (Again, the practical argument that I had never, ever broken down on the road and needed to call for help was not entertained.)

So, like every other driver in America, I went on down to Radio Shack and bought one.

For weeks, I listened in on some guy with a base station who must have had 10,000 watts of power, as he talked to darn near every trucker who rumbled down I-5 and I-90.

A couple of times I was tempted to get on and talk, but, (and I know this is hard to believe) I couldn't think of anything to say.

Once I actually pressed down the microphone button but I choked up and no sound would come out. Mike fright. Me. And I used to be a deejay. Plus, I couldn't think of a clever name to call myself.

I actually took the radio with me on a couple of trips, but my mike fright was so complete, that eventually, I just stopped.

So now my CB radio sits on a shelf in my garage, a testament to my inability to deny myself a fad gadget. It sits up there next to my Ginsu knives and some parachute luggage I don't use much anymore, and my slicer-dicer.

It was stupid to buy those things. Not at all like this new gadget they're advertising on television, where you buy your food in bulk at really cheap prices and then bag it with this device that vacuum seals it so it stays fresh forever. You can save hundreds of dollars a year with it, and even vacuum seal your clothes and silverware and first aid kits.

Now that makes a lot of sense.

This is one thing I need. I would use it, a lot. Really. I would. And it's only $300.

The only thing is, I'm not sure I have space in my garage for it.

Cool Roof Racks

In 1968 I bought my very first car, a Volkswagen bug.

Before I took it home to show my parents what they had co-signed for, before I took it to my girlfriend's house to show her the right seat where she would spend, I was sure, countless blissful hours, even before I took it for its maiden cruise of my Seattle haunts of Shilshole, The Bluff, Zesto's, and other Ballard hangouts, I took it to the local sports shop and bought an A&T ski rack for it.

And I put it on.

This was in August.

I didn't actually go home and load up my skis, although I was tempted. Intuitively, I knew that other skiers would recognize our brotherhood simply by the presence of the rack. Those who didn't understand the significance of a ski rack were not worth trying to impress. Perhaps they would be impressed by the car.

As everyone knows, a car is not mere transportation. It is a statement of who you are, of your status in life, and a lot more. The significance of the car you drive is almost Biblical; after all, we buy a car in our own image and likeness. We make our choices based on what we can afford and what we want people to know or think about us.

And the system works. There is a nice symmetry to it. It's like two coordinates on the social status map of life: How Much Money You Have and What You Buy With It.

Between the two, you can plot just about anything you need to know about anyone else.

You know what I mean: a Mercedes says you have money, a BMW says you have intelligence. A Volvo says you have both. A used Chevrolet station wagon says you have neither. It's all a very clear way of communicating a pecking order, and it works everywhere.

Everywhere except in the Northwest, that is.

Here, we're above all that. Just above. In Washington and Oregon with a wealth of opportunity for wind surfing, skiing, kayaking, bicycling, fishing and camping, it's not so much the car that projects your status, as the roof rack on top of it.

And not to put too fine a point on it, but if you're really into roof rack status, real status is denoted by how many attachments your rack has.

Unlike other parts of the country where you are what you drive, in the Northwest, you are what you drive *under*.

That's why it was so important for me to have my ski rack in place as I tooled around Ballard looking for a familiar face to honk at in my new Volksie; I had more identity at stake as a skier than I did merely as the owner of a new car. But the two together – a new rack and a new car, that was truly Nirvana.

Using roof racks as a status symbol is something of an out-doorsman's tradition. And as a dedicated roof racker, naturally I'm all for it.

The fact that it plays havoc on the entire automobile-based status system by which we all make our snap judgments about people is, according to roof-rackers, at least, a small price to pay.

What roof rackers are saying with their car and rack is quite different from non-rackers. Money is not the point. At least not the main point. Rather, a roof rack communicates an elitist, healthy, sports-oriented, granola based lifestyle. We think.

Instead of telling the world, "I make enough to afford a BMW," we roof -rackers are telling the world we pass, "This is what I do," and then we look at those without roof racks and add to ourselves, "and you don't."

That makes us feel infinitely superior. Which, of course, is what displaying your status is all about.

The nice thing about roof racks is they level the status playing field.

Any roof-racker will tell you that a beat up Dodge Valiant with a Yakima rack and a kayak on top confers the same status as a bald 450 SL. In roof-rackdom, that's just the way it is.

When one combines a beater car with an expensive rack, you get a kind of reverse snobism with a heavy dose of swagger thrown in. The roof-rackers sit there at the light, scoping out the expensive cars next to them, muttering, "Yeah, you may put pig valves in people's hearts, but I can do a water start in a forty knot wind in The Gorge, and which do you think makes for more scintillating party conversation?"

Like everything else in life, macho roof-rack-one-upmanship is not entirely fair. It favors activities that require bulky equip-ment.

You don't get much more gutsy than rock climbing, but unfortunately, roof racks don't come with piton holders.

And consider the world's runners: what are they to do? Strap their Nikes to a cross bar? And how would you like to see someone's Speedo stretched from rack to rack? How would you like to be down-range when it twanged off?

Clearly that's a market waiting to be developed. In the meantime, those folks will just have to rely on bumper stickers to assuage their identity crises.

Today, you don't buy a rack so much as a system. By changing the attachments, you can leave a rack on all year long. In this way, the rack becomes a permanent part of the top of your car, which, given how much you can spend for all the attachment goodies, is just fine with most roof rackers.

There is a downside, of course. All these spendy options have created an internal pecking order among roof rackers themselves. It's not unusual to hear a Yakima racker explain why the equivalent Thule is not satisfactory, and vice versa.

The nuances of bike racks illustrates the point. These are the ones that look as if they're made of short lengths of gutter, or like you're hauling around an upside down ironing board on top of your car.

Among the most popular configurations are the kind where the bike sits up on top with both wheels on and the kind where the front wheel comes off and the bike sits low in front at a rakish angle. A Fork Mount System, to those in the know.

"This is the kind to get," a friend assured me, patting his fork mount. "It's fast, it's clean. It looks neat. The other kind looks like some nerdo parked his bike on top of your car."

"What kind of bike do you have?" I asked.

"I haven't actually bought one yet," he said. "After I bought the rack, I couldn't afford one. But I've got my eye on a mountain bike."

It's a point well taken. Once you've entered roofrackdom, what the rack actually carries is somewhat secondary to the image it projects every moment it sits on top of your car.

A kayaker told me how relieved he was to finally get a set of boat cradles for his rack. "Now I don't have to carry my boat around for people to know I white-water," he said.

I knew just what he meant. For years, my kayak was a permanent fixture on top of my Volksie. If people thought I had just come down from running the Middle Fork of the Snoqualmie River, well, that was okay with me.

In fact, like driving a car you can't really afford, sometimes that's the whole point. Like any automobile status symbol, roof racks can be used to deceive as well as haul.

My VW was sold after ten years of dedicated service. The ski rack and roof rack went with it. Every now and then I see it. The person who owns it now has a nice Thule rack with a wind surfer permanently mounted on it.

It looks just right.

Global Warming

I'm suddenly very concerned about global warming.

I'm also a bit embarrassed about global warming. And I'll tell you frankly, I'm a little afraid. And if you're a man, especially a married man, you ought to be afraid, too.

By now, you've probably heard about the cowpie case?

That's the lawsuit where some environmental group in Washington D.C. is suing the United States Department of the Interior, The Agriculture Department and the Energy Department. The theory is the sheep and cattle out there on the lone prairie may account for as much as 15 percent of atmospheric methane. Methane, you may remember from your high school chemistry and biology class, is a gas produced as a by-product of digestion. It may also be a contributor to global warming, which is the subject of the lawsuit.

Why a group in Washington D.C. cares about sheep breaking wind on the pampas of Wyoming is another question, and one for which I don't have an answer. You'd think they'd start with a suit naming members of Congress and the federal bureaucracy for their nauseating output, wouldn't you? But that's another commentary.

The suit says, basically, that these departments have failed to evaluate their programs in light of this startling scientific information on what all this methane produced by all those sheep and cows grazing on all that United States-owned prairie land may be doing to speed up global warming. And that that's intolerable and has to stop. Or start, depending upon how you phrase it.

(This is an aside, but one of the wonderful things about living in the United States is that we have all these high-priced lawyers and judges grappling with problems like this. I mean, can you imagine anybody in the Soviet Union bringing a suit like this? Not that their legal system would allow it, but even if it could, they are so backward, even in the 1990s, that they can't even get a halfway decent crop out of the field and into the stores. And here we are, in a nation where we not only get bumper crops off the field, but we've got enough time left over to argue about whether or not cows grazing on government lands are passing too much gas! In a thousand years, historians may well point to this lawsuit as the zenith of American Agri-business. "Having fed the world, they turned their attention to the problem of bovine gaseous emissions." On the other hand, the Russians may hear about this, and just conclude that we're all nuts.)

But, back to the subject at hand.

So, why should we men be concerned about this lawsuit?

Well, figure it out.

If all the flatulent sheep in Wyoming are contributing to global warming, how long do you think it's going to take for them to ask the same question about all the husbands in, say, Los Angeles, or Seattle, or Spokane? Or, for that matter, all the men west of the Mississippi?

And if they are right about the effect of methane on the atmosphere, I will be the first to admit, that I have been a contributor to global warming myself. And I feel real bad about that.

But this lawsuit; can you see where this is going?

It could change the whole social landscape.

Think back to when you were first dating. Did you do any global warming in the presence of your dates? Of course not. I mean, unless you went to WSU or something. But I mean, generally speaking, men don't do that in front of their dates.

We have some couth, after all.

But then you got married. And things changed, didn't they? It starts innocently enough. You share a bathroom in your first apartment. She puts on her makeup in front of you. You brush your teeth in front of her. The little mysteries between men and women begin to break down.

And then one day, about the time you discover that she really prefers to sleep in flannel, she discovers that you can warm the globe. *On demand!* And not only that, it's a talent you're kind of proud of.

And the next thing you know, you don't care if she's in the room or not when you feel like warming the globe. Or maybe you care, but global warming is something you just can't seem to do much about.

You really know that you are married, and all the mysteries are gone, after dinner with friends. It's been a wonderful evening with good food and wine, over in someone's tiny little apartment which the women have all decided is "darling," as in "Oh, those curtains are so darling," and when you finally leave, you get in the car and you can hardly bend because your stomach feels like a timpani with the skin stretched a bit too tight. When you tap on your tummy, it sounds like this: Toongk, toongk toongk.

Clearly, it's a little time for some global warming. Right then and there. In the car. Baby, the honeymoon is over.

"Do you have to do that?" your bride says.

"Yeah. Why, don't you?" you ask.

Of course, the answer is, women don't. At least, not as much as men. Men warm the globe the first thing in the morning, after every meal, during football on TV, and anytime they have had to sit for more than fifteen minutes at a stretch. Nobody knows why this is.

But here's the point: If this lawsuit wins, all husbands are at risk.

If this lawsuit wins, your wife might be able to slap an injunction on you every time you feel the need to heat up the globe a little bit. "Don't do it, George, don't make me call the police."

This group in Washington that is bringing the suit wants us to stop eating beef. I'm not sure what they think we are going to eat when we all have our kebab attacks, or what they're going to put in the middle of a Big Mac, but that's not the point. If they succeed, can husbands, as a target to be eliminated, be far behind?

Will young men who want to be married have to go through some sort of testing like cars now do in this state? "Just pull up to the yellow line, keep your heart going at a fast idle, and we're just going to measure your carbon monoxide output. Whoa! You must drink a lot of beer!"

Will couples who want to have baby boys have to file environmental impact statements first?

Clearly there're a lot of unanswered questions here.

Now, understand, I am against global warming, and I apologize if I have inadvertently contributed to it. But I think this lawsuit takes us in a dangerous direction.

After all, if they make global warming illegal, what will we men do first thing in the morning?

Asking Directions

In virtually every culture in the world, men have some rite of passage into adulthood. The passage defines what it is to be a man. In America, being a man means never having to ask for directions.

We can take direction. Men stay in school and learn and learn and learn – some would say right up to the moment when we know everything.

And all athletics is based on the giving and taking of directions. That's why we have coaches.

Speaking of coaches, and taking directions, how many of you men have been lucky enough to be your wife's "coach" for Lamaze? It's kind of a misnamed position, isn't it?

You: "Breathe, honey."

Your wife: "I AM breathing, you bolt."

The problem with Lamaze is they call you a coach when, in fact, you're really sort of a useless assistant. If you were a coach, you'd wear a whistle and start every sentence with, "Okay, listen up!"

You say that to a woman in hard labor with contractions coming every three minutes, and she's going to tell you to stuff it, whether she loves you or not.

It's a wonder of nature that in the middle of the miracle and spiritual event of child birth, a woman is able to give her Lamaze "coach" clear and precise directions like, "Shut up. And while you're at it, why don't you grab your upper lip and pull it over your forehead and see how good this feels? Now, go find a doctor and get me some drugs."

Which, as the useless assistant you are, you do. Which proves a simple point: men can follow directions.

But will a man ever ask for directions?

Not voluntarily.

And I don't mean just driving around looking for an address that doesn't exist or looking for a freeway exit your wife knows you passed four miles back, either.

Just ask an experienced surgical nurse how often doctors get lost doing surgery and won't ask for help when they should.

Personally, I think it's a hormonal thing. I think testosterone blocks our ability to ask for help. We see it as a sign of weakness. And most men would rather be dead than weak.

It certainly isn't new. Some people believe that Moses wandered in the desert for forty years with the Children of Israel because he refused to ask anyone for directions.

Typical man.

Makes sense to me: look at the map. It's just not that far from Egypt to Israel. You could crawl across the Sinai in less than forty years.

I wonder if Moses said to his wife, "What do you want me to do? Ask the locals? What's a Bedouin know about The Promised Land? For all we know, they're the Pharaoh's soldiers out here for a little R and R. And what am I supposed to ask? How far is the Red Sea? And do you think we'll need reservations when we get there? There's about six hundred thousand of us. And while we're at it, have you seen any unexplained burning bushes or stone tablets with Hebrew writing laying around?"

And I wonder if Moses' wife ever said, "Never mind. Pull over. I'll ask."

The Bible is silent on that question.

Most of the time, not asking for directions is just plain dumb. But it probably has a good side to it. Serendipity. You know, discovering things by accident. Like discovering the world's most powerful antibiotic while you're looking for Superglue but not following directions.

After all, if we all asked for and followed directions, it wouldn't take that long before we would all be piling up at the end of the road of human knowledge, would it?

Did Christopher Columbus ask for directions? No way. It was Isabella who kept saying, "You want to go east by sailing west? Chris, why not just go east by sailing east? Wouldn't that make more sense?"

Not to a man.

Of course, it was the ever practical Isabella who gave him three leaky ships and prisoners for a crew. That would be like NASA getting astronauts from San Quentin. "So what if he sails off the end of the earth? That'll teach him not to ask for directions."

But he didn't.

He didn't get to India, either, but we men like to consider that a relatively insignificant point in the story.

I wonder if Isabella knocked him down on his performance rating for that?

"Thank you for the new continent and all it's wealth, but you were after SPICES!"

I don't know what it is in a man that makes it so hard to ask for directions. I don't even know why we find it so hard to even look at directions.

Is there a man who has ever put a Christmas toy together without a few parts leftover? I doubt it. (When I put together a Christmas toy, I am like a surgeon: "Phillips head screwdriver. Crescent wench. Ball peen hammer." My philosophy is whatever won't go together with a screwdriver and wrench will with the help of a ball peen hammer.)

My wife and child like to suggest that I look at the directions, but I'd rather look at all the parts and just jump right in. It's the man in me.

Most of us don't even read the safety directions that come with the power tools we cherish so much. That could account for why any given number of men is apt to have fewer than the allotted number of fingertips than an equal number of women.

Maybe it's as simple as a man's got to do what a man's got to do.

Yeah.

Even if he doesn't know what it is, where it is, how to get there, or how to do it.

Big Boys' Toys

The bumper sticker read, "He who dies with the most toys, wins."

Now, that's a philosophy of life I can get a handle on; I can understand it right down in my bones. Plus, it seems uniquely American, somehow, and that makes me feel good, too.

It's not wishy-washy like "Don't worry, be happy," which has a nice ring to it, but, when all is said and done, really doesn't tell you what to do when you see a competition water-ski on sale for only two hundred thirty-five dollars.

"Don't worry, be happy" sounds like something Aristotle might have said had Alfred E. Newman been his teacher instead of Plato.

One can only wonder what Plato and Aristotle might have come up with had they had, say, a middle class, 1960s California upbringing, a surfboard and a mountain bike.

The collecting of toys is, I admit, something of a middle class, capitalistic, and hedonistic approach to life, but most of us baby-boomers don't have any great problem with that. After all, we were raised in the I-want-it-now, instant gratification '60s and the I'll-pay-for-it-later '70s, and hedonism was a big part of that era.

Remember, "If it feels good, do it."

Of course, now that we're all adults, and we have children of our own, we have all recanted that particular philosophy. Now we say something more like, "If it feels good, wait until you're an adult; and then, maybe, you can do it in moderation."

Kind of like what our parents told us.

The same thing is happening with rock and roll.

I find myself wincing a little bit when my favorite oldies station plays Jan and Dean singing about racing to Dead Man's Curve, and the Beach Boys sing, "She'll Have Fun, Fun, Fun Till Her Daddy Takes The T-Bird Away."

Somehow, songs about drag racing, lying to your parents and driving off cliffs into oblivion seemed okay when I was 18, but now that I have an eight-year old of my own who will be driving someday, I would just as soon those songs disappeared from the air forever, and the sooner the better.

But back to toys.

I think there's a lot of truth in the old saying that the only difference between a boy and a man is the price of his toys. There are other differences, of course, but they pale in comparison.

I think in a thousand years, what they're going to say about this time in America is, "Boy, did those guys know how to play." The Ancient Romans may have invented partying, but it was the baby boomers who raised playing with expensive toys to an art form.

Take water sports, for instance: as recently as the early fifties, there was a limited choice in boats. Boats were cruisers, or oversized rowboats mostly used for fishing. What we might call a ski boat today didn't really exist then.

Today, boats come in all sizes, shapes, materials and prices. You can buy boats that are only good for pulling waterskiers, or boats made just for catching bass. If you want to do it on the water, there's a specialized boat for it. And boats only begin to cover water toys.

There is a whole class of jet ski's, a myriad of wind-driven things, from sailboats to Hobie's to windsurfers. Even water skis have evolved into kneeboards, wave runners and who knows what.

Now, I ask you, do the Russians have anything like that? I don't think so. Would they like to? Of course they would. Fun is fun. And we're way ahead of them in this category.

So, I think we should export our mania for toys. After all, we seem to have exported other parts of our culture: McDonald's hamburgers, Levi's 501 jeans and rock and roll, to name a few. I think there's an opportunity here to corner the Black Sea market in open bow boats or be the Jeff Jobe or Wally Burr of Mother Russia.

If we exported our toys instead of things like weapons technology, we might be able to help some of those countries where the male population is wound a little too tight, you know what I mean?

For instance, imagine the effect if we gave every child in the Middle East an American-made skateboard, a frisbee, a Walkman and a tape of The Beach Boys' Greatest Hits. Pretty soon they'd all be saying, "Surf's Up" and calling each other Big Kahuna and stuff.

If we gave every man under 50 an all-terrain vehicle, on their days off they'd all be out there tearing around the desert, having a great time, and the idea of becoming a martyr in a war with the Great Satan, who, by the way, has all the spare parts for all the toys they are now addicted to, might not seem like such a hot idea.

Plus they'd want to buy lots of big 4 x 4 pickup trucks from Detroit to carry their toys back and forth in, and then they'd need big Koss speakers from Milwaukee for the rock and roll they'd want to play in their tape players, and pretty soon they'd have huge rock concerts, where they'd all get permanent ear damage, so a whole lawyer class would have to spring up to sue all their rock and roll stars and promoters, and with a burgeoning lawyer class, everybody would be suing everybody like we do here, which would open up a huge growth market in liability insurance ... well, before long, it would be just like America, wouldn't it? A nation of big toys.

I think somebody should talk to President Clinton about this. I think we're on to something here.

Big boys' toys. For peace.

That has a nice ring to it, doesn't it?

Tipping

I watched his young eyes scan his surroundings. He was trying to get interested in the crayons and coloring project the waitress had left behind, but something on the uncleared tables had him much more interested.

While his parents pondered whether the hunger demon inside wanted sausage and eggs or a waffle, he slipped off his chair and made a quick tour of the almost empty non-smoking section.

You could see the amazement in his eyes. There was money on these tables! Just … lying around.

He moved closer. The table was about eye level to him. It was clear that he had been taught that you didn't take things that didn't belong to you, but he knew a different rule applied to stuff you found.

The question was, was that money left on the table there for the finding? He had probably found money on the floor before that his parents let him keep. Wasn't this the same thing, sort of?

Before he reached for the dollar bill and change he took a last look around.

He and I locked eyes. Slowly and deliberately, I shook my head no. Don't do it, son, my eyes said to him. A little man-to-man communication that said it may not be mine, but it's not yours, either.

He went back to his chair, tugged on his dad's sleeve and, I'm sure, got his first explanation of the curious social custom called tipping.

The same explanation we all got from our parents at about the same age.

The first time I left a tip was probably on a date. In those days, 10 percent was the regulation amount. That was good. I could figure out ten percent of anything. Whether I wanted to leave it behind or not was another question.

And it is a question that has plagued me since.

I have never quite known if leaving a tip is voluntary or obligatory.

And how much is enough? How much is too much? Is there such a thing as too much? (Service workers everywhere are screaming "No! No!, There's no such thing as a tip that's too much.")

Now 15 percent is considered minimal. I wonder who decided that? Dear Abby? Miss Manners? Federated Food Servers of America? I went from being an okay tipper to something of a tightwad overnight. 15 percent? Are you sure? Sure seems like a lot.

Plus, it's harder to figure out.

In some countries, they just add the tip in for you. The gratuitous gratuity.

The first time I saw that, I remember thinking, why don't they just add it to the cost of the food and be done with it?

Personally, in those situations, I'm never sure that I'm not supposed to add a little voluntary tip to the involuntary gratuity that has already been added onto my bill. You'd think by this time in my adult life, I would know this social stuff, but I don't. But then, I don't get out of the country much, either.

In general, my wife and I tend to believe that leaving a tip (in tipping situations) is obligatory, but the amount is discretionary.

That makes tipping, in our case at least, like a little job performance review. If you've ever been though one of those, you can be grateful we don't have to explain our tips.

"Bob, we wanted to go over our tip amount with you. We do this so that you will become a better employee of this establishment and to dispel any notions that you may have that the amount of our tip is in anyway influenced by your sex, race, creed, national origin, sexual persuasion, or, in your case, those dangly earrings.

"Bob, both my wife and I were impressed with the concern and caring you showed when you introduced yourself and asked if we were having a nice day, however, my wife felt that showing us pictures of your kids was a bit much.

"You were a bit slow in getting back to us when we were ready to order, and your explanation of the daily specials was, well, perfunctory, at best, Bob. You did a good job keeping our water glasses filled, and the food was nicely presented. It was a bit slow in coming, but we didn't dock you points for that, even though we felt you could have kept us better informed of the progress of our meal, especially when it got bottlenecked behind a slow cooking fettucini.

"My wife and I split on the compliment to her hair; she liked it, I felt it was obsequious.

"You cleared well and kept the coffee hot for a strong finish in a performance that overall, we felt, lacked polish and real enthusiasm.

"Therefore, we're leaving you 13 point 8 percent. Besides, I don't have any more change, and if I leave another dollar, that would bump you up to 16.5 percent, and, in light of your performance, that hardly seems appropriate, does it?"

Thank goodness we don't have to go through that.

Like everybody else, we just leave the tip, and if we're unhappy about the service, it's low, and we let the server try to figure it out for himself.

Tipping in bars is an altogether different matter, which has more to do with amounts of change left over than actual percentages. Some people feel they win if they manage to drink up all the change so there's nothing left to leave behind.

Not me, of course.

Given how hard waiters and waitresses and barmaids work, I am inclined to tip the full 15%, when I can figure it out, and I try not to penalize the server for things that aren't their fault, like inexperience or bad food. Like most of us, I'm not a big tipper, but I'd like to think that I'm not considered a jerk, either.

Or course, I'll be able to live with being a jerk when the appropriate tip is bumped to 20 percent.

Certification

I had a revelation the other day that made me feel inadequate.

And of all the things that I don't want to feel, inadequate ranks right up there at the top. In fact, being inadequate is just a little worse than being deemed "adequate."

The revelation was I'm not certified.

I can practically hear the collective gasp of amazement out there: you mean, you don't have any letters following your name that start with "C"?

No I don't, but I do have a plan to change that. I'm going to open Doug's Certified Certification Clinic, and I'm going to be my own first customer.

I realized I wasn't certified when one of our former clients, who moved away and has a degree in marketing and used to be the promotions and advertising manager for a major local mall, started adding the letters CMM to his signature. For a while, we all thought it was shorthand for "Call Me Monday" – you know, sort of like, RSVP.

Turns out it stands for Certified Mall Manager. Now when people ask him what he does, he can say, "I'm a CMM." Sounds like maybe he took care of an inadequacy problem, too.

I'm not sure who started all this certification stuff. Perhaps it was accountants. After all, for as long as I can remember there have been CPA firms. Being a CPA differentiates some accountants from other accountants who are not CPAs and who are known condescendingly as "bookkeepers." (That's to their face. Behind their backs they're all called "bean counters" no matter how many letters follow their name.)

About the time I had to send in my first 1040 form, I asked what the difference was between a CPA and a bookkeeper; and I was told the primary difference was $40 and hour. And, you didn't want your taxes done by a bookkeeper.

That was elucidating.

Maybe certification came about because in a lot of professions, you don't need any qualifications to get in.

Advertising for instance. Most of the ad agencies in this town are headed up by people who said, "Gee, today I'm a media salesman; tomorrow I think I'll be an ad agency." And they were. Are.

There are other professions like that. I bought my life insurance from a friend who used to be a bartender. One day he made great coffee nudges. The next, he was figuring out how much money my widow and her new husband would need to live on if I should die.

Made sense to me.

At the time, though, he didn't have any "C" letters after his name; and I must tell you, I didn't miss them. Shows what I know. Now he's a CLU, which I think stands for Certified Life Insurance Understander, which means he understands the difference between term and whole life.

I feel much better now that he's certified so long as he doesn't charge me more for it.

I also feel much better when I take my car in for service and I see the guys in there wearing shirts with little patches running up and down the sleeves declaring that they are a Certified Break Specialist, Certified Front End Specialist, Certified Torque Wrench Specialist. (Some of these guys have to have pretty long arms to wear all the patches that tell you what they are certified to work on.)

All this is reassuring right up to the moment when you're standing there talking to the guy with the clipboard, and you hear one of the mechanics say to him: "Hey Ernie, can I borrow one of your shirts again? I got oil on mine when I took that thingy off that Chevy over there."

Actually, I am a certified volleyball referee. We used to wear patches that indicated what level of play we were qualified to officiate. This year, the national association declared that the patches are gone; and stitched right into the shirt, it says, "Certified Volleyball Official." We're certified apparently, by virtue of wearing the shirt.

So much for certification.

The one thing I have figured out about all this certification stuff is if you're going to be certified, the certification title has to have a ring to it.

Loggers become Certified Tree Fellers. Stockbrokers become Certified Financial Planners. (Well, when you think about it, what else would they be? "Certified Stockbroker" just sort of lays there and dies. And even though everybody invests to make money, "Certified Money-Maker" over-promises and "Certified Money-Loser" more closely defines the investor than the investee. No, Certified Financial Planner is just right.)

Doctors have carried certification to a higher level of sophistication; they are Board Certified in their chosen specialties. Board Certified. Now, that has the ring of authority, doesn't it?

This begs the question: certified by whom? And who certified them to certify someone else? I mean, who is the big Poobah of certification? And if certification means you now know what someone else knows, does that mean certification leads to calcification?

These are deep questions about the C word that, frankly, and certifiably, I don't have the answers to.

I only know a trend when I see it, and adding the word Certified after your name to differentiate yourself from the great unwashed who may have accidentally wandered into your profession is certainly the trendy thing to do.

And for all I know, it may actually mean something.

But that's a finer point I'd rather didn't get in the way of Doug's Certified Certification Clinic, where we will guarantee that all people who successfully pass their certification tests by paying the requisite amount of money (I figure about $500 bucks is just right) will be deemed "board certified" with an appropriately distinctive sounding title.

McDonald's employees will become Certified Culinary Facilitators; newspaper reporters will be Certified Factological Deseminators; elevator repairmen will be Certified Interfloor Transportation Specialists; photographers will be Certified Image Counselors – no, that's already taken by Mary Kay salespeople (or is it the fake fingernail people?). Well, we'll figure out something for photographers.

After all, our motto at Doug's Certified Certification Clinic will be, "To each his own credentials; according to his ability to pay."

Love and Money

My stockbroker sent me a book the other day. It was all about how to invest in stocks and die wealthy (assuming, of course, that you don't first lose your health insurance and then your health, in which case you die poor, no matter what).

The basic premise of the book is that if you buy stocks regularly, over time they will go up, and the compounding effect will make you rich, sort of.

I'm not sure why my broker sent me the book. Maybe she took a look at my account and decided that the $123.78 I invested nine years ago wasn't performing well and it was time I gave her some more money.

She's probably right. According to the book, investing $123.78 in a losing stock once every nine years just isn't regular enough.

I would invest more, but I can't.

And it's not my fault.

I have low self-esteem.

Just kidding. My self-esteem is okay. Except in certain areas, like sex, parenting, income, and looks.

No, the reason I can't invest regularly is the same reason none of us can. Because of the Baby Boomers Fourth Law of Financial Ineptitude, sometimes known as the Men, Money, Love and Chaos Law, which states that when men fall in love, it causes chaos with their money.

(There is a parallel law for women boomers having to do with Nordstrom, fashion cycles, black clothing and the effect of the word "sale" on the pituitary, but I don't want to get into that right now.)

Normally, we men are very prudent with our money. Everybody knows that.

For instance, have you ever known a man who just pulled into any old gas station without regard for the posted price of unleaded self-serve gasoline?

Of course not.

That wouldn't be financially prudent, and we wouldn't die rich if we did that, so we keep driving, looking for another gas station where we can buy gas for maybe a penny a gallon less.

Hey, that's 15 cents a tank for some people. According to the book, if you invest that in the stock market on a regular basis, you will eventually have a lot of money.

But what happens is you've been driving all over town, saving fifteen cents here and fifteen cents there, and just about the time you have a little nest egg to send off to your broker for a little chunk of Disney, you fall in love.

I have to confess, this happened to me just the other day. It shouldn't happen to me. I mean, I'm married, I have a child, I have responsibilities, but ... she was so sexy.

Blonde, good looking, solid body. I mean, I knew I should have stayed away, that she could only mean trouble, but I held her, and she felt beautiful in my arms, and with her voice ringing in my ears, that thing that happens in a man happened, and I knew I had to have her. To hell with my daughter's not-quite-started college savings plan and to the goal of dying rich.

I had to have that guitar.

This is where the chaos comes in. You see, you can't be buying $700 guitars from guys named Gonzo without causing a little chaos in the family budget.

Now, this is made all the more complex by the fact that I don't really play the guitar. I know about three chords. So buying a new guitar doesn't make a whole lot of sense.

But that kind of rational thought rarely gets in the way of a man in love.

My wife was standing with me at the time. She's pretty good at spotting when I'm falling in love, and she knows exactly what to say. Now, if I were her and she were me in this situation, I would say to me, "Look, let's talk about this. First of all, you're not Jimmy Buffet, and you're never gonna be. Second, you don't play this thing. Third, you're darn near tone deaf, and fourth, if we were to take your long-term musical potential and then double it just for good measure and then match that with the quality instrument you should play, you shouldn't spend more than 75 bucks on a guitar, which makes this purchase nominally a thousand percent over budget. And lastly, I'm sick and tired of you buying stuff that means I'm going to die poverty-stricken in my old age!"

But instead, she says, "If you want it, get it." I hate it when she does that – making me completely responsible for my own spending.

About this time, Gonzo, who has done this before says, "This is an investment grade guitar. It will only go up in value."

"Did you hear that? An investment grade guitar! Not some piece of trash! It'll go up in value. It's better than investing in stocks. Plus, if I learn just two more chords, I'll be able to play "Cheeseburger in Paradise" on it and be just like Jimmy Buffet. I'll probably die young, anyway, so who cares about being rich?"

It could be worse, I suppose. Some men have that kind of reaction when they walk into an Acura showroom. "$35,000 for a Legend? I'll take it! It's Japanese! It'll last forever and go up in value! It's better than owning 35 thousand dollars of General Motors stock!"

Tolstoy once said, "Where there is love, there is God." Writing today, he would more likely say, "Where there is love, there is financial chaos."

I should tell you that I didn't buy the guitar. I have learned that it's better if I don't buy things when I'm foaming at the mouth like a horse that's been ridden too hard.

But I think I'm going to, and here's the justification: About four years ago, I wanted to invest a thousand dollars in Chrysler when it was trading at about 34. Today, it's down to 8. By not investing, I've saved 750 dollars. And it's with that money I saved, that I'm going to buy the guitar.

I figure when you're a savvy investor like me, you can afford some of the nicer things in life.

Besides, I'm just sure I can learn "Cheeseburger in Paradise" with that guitar.

Old Husbands' Tales

Why is it, in this day of sexual equality, that old wives still get all the credit for passing along faulty information?

How come there are old wives' tales but not old husbands' tales?

Historically, some of it makes sense. For instance, I can understand how old wives get tagged with the old wives' tale that getting chilled causes colds, because for centuries old wives were the caregivers of the kids with those colds.

Now we know that bad morals, evil thoughts and passing germs by contact causes colds. But the old wives' tales about getting chilled persists.

(Personally, when I hear an old wife say to her child, "Put on your coat! You'll catch cold!" I figure old wives deserve the abuse they get from old wives' tales.)

But what about "A clean car runs better?"

Why should old wives get credit for that little bit of arcania? Do you see old wives outside on Saturday morning before a rainstorm hosing down the family minivan, telling their daughters, "A car runs better when it's clean"?

Heck no: that is clearly a male thing, an old husbands' tale, and I think it's time we old husbands got credit for it.

There's a lot of old husbands' tales floating around that we don't get credit for. For instance, there's an old husbands' tale that says that hair you buy in the store looks as good as the hair you used to grow. Or, that store-bought hair looks better than simply being bald. This old husbands' tale persists even in the face of irrefutable visual evidence that indicates that false hair looks like, well, false hair.

Then there's the notion that says that bald men are more virile. Virile than whom? Men with hair? Than themselves when they had hair? Clearly, this is an old husbands' tale. (Although, I've got to tell you, the more my forehead creeps back to meet the bald spot on the back of my head, the more I am inclined to believe this virility thing just might be true.)

A lot of people think there's an old husbands' tale that says that coats and shoes left on the living room floor are invisible.

Well, there isn't.

It's the truth. I certainly never see them. Do you? I'd be willing to bet you don't if you're a man. Or a child. I know my daughter never sees anything on the living room floor – coats, shoes, school bags, candy wrappers, stuffed animals, Teen Magazines, empty cassette holders, half-eaten bowls of macaroni and cheese; the list goes on and on. She doesn't see any of it. It <u>must</u> be invisible. It's the only explanation for that stuff being there.

Some old husbands' tales are pretty benign, but others aren't.

Those are the ones that die very hard.

When I was growing up, little girls couldn't play in Little League Baseball. And there was no such thing as girls' basketball. And the thought of girls playing soccer, which not even very many boys did, was unthinkable. This ban on girls in sports was generally upheld by invoking the old husbands' tale that sports wasn't good for girls. It was bad for their female bodies.

This, in the face of the assumption that sports was good for boys and not harmful to their little bodies.

Now, of course, most everything that boys do in sports, girls do. Still, there are some old husbands out there who cling to the notion that there is something not quite right about girls doing sports. It's like your mom: "Put on your coat; you'll catch cold."

Along with sports, we grew up with a lot of old husbands' tales about what was and what was not women's work.

Cooking, cleaning, doing the dishes, shopping for groceries, taking care of the kids, that was all women's work. This was one of the great all-time old husbands' tales, because it not only kept women in certain occupations, but it also kept them out of others.

Now we look at those old husbands' tales and just shake our heads that they were generally accepted as Truth.

We know that there really is no such thing as women's work or men's work; there is just work. Or should be. And whoever does it, does it. Of course, if a woman does it, she gets paid less for it.

There are exceptions to this work thing. Military combat, for instance, which is still men's work, because everybody knows it's much too dangerous for women. Right. Maybe someday we'll refer to that as an old general's tale.

Hey, general, put on a coat; you'll catch a cold.

A lot of old husbands' tales are passed along from father to son for generations. There's a whole slew of old husbands' tales that have to do with how we measure up as men. "Real men don't cry." "Men don't let their emotions show." And this – the most damaging of all old husbands' tales – "A man is measured by the size of his income."

Well, at least by other men.

And when you've got a little, tiny income, it doesn't help to hear someone say, "It isn't the size of the income that matters; it's what you do with it."

This passing along of old husbands' tales is truly unfortunate, because a lot of them limit men from things in the same way that they limit women.

I was surprised to find out recently that a new father I know was not sharing all the parenting; he was leaving his wife to do the changing, feeding, getting up in the middle of the night, all that sort of thing. Probably responding to that old husbands' tale about babies being women's work.

Too bad. When a man lets an old husbands' tale like that get in the way of being a participating parent, he not only cheats his wife and child, but he cheats himself. Himself, most of all.

Hey daddy, put on a coat; you'll catch a cold.

You'd think we'd learn.

FINDING TRUE LOVE IN THE WANT ADS AND OTHER THINGS I DON'T QUITE UNDERSTAND

Speaking in Code

Do you think a thousand years from now, linguists and historians will know that we talked in code? That often what we said isn't what we meant?

Or more precisely, that what we meant had a different meaning from the words we said?

I was first struck by this while vacationing. Looking for a restaurant recommendation, we asked another vacationing couple if a particular restaurant had good food.

"It's not too bad," was the coded reply. Unsure what that meant, we asked about another restaurant. The woman scrunched up her face in deeper critical analysis and said, "It's not too bad,"again.

This was code for something, but I didn't know what. I could tell by her inflection that the restaurants, clearly, were different. But was one great and "Not too bad" was high praise? Was one bad but not awful? You know, not <u>too</u> bad – you could eat there and not die? I didn't know. And I mean I didn't have a clue.

I resolved to drop the phrase "not too bad" from my descriptive repertoire.

But we all speak in codes, all the time.

Teenagers speak in nothing but code.

(We can be grateful that Shakespeare was not born at this moment in history. If he was, the play Hamlet might not open with the prophetic "Who's there?" but with "Hey man, wassup?" and when Hamlet says to Ophelia, "Get thee to a nunnery," she might reply "As if!")

Men and women speak in codes to each other all the time. Married couples go so far as to develop their own codes.

For instance, when your wife says, "I see your point," what she's really saying is "I can't believe your making such an idiotic argument."

When she says "It was on sale at Nordstrom," what she means is "I could have spent more, but didn't. But if you earned the kind of money you're supposed to, I wouldn't have to shop at Nordstrom only when there's a sale on, which is what I do, but wouldn't have to be doing if I had married that guy I was dating just before you came along."

And when you look at the sale items and reply, "Great!" what you mean is "Thank you for exerting at least some spending damage control which will be necessary for the rest of our married life because I am turning out to be an abject failure in the earning department; but at least I am not the complete dork you were dating when we first met."

And when she asks, "Do I look fat in this?" she is asking in code for affirmation that her personhood, with all it has to offer the world in its many and varied facets, is not lost because the temporal body in which it currently exists is, in the language of medical science, a tad obese.

So, of course, you must answer in code. The coded answer is "No," which means, "Your wonderful selfhood transcends the body it finds itself in, and the outfit is a perfect expression of your vibrant and all-encompassing passion for life, which explains why you haven't had time to lose the forty pounds you gained after you had the last baby. Which was eleven years ago."

(You new husbands should know that "Yes" to the question, "Do I look fat in this?" is code for "Yes.")

When you tell a life insurance agent on the phone that you're too busy to schedule an appointment, that is code for "Go away and never come back."

But now, in the interest of political correctness and lawsuit avoidance, we have moved codes to a new and higher level of sophistication.

Case in point: the reference letter.

Knowing you can get sued for saying anything derogatory about even the worst of employees, we have invented a new code.

For instance, "He found the work challenging" is code for "He's an idiot who couldn't figure out the phone book."

"She was always cordial to her co-workers" means, "We hated her."

"She was never tardy and finished her work on time" means, "We really hated her."

"He's got an old-fashioned work ethic" is code for "He's a walking sexual harassment suit waiting to happen."

"She would be an asset to any organization" means, "Hire her, then maybe she'll be your problem and won't sue us."

In its extreme version, former employers just give the dates of employment, which is code for "If you can't figure out this code and hire this person, you deserve all the grief you're destined to get."

Credit Card Fees

It was almost thirty years ago.

I was in college.

I needed to buy my first television, but I didn't have the money.

I needed a television so I would have an excuse to invite my future wife over to my apartment, and there would be a pretext for her to say "yes." This is because I didn't have the nerve to just say, "So, you want to come over to my place and get naked?"

I did have the nerve to say, "So you want to come over and watch television or something?" ("Or something" being the college-ese for "and maybe get naked?")

So I went to my local Seafirst Banker, who told me they don't do consumer loans for $200, but I could apply for a credit card, if I wished.

I wished. With my true love sitting beside me, a TV waiting at Sears and an empty apartment down the street, I wished with all my heart.

And then he said the magic words: "If you pay it off every month, you won't have to pay any interest."

What I should have said, but didn't because I didn't want to offend the man who held the card to my happiness, so to speak, was, "If I had the money to pay it off every month, I wouldn't need the card, would I?"

So I got my first credit card. And wife, as it happened — but that's kind of a different story.

What he didn't tell me was that some few years hence, Seafirst would try to charge me $12 a year for the privilege of using their card.

Indignant that they would try to fleece me like that, I switched banks. Not just credit cards, mind you, but my whole banking package.

"I'm taking my slightly overdrawn checking account and my $244 in savings elsewhere," I announced; and I opened an account at Washington Trust Bank.

I showed them.

Since then, not paying a credit card fee has been a matter of principle. And as soon as I could, I made it a point never to charge more than I could pay off completely at the end of every month.

I recognize that when I pay off my balance (which, to be completely honest, isn't as frequent an event as it used to be before there was a teenager in the family and a Hastings Records and Tapes nearby), the banks don't make any money on me; but I always figured it was a fair trade because they also didn't have to send me nasty letters or phone calls to collect my money, either.

I was wrong.

GE Capital Credit Corp., which issues the GE Rewards MasterCard, announced that it is going to start charging people like me $25 dollars a year for their card.

There's a reward for you.

"To our scumball customers who have neither the self-control nor brains to live within their means, are a significant credit risk because they can't seem to control their spending, and run up huge credit card balances which they can never hope to pay off in a single lifetime, we at GE Rewards would like to say, 'We love you, Man'."

"To those of you who have the unmitigated gall to not carry a credit card balance: Take a hike. We don't want your kind around here. No debt, no balance — no service. We're GE: We bring good things to *our* life. Like undeserved credit card debt that *we* collect."

Their reason for charging this fee is pretty simple: They want to make more money.

Now, even though I would be one of those customers that they don't care if they lose if I had a GE Card, which I don't, as a marketing guy, I kind of admire the brazen way they just decided to shake down their customers.

I mean, who's next? Nordstrom?

"Hi. With our legendary attention to detail and customer service, we couldn't help but notice that you haven't bought anything recently. So we're charging your account $50. Next time we have a sale, we suggest you be there. And buy something."

And it doesn't have to be retail. I mean, where is it written that your doctor or dentist can't boost income this way? "We are pleased to announce that people who miss their annual checkup will only be charged 75 dollars."

From a marketing standpoint, this has real potential. Car mechanics already charge you for looking at your car and not doing anything. (They call it a "diagnostic fee." "My diagnosis is it's broke. That'll be forty bucks, please. You want me to work on it?") Now they could charge you for not showing up.

As a consumer, do I like it? Not for a moment. If my Visa cards start charging, I'll just write more checks. After all, I've got one of those free checking accounts so it doesn't matter how many I write.

At least, that is, until they start charging twenty-five bucks a year for free checking.

Eating your Vegetables on Vacation

I just got back from vacation, and almost as a cosmic sign that I may have done the whole thing wrong was an article in the paper about eating a low fat diet while on vacation. Above the article was a photo of a plate with five asparagus spears, a circle of butternut squash with creamed spinach and a single breaded chicken breast. A lemon wedge and sprig of parsley garnished the plate.

When I looked at the picture, I thought — and this is a quote — "bleeaack."

The gist of the article was that if you tried, you could avoid red meat and high fat foods and eat vegetables five to seven times a day while on vacation.

Excuse me? Eat your vegetables on vacation? Why? Is your mother coming along or something? What kind of vacation is that?

Which gets us to the first essential vacation question: Are you vacationing to something or from something?

You take a vacation <u>to</u> the Grand Canyon; you take a vacation <u>from</u> work.

The writer of the eat-your-vegetables-even-though-it-is-a-lot-of-work-and- everybody-in-the-family-will-be-mad-at-you-because-they-can't-have-red-meat article obviously wasn't taking a vacation from her diet.

And her family wasn't going to, either.

Which gets you to the second essential vacation question, which is; if you're not going to take a vacation from some of those things that make you miserable (and I don't know about you, but I put butternut squash with creamed spinach on it right up there at the top of that list), what's the point?

Now, the to/from questions are not mutually exclusive, of course. On any vacation, you are going to do a mixture of both.

The younger you are, the more a vacation is a vacation to somewhere. Disneyland, for instance. Or Cannon Beach. Or, if your parents are vacation challenged, Moses Lake.

But all that changes when you enter the work force, doesn't it? Then, in almost equal measure, you're not only vacationing to somewhere, but also from work.

"Where are you going on vacation?" you ask your young employee.

"Anywhere you're not," comes the reply.

"Maybe you should take some of that time and look for a new job," you think but don't say.

It is the to/from question, however, that sows the seeds of what may be called the family vacation conflict syndrome.

For instance, it is not too unusual for a man to want to take a week off work and stay home and do something like build a deck. This gets you away from work and, if you're using power tools, has an element of danger involved, which we men like.

If you're a woman, however, watching your man put his fingers at risk with a circular saw for five days may not be your idea of a good time on vacation.

The older you get (and your kids get, I might add), the more your vacation is likely to be a vacation from something. Like shaving.

"Honey, I've decided that this year, I'm going to take a vacation from shaving, wearing deodorant and washing my hair everyday."

"Really? Well, in that case, maybe I'll take a vacation from putting on makeup, doing my hair and having sex."

"Oh. In that case, don't forget to pack my razor, okay?"

These days when I go away on vacation, I also take a vacation from newspapers, regular exercise, the rational intake of alcohol, normal spending constraints, and anything that smacks of having to be on a schedule.

And, I might add, of anything like restraint in a restaurant. "I'll have a filet mignon — rare — pasta primavera and mud pie, please."

"For breakfast?"

"Yeah, you're right. I better have an egg with that."

The lady who wrote the article about eating all those vegetables while on vacation says she follows the food pyramid.; I do too. It's just that on vacation, I eat from the top down.

I do have to wonder what her husband thought about eating all those vegetables on vacation, though.

Probably what you and I would think.

"Maybe it's time we took separate vacations."

The Accident

A few months ago, I had to go work on a Sunday. It was a clear, bright day, and work was the last place I wanted to be, so I was feeling very put upon.

I was feeling quite sorry for myself as I turned and headed down Regal Avenue toward town.

What got my attention off me and onto the task at hand, which was driving, was that a car coming at me, about two blocks away, lurched across the center line and then back again.

"That's weird," I said aloud.

The car didn't drift over and back like a drunk was driving it (which did cross my mind - I've been paying attention to the ads); it swerved hard, like someone grabbed the wheel and yanked it. And there was something else: The people in the front seat were fighting or something — I couldn't tell exactly.

What I did know was it wasn't normal.

As the car, a big old Dodge, proceeded to come toward me, it went off the road to the right, up over the curb.

"That's <u>really</u> weird," I said.

There were a few cars behind me, but no one in front of me. I may have let off on the accelerator and let my car kind of drift for a moment as I watched the big Dodge.

By this time, he was a block away; and I thought, yeah, somebody's fighting in that car, a guy and a girl, and she's pounding on him, and they're fighting for the steering wheel; and all of a sudden, the car swerves back across the road and starts heading straight for me — or at least for where I'm going to be in about 3 seconds.

And it was picking up speed, fast. Whoever was in that car was standing on the gas pedal, and that Dodge is going to come through the left door of my Subaru unless I did something real quick.

At the moment I realized he was coming across the road and going to hit me, I considered stopping. (Yes, that's an option: I think I can stop, and it looks like his trajectory will have him pass in front of me and down the side street he is sort of, but not really, heading for.) But then I think: But what if they stop fighting long enough to lurch back like they did a moment ago?

They hit me head on, that's what. And I die. I eat his fan belt as his land boat comes crashing through my compact car windshield; and I'm here to tell you I'm not that hungry.

There's no place to my right, and going left into oncoming traffic is a bad choice.

My only option is to go straight ahead. Fast. I've got to beat him past that point where, as of this moment, we are going to crash.

All of this calculating takes about 3 nanoseconds.

So I accelerate, hard. As we come together, time starts passing so slowly, that I have time to cheer for myself as I realize my front fender is clear of being hit, then my door is clear, then my back door is clear, and I think, "Yes! I made it," just before I hear the thunk of him hitting my back fender, at which time I swear.

This really makes me mad.

I'm glad he didn't total me, but mad the jerk hit me.

First I have to go to work, and now this. Because he hit me, I have to go back and get his name and all that. Now we have to get the police and insurance companies involved, and who needs that on a Sunday?

And there is something else. When they almost came through my door, I got a really close look at what was going on, and I know that something very strange was happening in that car when it tried to kill me.

I look in the rear-view mirror. The car has gone through a fence, into a back yard.

At this point, I really wish I wasn't involved, you know what I mean? I wish I could just drive away. But I can't. I'm not sure I would have if I could have, but I couldn't anyway, so I went back.

The car has gone through a fence, across fifty feet of yard, knocked down a small tree and demolished a swing set. It is stopped. There's a girl screaming hysterically inside the car.

It's not an injury scream, understand; it's a scream of someone who has just been taken for a ride across four lanes of traffic, hit a car, gone through a fence, sheared off a tree and landed in a swing set, and she's upset about it.

To be honest, I thought they were *still* fighting, and he was beating on her, and they hadn't noticed where they stopped.

"Terrific," I thought. "Domestic violence. He's beating on her, he's wrecked his car, and I have to ask him to stop so I can get the name of his insurance company."

On the other side of the fence that he didn't drive through was a group of eight or nine kids, all Cambodian or Vietnamese or Hmong or something. I don't know where they were playing when this car came at them, but it must have been interesting. Now it was in the neighbor's yard.

They were staring at the car in the swing set. You could see them thinking, weird place, America.

As I got nearer the car, I could see that the people inside weren't fighting. He was sort of rigid. She was trying to get a response from him, but all he was doing was gurgling.

On the one hand, I thought, "Hey, great, I'm not going to get my lights punched out," but then, "Not so great. Someone's got to help this guy, and I'm the only one here."

I turned to the Cambodian children. "Call 9-1-1," I said.

They looked at each other. "911? 911? Oh, 911. Ahhh, 911." Pretty soon they were all nodding and saying, "Ahhh, 911." Nobody moved. I wondered for a moment if 911 meant "Don't anybody move," or something, in Cambodian.

Finally, a neighbor came out and asked if she should call for help.

Oh, yes.

I went back to the car. The girlfriend was still screaming. What a set of lungs.

"Are you hurt?" I asked. She looked at me with a kind of blank stare for a second. "Please speak English," I thought. Then she said that she wasn't, but that Richard wasn't breathing, and she started to scream at him again.

I'll tell you what: If you could jump start a heart or brain through stimulation of the auditory nerve, Richard would have been on his feet again in no time. As it was, Richard didn't look so hot. He was still making gurgling noises. He was, to use the proper medical term, gorked out.

Somebody else came along side. "Should we move him?" he asked.

Yeah, I said, having no idea if it was the right thing to do. He didn't look injured, and if he needed CPR or something, we couldn't do it in the front seat of a '73 Dodge.

We dragged him out onto the ground.

He was really gorked out.

Heart attack, I think. CPR time.

I know from past experience that when I panic, I tend to become non-functional and fail to do what might otherwise be painfully obvious. So I try to collect myself and think very hard about the CPR class I took once several years ago.

"A,B,C," I tell myself. Or is it "1,2,3?" Sounds like a Jackson 5 song. Pulse, that's the main thing. Then breathing. Find a pulse first. I tried to get a carotid pulse by jamming my fingers into his neck, but all I did was bruise his neck. And my heart was beating so fast now, I couldn't tell if I was feeling his pulse or mine.

Okay. Forget the pulse. A pulse isn't really important, I decided. Next check for breathing. I looked at Richard, who was still gurgling. I wondered why, if I had to give CPR to someone, why it couldn't be to a cute female aerobics instructor? Why did it have to be to Richard who was gurgling?

I tried to check his airway to see if it was clogged or any-thing, and it didn't seem to be. I was about to make a final deci-sion about whether or not I was going to have to give him mouth-to-mouth, and whether or not it would be uncool to ask if anybody else wanted to give it a shot, when it occurred to me that his gurgling was caused by breathing.

In fact, he was breathing real good now.

Terrific. But now what? I heard somewhere about gorked out people puking and choking, so we rolled Richard onto his stomach.

Don't throw up on me, okay, Dick? I'm just the nice guy you just missed killing. About this time, he started to come around. First some arm movements, then leg movements. I was ecstatic that all I had to do was make him comfortable.

The girlfriend was still shrieking.

A woman came over and asked about his eyes. Were they fixed and dilated?

"Darned if I know, let's take a look," I said. We looked. As I looked at his eyes, it occurred to me, for the first time in my life, that I didn't know what fixed and dilated looked like, so I wouldn't know if they were or not. What I did know was fixed and dilated meant you were on your way to being dead, and Richard certainly wasn't that.

By this time, Richard was thrashing about all over the place; and keeping him calm until the medics arrived was starting to look like a chore. He was a pretty big guy.

Then the lady who asked if his eyes were fixed and dilated did a neat thing: she took the hysterical girlfriend aside and began to talk her down from her hysteria. When the girl looked at Richard, her fiance', helpless and in distress, she started to lose it again; but the woman kept talking and kept soothing her, and finally the girlfriend got back into control.

Of course, by this time, most of us were deaf in one ear.

About this time, the fire department arrived, and the police arrived, and medics and a few more Cambodians arrived (all pointing to Richard and saying "Mmmm, 9-1-1"); and I turned into Chief Witness.

I told my story about a dozen times. Richard woke up and wondered what all the fuss was about and how his car got into the swing set in the backyard of a daycare place, (fortunately empty on Sunday), and why was everybody so interested in who his insurance company was.

He had no memory of what we all agreed was some sort of seizure.

After a while, they convinced Richard that he should go to the hospital and see if they could find any obvious reason for his seizure, and he left. Then the other aid people left, and the neighbors drifted back into their homes. Finally the police left, leaving me, in the wreckage of someone else's backyard, to contemplate the fact that that fifty feet from where I stood, forty minutes before, I came within about eight feet, moving at forty-five miles per hour, of getting killed.

Killed. *Me.*

I did some quick math and figured the margin of Richard coming through my door or missing me at that moment was about one-tenth of a second.

But I didn't get killed, and neither did anyone else — also a stroke of good fortune. All in all, no one even got hurt, much. And any damage I sustained would be covered by insurance.

Whatever my problems were earlier that morning, all of a sudden, they didn't seem so bad anymore. Especially compared to Richard, who had something wrong in his brain, and who was going to have to find out what it was. And then live with it.

The moment became very surreal. Eight feet. A tenth of a second. You live or you die. And forty minutes later, one way or the other, life goes on.

On oddly wobbly knees, I got into my car with its freshly dented bumper.

Suddenly, the idea of being able to go to work, whole and healthy, seemed rather like a privilege.

Even on this very, very beautiful Sunday morning.

Assault With a Deadly Strip of Bacon

It is rare in the lives of human beings when we are witness to a moment that combines deep theological questions about the will of God and the care and feeding of animals in their natural habitat, all in the context of an attempted murder.

But last week, the Spokesman-Review reported that such an event took place up by Loon Lake when Tracy Walter and Randy Thomas tried to kill their friend, James Peterson.

First they tried to shoot him, but the gun misfired.

Taking this as a sign of Divine intervention, the message being that killing Peterson was okay but that God didn't want them to use a gun, Walter and Thomas tied Peterson between a couple of trees and left him to be eaten by bears and wolves.

To make sure the bears and wolves understood that Peterson was to be considered a meal, they garnished him with bacon.

"I never can remember. When you're feeding humans to bears, does the bacon go on the left or the right? And do you serve the human sunny side up, or what? Hey Jimbo, I need you to roll over."

It makes you wonder if, when they all got into the car together that night, they didn't say, "Hey, Jim, you don't happen to have any sour cream and chives on you do you? Ha ha. Just wondering."

And as I said, all of this happened near Loon Lake.

How appropriate is that? Personally, I always thought the Loons of Loon Lake referred to the birds — not the local criminal population.

Now, while we can appreciate Walter's and Thomas' concern for the care and feeding of bears and wolves, there are a few problems with this whole incident. And I'm sure you can see what they are.

First of all, and this is just the most obvious problem, there are no wolves up there. So if you are going to kill your friend and feed him to the wolves — speaking in the literal rather than the metaphorical sense for once — you need to do it closer to, say, Yellowstone Park, where the wolf has been successfully reintroduced.

And the other problem is bacon. Bacon? This is very disturbing. Do you know how much fat there is in bacon and how bad bacon is for bears? I mean, right now, there are Federal wildlife agents who are probably stoking out over the very thought that someone would deliberately feed bacon to wild bears.

And there are other problems.

I am not a theologian and would never presume to know the will of God, but even I have to wonder: Didn't these guys pay *any* attention in Sunday School?

While we can applaud their tenacity, where did they get the idea that "God helps those who help themselves" includes attempted murder and cancels out "Thou shalt not kill?"

And why would they think their gun misfiring was an act of God? Come on. If it had been, wouldn't there have been the jawbone of an ass lying around? God is a lot of things, but careless isn't one of them.

It kind of makes you wonder what they're smoking north of Deer Park.

But we all know the real problem here, don't we?

The real problem here is their choice of bacon as a murder weapon.

Because you know as well as I do that our legislators, in their zeal to protect us from ourselves, are just not going to be able to let this one go. And the next thing you know our constitutional right to bear bacon is going to be threatened.

Oh, they'll start small, with little changes in the law that will disguise their true intent, which will be to take away everyone's bacon.

First they'll make it a crime to be a felon in possession of bacon.

Then they'll make it illegal to carry concealed bacon without a permit.

Federal agents will patrol Safeway parking lots. "You got a license to carry that slab, lady?"

Bank tellers will get notes: "Put the money in the bag. I've got a strip of bacon in my pocket, and I'm not afraid to use it."

SWAT Teams will have to adopt new tactics. "Put the bacon down and nobody gets hurt."

The ATF will have to become the ATFB: The Bureau of Alcohol, Tobacco, Firearms and Bacon.

Pretty soon, military surplus bacon will be illegal to buy. "This kind of bacon has no sporting value whatsoever," the bacon control lobby will say.

The National Bacon Association will be formed and will hire Charlton Heston as its spokesperson and give thousands of dollars to George Nethercutt for his support of repealing the ban on assault bacon and the Bacon Brady Bill which mandates a three-day waiting period and background checks on everybody wanting to buy Saturday night specials on bacon.

Schools will get new signs: "This school is bacon free."

There will be a zero tolerance policy; and in Seattle, a third grader will be sent home for bringing Bacon Bits to school. In an effort to be safe, even ham, spare ribs and pork chops will be suspect.

There will be new bumper stickers: When bacon becomes criminal, only criminals will have bacon.

Well, you get the idea. It will be a mess.

Of course, for years dieticians have been telling us, "When it comes to bacon, that stuff will kill you."

I guess they're right. At least around Loon Lake.

Wedding Pictures in the Paper

Of all the pictures anybody has ever taken of you, which one would you most like to have back?

I know which one I'd like to have back. The one they took at my wedding that wound up in the paper.

I'm not even sure when they took that picture, but I can tell you one thing. I'll bet everybody who saw it took one look at my wife, in all her bridal loveliness, and one look at me, looking like Sonny Bono was the biggest influence in my life, and concluded that my wife was terminally nearsighted. Or maybe legally blind.

Anyway, poor thing; she lost.

Winners and losers. That's what the bridal page is all about, isn't it?

I know it sounds elitist and snobbish, and it is, but be honest now — don't you look through the pictures of the newly-weds, and setting aside the people you know, render judgments on who won and who lost and who came out even in the marriage sweepstakes?

Sure you do. We all do.

At work the other day, as the coffee was perking, several of the ladies I work with were going over the latest batch of wedding pictures and making their calls.

"She lost."

"She got an ugly one."

"He's cute, but look at her!"

"Maybe it's just a bad picture of her," I offered.

No, they all agreed. He's cute and she's, well, dumpy. Not a match at all. Clearly a couple destined for a divorce.

I suspect all this has to do with the fact that people, like water, tend to seek their own level. Sometimes it's a cosmetic thing, and sometimes it's much more complex, having to do with self-image and value systems and things that aren't necessarily photographable.

On the other hand, maybe those things do show up in a photograph. Maybe you can look at a picture and see the imbalance that will one day scream to be corrected.

And a lot of people get married for the wrong reasons, and maybe that comes out in the wedding picture, too.

"She tans too much," they went on, looking at more pictures. They critiqued things I never thought of looking for. "They're too young to get married."

I looked at the doomed couple. I couldn't help thinking they were right.

"Here's a couple that looks like they deserve one another," they said.

I looked. "Hey, I know this guy. That's his third wife."

They looked at me. "He's had two tries, and this is the best he can do?"

"I don't think he learned a lot from his first two marriages," I offered.

I wondered again what they would have said about my wedding picture. Would they look at that stupid grin and hair that looked like I wanted to be one of the Monkees and conclude that I was caring and sensitive?

I didn't think so. I suspected that they would have taken one glance at me and the word "unemployable" would have come to mind.

The scary thing is, they would have been pretty close to right.

Like any photo, a wedding picture not only captures the event, but also the attitudes and opinions and styles of the times. These are things apt to change over time, and look strange in the years to come.

They continued on down the page, tallying the winners and losers and which ones looked like they deserved one another. Half were destined for divorce, they concluded.

When you see someone on the page that you know, you know if it is a good picture or not. In these cases, you charitably suspend your judgment.

A young couple I know married recently; and even though both of them are spectacularly attractive people, their picture didn't show it. They each looked like they'd just chugged a bottle of Annie Greensprings, and someone asked them what day it was, and they were both saying "Huh?" when the picture was snapped.

I grew up in Seattle, and there was a time when, if your parents were somebody important in Seattle society (if that isn't an oxymoron), you got a bigger picture in the Seattle Times than the rest of us. Those tended to be better pictures, as I recall, giving rise to the impression that the socially connected and rich tended to be better looking than the rest of us.

(A friend of mine was dating a girl from Tacoma at that time. He said that because Tacoma didn't have anybody who was either rich or socially connected, if your father was a longshoreman or better, you got a big picture in the paper when you got married. I've always wondered if that was true. He married someone else, so I never got to find out.)

But since then, democratization has come to the wedding picture page, and now everybody is treated the same. Which makes it nice; you don't have to let money clutter up your superficial, catty, cosmetic judgments.

It seems like with all the money people spend for wedding pictures (not to mention the wedding itself), you'd think that couples could get a picture in the paper that looks better than a snapshot taken when the groom was trying to remove a piece of wedding cake from between his teeth with his tongue.

Perhaps a wedding picture is an act of God. And we've all seen what a curious sense of humor God has at times, haven't we?

Perhaps a flattering picture of two young people who haven't a chance is God's way of saying, "Here, start your life together with the positive feelings of all the strangers who look at this picture in the paper and can't know you're mismatched."

And maybe a bad picture is God's way of saying, "Even though you're perfectly matched, never forget that you're human, and that things are going to go wrong — starting with this picture. By the way, you've got cake in your teeth."

Of course, it's possible God looks at the pictures like you and I do, and says, "He lost. He won. She lost."

And on occasion, "Wow. Look at this one. A Sonny Bono wannabe. She must be nearsighted. I must remember not to let her get contacts."

SWM, *Looking for True Love in the Want Ads*

The other day, one of my co-workers came in and wanted to know if I happened to have a swimsuit he could borrow. He needed it right now.

As I dug out an old pair of exercise shorts I happened to have stashed in my desk, in the unlikely event that I might suddenly feel the need to go run a mile, I asked what he wanted them for. Some new, creative idea? A clever pitch to a prospective account? A strange lunch date?

It seems he was responding to a want ad. A personal want ad.

It read, "SWF, 20, Blonde, 120 pounds, very fit, in town for summer. Loves boating and skiing. Wants to share summer with fun loving guy(s)" (apparently groups of respondents were okay), "19 -25. Your swimsuit photo gets mine. Chris."

There was a box number at the paper.

He took a great Polaroid picture of my swimsuit and sent it off with a short letter that very day. No one was in the swimsuit, of course; she didn't say anything about seeing a person in the swimsuit, and we didn't figure she'd know it was mine and not his.

Well, this got me to thinking about finding true love through the want ads.

Does it seem a little strange to you? It does to me, too. Sort of a modern day equivalent of the mail order bride of a century ago.

The key to success, I should think, is in the writing. How you express who you are.

Like any writing, if you're going to write a want ad for yourself, there are certain rules you have to follow.

First of all, you have to identify yourself – Single White Male; Divorced Black Female — that sort of thing. These identifiers you abbreviate with capital letters: SWM, DBM, etc. (In some areas, it's acceptable to put DW?, but you 'd better be ready for some weird responses and very strange photos.)

Next comes your age and weight. You can lie, of course, but is that any way to start a relationship?

It also is required that you qualify your looks. Even though this is a subjective area, I suspect that this is where the truth starts taking a beating. I have yet to see one that says, "I'm ugly as a stump but I'm nice, and ... "

But let's face it. If you were wandering through the want ads, looking for someone who likes to take romantic walks in the rain (walking in the rain romantically is a biggie with personal want ad writers), would you respond if someone said they were ugly? Heck no.

So everybody sounds pretty good.

In fact, everybody sounds darn near perfect. Which makes you wonder what they are doing in the want ads.

Anyway, then you have to specify what you want in a person.

There is an abbreviation NSTD, which means no sexually transmitted diseases.

I'm not sure if it means the writer doesn't have any or doesn't want any.

Probably both, now that I think about it.

Ordering up a person you want to meet in the want ads is not a lot different than ordering at McDonald's. "Let's see; I'll have a SWF, with lots of sports activities, romantic, 18-22, good shape, financially secure, and ready for an honest relationship. Oh, and throw in a good sense of humor with no hangups, and hold the eating disorders, please."

Sure. Right. Coming right up. You want fries with that lady?

And then the question is, because everybody sounds so humorous and so sensitive and so caring and so attractive, will anyone believe you? Perhaps more important, are you going to believe anyone who responds to your ad?

And how do you keep the whole thing from sounding like, "Do You Like Pina Collada's ... ?"

The answer is, you can't.

Unless, of course, you are prepared to write something honest like DWM, balding, small drinking problem, 60 pounds overweight, misogynistic tendencies, card-carrying NRA member who loves to shoot small birds, big deer and the occasional person strolling in the woods during hunting season, seeks woman, 18 to 20, with high disposable income and Farrah Fawcett or Dolly Parton looks. Must be immune to Swine Flu and hypothermia."

Honest, but I wouldn't be expecting a lot of responses.

No, the problem is advertising for yourself in the want ads and projecting clearly who you are in all your many complexities is just about impossible to do. It's a limitation of the medium. It's tough enough doing that in person, much less in two column inches at 30 cents a word.

My advice to someone writing one of these want ads is to have someone else write the ad for you. Make it sound like a blind date. Perhaps it might read, "I have a friend who is recently divorced, great looking, and ready to party. Having been married for twenty years and suddenly thrown out, he's rebounding like a racquetball, but my wife says he's cute, so if you know someone who sounds right for this guy, maybe we should get them together. Send me something about your friend to make my friend interested, and I'll be in touch."

Now that's an ad you just might respond to.

(I know somebody like that, by the way. Be kind of funny if I ran an ad for him and his ex-wife responded, wouldn't it? "Hey, fancy meeting you in the want ads. Have I got a date for you.")

Well, presumably, if you're in the want ads, you've tried the bar route and found it wasn't for you. And even though want ads are a less than perfect medium for meeting people, I certainly don't have any better suggestions.

Oh, and by the way, if you're the SWF, 20, blonde, in town for the summer who got our swimsuit picture, we're still waiting for our picture of your swimsuit.

You don't have to be in it.

The Implausible Awards

There are a lot of advertising awards out there: everything from our local awards to national and international awards. And like the Emmys or the Grammys or the Oscar, they all have names. Perhaps the best known is the Clio.

Having watched my share of commercials lately, I think we need one more award. I would name this award The Implausible and award it to commercials that have nothing to do with reality (as you and I know it), showing us instead something totally implausible.

Not impossible or, heaven forbid, untrue, just, well, implausible.

Now, it should be noted that all of these commercials nominated for the Implausible Awards follow the Television Advertising Law of Implausibility and Budgets, which states, "The bigger the production budget, the more you can make an implausible situation look real." So all of these commercials look great. And because they look great, you are apt to overlook the fact that they don't look anything like real life.

My first Implausible goes to Hidden Valley Ranch Salad Dressing!

This is the commercial that shows the world's longest green salad going by the camera while enough Hidden Valley Ranch Salad Dressing pours on to gag even those of us who still think that a salad bar where you can really gob on the dressing is the zenith of culinary achievement. Plausible? I don't think so, not even if you buy your Hidden Valley Ranch in fifty-gallon drums at Costco.

Another Implausible goes to the cat food that mixes shots of some babe in an evening gown preparing cat food on a sterling silver platter with sterling silverware. I can't tell you the name of the product because each time they show the fork going through this oil-based cat food, it suggests the woman is going to eat it; and it activates my gag reflex, and I have to leave the room to retch.

And feeding your cat in a white evening gown? You can almost hear the director arguing with the agency guy that no woman in her right mind would do such a dumb thing. And the agency guy replying, "It's classy. And we're not selling cat food, we're selling classy. Cat people are like that."

The "Little Slice Of Life At Christmas" Implausible goes to Sears, which shows happy families gathering around all the presents they got at Sears. The message is clear: Buy this stuff, and everybody will be so happy on Christmas morning. Mom will even fire up the new home computer.

Now, if you don't find this little scene implausible, you haven't been paying attention at Christmas.

Where are the self-absorbed kids? Where is Dad looking around and wondering if that's all he got? Where is Mom crabbing about everybody making a mess and telling the kids to stop fighting? Where is Grandma carefully picking up used Christmas wrapping paper and folding it for later use, just in case there's another Great Depression? And why is the whole family gathered around the computer? And how come Mom, who has apparently just discovered the miracle of turning on a computer, isn't saying, "What does 'Windows' mean? Why does it say that? Make it do something!"

Stetson Cologne wins the Pandering to Our Baser Instincts Implausible for their ad showing a guy and a gal on a horse out in the snow. This ad is the one that ends with them apparently not in the boonies of Wyoming, but in the boonies of Central Park in New York City. And even though being in Central

Park on a horse in a snowstorm is pretty implausible (and a whole lot more dangerous than being lost in a snowstorm on horse in Wyoming), that's not why it wins.

The reason it wins is there is a chorus of women singing what at first seems to be the refrain from the "Little Drummer boy, pa-rom-pa-bum-bum" Christmas song. But really they are singing the words, "Easy for you" like some sexually perverted choir of angels.

Come on, Stetson. "Easy for you?" What's easy? Me? Her? Him? The horse? Splash on a little stud muffin juice and suddenly it's easy for me? Do the Stetson people think we men can be so easily manipulated?

Implausible! (I bought myself some — just in case, you understand — but it's still implausible.)

But this year's grand prize Implausible goes to Chevrolet.

Now car commercials are almost always implausible — that just goes with the territory. We know it's implausible when happy people look at Toyota sticker prices and don't faint; that cars in commercials always seem to drive on wet roads, stop on top of water (and just what is the Biblical significance of a Jeep Cherokee that walks on water, I'd like to know) and the voices of actors we know but can't quite place tell us stuff like "Pontiac builds excitement."

But this year, Chevrolet gets the Sterling Moss/Mario Andretti Implausible award for their commercial that purports to show how good the suspension is on their Chevy something or other.

We open on: engineering drawings. Cut to: an old truck with crates and boxes stacked so impossibly high, the driver must be on acid. Cut to: a family getting into their Chevy station wagon. Cut to: a computer screen showing how the engineering drawings would really work. Cut to: the truck with the crates weaving down the highway. Cut to: our family, coming the other way. Cut to: the underside of the Chevy. (Implausibility number one: it works.) Cut to: the truck. (Implausibility number two:

It dumps its load of boxes into the — you guessed it! — oncoming lane!) Cut to: ...

Time out! What do you do when you see something drop off a truck onto the highway in front of you when you're doing sixty?

Right. You scream an obscenity and try to push the brake pedal through the floor, past the firewall, and up to around the headlights. Meanwhile, your kids have gone face first onto the back seat floor, and your wife is either screaming at you to do something ("I <u>am</u> doing something: I've locked up all four wheels, and I'm about to leave the road backward!") or she's gone totally catatonic.

If you don't roll it, you plow into Acidhead's boxes and demolish your front end.

That's reality.

What does our Chevy driver do?

Suddenly, he's Sterling Moss, and this is Sebring. Without so much as a peep from his wife and kids, he starts weaving around these boxes like they're pylons on a test track. He doesn't even brake. "Look Ma: I don't even have to slow down with this great Chevy suspension."

I don't think so.

Being in advertising, you're probably thinking that I object to all this implausible reality in commercials. Actually, that's not the case. After all, if advertising couldn't use a little implausible reality once in a while, we'd have to look at everyone's products being used in real life situations.

Now there's a plausibility I'd rather not have to face.

Tanning Booths

I ran into an Orangite yesterday.

At least, I think it was an Orangite.

It might have been someone who just got back from vacation in some sunny part of the world, but I don't think so. I think she just got back from a tanning booth.

While the rest of us turn pale as fall turns to winter, the booth tanners stay a kind of perpetual brown But by my way of thinking, it's not like a real tan from the sun. It's more like they've been dipped in Formby's wood stain. Maple to Walnut, take your pick. Which is okay, I guess, if your father was, say, a Mandarin orange.

It reminds me of the time in eighth grade when Jim Kennedy smeared a product called ManTan all over his body. ManTan came after sunlamps, which now have been relegated to keeping your bacon and eggs warm at Dennys. If you didn't put ManTan on evenly, it streaked and made your skin look like it belonged in a National Geographic article about the Tasaday Tribe or something. That's what Jim looked like. I decided to pass.

I'm passing on tanning booths for the same reason.

I may be in the minority about this, but I think too much tan in the winter, especially the tan from a booth, the kind that doesn't leave the same kind of sunlight-from-the-top-down-highlights and subtle shadowings the real sun does, looks strange. It looks not quite right.

On the other hand, I can see why you might not want to go around looking like Madonna all winter, too. It's all subjective, of course.

There's a curious paradox at work here, I think.

A summer tan speaks of time spent outdoors, of doing those healthy things that one does outside in the summer sun. It also speaks of being a little sun-stupid, given what we now know about the damage the sun can do to our bodies. But around here, with the limited amount of sun we get, who cares?

But a winter tan, that's something else, something out of place. A winter tan is something quite different.

So a whole different standard of judgment comes into play.

And that's where we come to the real problem with tanning booths.

You see, the Orangites, these people walking around looking like they've got a terminally high bilirubin count, are also the people who have absolutely devalued a Hawaiian or Mexican winter vacation to zip because, in the past, in the time before tanning booths, a winter tan was unspoken proof that you went someplace where there was sun.

And you got to stay for at least a week.

It wasn't that long ago when you could save up for a year, gather up your various charge cards, and head out of town in February for five or six glorious days of sun in Hawaii ("The Islands" in the vernacular) or Mexico ("P.V." to those in the know) and have the white-skinned people you returned home to absolutely green with envy over your tan.

(Black people, I've noticed, tend not to gush over white people's tans.)

A tan was proof that you had spent time in the sun. You could take great comfort in the fact that the closest thing anyone in Minnesota got to that was retina burn from watching a blow torch while they thawed out frozen pipes.

Now, that was a vacation worth taking, and it made coming back almost worth it.

But now you come back and what happens? No one says a word because your tan doesn't mean what it used to.

People look at you and think that maybe you've been someplace fun, or maybe you just like to hang out in a coffin with blue lights to assuage a minor defect in your personal self-image.

Nobody knows and certainly few people are about to ask, because it's embarrassing to ask someone admiringly if they got their tan in Hawaii or Puerto Vallarta and find out that no, they got it in a health club by pretending to be a slice of human Wonderbread in a high-tech toaster with the control set on "dark."

Of course, it's equally as gauche to venture the opinion to someone that maybe they've been spending a bit more of their off-duty time in the tanning booth than they should, and find out that what you thought was table burn was had for several grand in Cancun.

The net result is nobody says anything.

What I find especially curious about all this is that the whole tanning booth phenomena is occurring at a time when information about skin cancer is at an all-time high. You'd think the two would work against each other, but that doesn't seem to be happening.

Which leads me to believe that the final word on all this will not come from people like me, but from the lawyers, about 20 years from now.

"Ahh, I see from your chart you have skin cancer, and now, between your sutures and your skin texture, your face looks like a football. Tell me, were you ever once in a tanning booth? Yes? Really. I think we have a case."

Well, like I said, not for me. If I'm going to have skin that looks like a flank steak that's been on the barbecue too long when I'm old, I'm darn well going to get it on a beach somewhere with a Mai Tai in my hand.

Besides, I don't think Madonna looks half bad.

Reading Divine Signs

One of the ladies I work with recently took a spontaneous day off.

"I got up, got ready for work, went out to get in my car and broke my key off in the garage door lock," she said. "Then my husband got up and his car wouldn't start, so we decided we weren't supposed to go to work. We decided it was a sign of some sort."

"Ahh. A divine sign?" I offered.

"Right," she said.

Getting your key stuck in the door is a divine sign to take the day off?

Kind of makes you wonder what <u>isn't</u> a divine sign.

I couldn't remember the last time I had a divine sign. But if a door that won't open is a sign not to go to work, maybe I just wasn't recognizing them.

For a while in my life, I used to get divine signs quite frequently.

Like whenever I went into Eagle Hardware.

"Buy that Black and Decker 3/8 inch Variable-Speed, Reversible Drill," would come a voice.

Well, not a voice, really. More like a thought.

"But I've got a drill," I would think back.

"You need another!" would come the next cosmic thought.

Nowadays, I hang around the riding lawn mowers hoping for some sort of signal, but nothing comes. Maybe because I don't have enough lawn.

I always tried to avoid the paint and wallpaper section of Eagle, especially when I was in there with my wife. I figured if I was getting buying signals while in the power tool department, it would be entirely possible for her to get a cosmic message to redecorate the kitchen while browsing through wallpaper books and paint chips.

I don't think my Eagle experience is too far out of the norm.

I've known people who get divine buying signals in Nordstrom. Especially during their half-yearly sale.

Actually, I know some people who contend that if you get to that sale early enough, you not only pickup your own divine signs telling you what to buy, but you also stand a good chance of receiving signals intended for someone else.

"Mary, I want you to buy that skirt and blouse at 40% off," comes a voice from above.

"My name's Susan."

"Oh. Well, whatever your name is, buy it anyway."

Some people look for divine signs concerning the major events of their lives, like getting married.

When you're an 18-year-old male, you're most apt to think you're getting a divine sign to get married every time you see a beautiful woman.

These signs are especially strong if you meet at a party and you happen to have been drinking.

"Marry that one! Do it now!" comes the voice.

"Like, shouldn't I meet her first?" you reply.

"No! Marry her before she gets away."

Later on you realize this is not a divine sign, but a sign that your hormones have gone permanently out of balance. An entirely different thing.

Every bit as compelling, but entirely different.

To be honest, I don't know many people who got married as a result of what they considered a divine sign.

Most people get married for practical reasons, like because all their friends are getting married, or they're pregnant, or they've seen a dress in Brides magazine they like, or most important of all, because there no longer seems to be any reason not to.

Actually, I would suspect that when it comes to marriage, a lot more people get divine signs telling them to cancel a wedding than to have one.

"Don't do it," says that voice.

"But the wedding's planned. "

"Don't do it."

"I'd have to give back all the presents."

"Don't do it! It's wrong."

"I've written all the thank you notes already!"

"Hmmmm. Let me think about this a minute."

Another biggie is house buying. Especially the first house. Did you look for some sort of divine sign when you bought your first house?

My wife and I sure did. I think that's normal.

You and your wife are about to take the biggest financial step of your young life, and you've got more doubts and questions about what it will mean than answers. I think it's pretty common to look for some sort of cosmic "go" signal – something beyond simply getting approved for the home loan, which for a lot of us, is pretty cosmic by itself.

When we bought our first house, my wife called me at work and told me she was looking at a house and to come by. I didn't want to buy a house, I didn't want to stop anywhere except the local tavern after work, and I certainly didn't want to commit myself to anything like the work a house would take.

But I went anyway. I wasn't inside the house ten seconds when I turned to my wife and said, "I could live here." That, plus the fact that I was there was sign enough for her. She turned to the owners and said, "Call the Realtor. Call right now." I think she thought the sign might go away and be replaced by an opposite message if she waited.

I guess some people are called to their profession by divine sign.

Since I'm a writer, I'm not sure how that happens.

Certainly I don't know of any writers who got into the business because of some cosmic signal. Most everybody I know got into writing advertising because they were unfit for a real job and it looked like a good way to not actually work very much.

Which gets you to the fundamental question, which is, how are you supposed to know whether your stuck key is a divine sign or just, well, a stuck key?

I sure don't know.

And if divine signs come in packages as small as stuck house keys, have we been missing them, you and I? Have we been looking for big signs when we should be looking for small ones?

I'd sure hate to miss one. Especially if it meant that I was supposed to take the day off. And especially if it happened on a Friday in the summer, when I could turn a sign like that into a long weekend.

Well. I'm sure we're all meant to go to work today. But I think maybe on Friday, I'll just try my garage door key, just in case.

I think I'll try my front door key, too. That one hardly ever works.

Re-Naming Things

One of the greatest things to hit America in recent years is the general re-naming and, in the process, redefining of all manner of unpleasantness, and in the process, making the unpleasantness go away.

Or at least seem to.

You know what I mean. People used to be handicapped. But then somebody, presumably somebody handicapped, came to realize that when people said the word "handicapped," they brought with it all kinds of negative baggage about what handicapped meant, creating an image of handicapped people which may or may not be at all accurate.

Hence, the handicapped became the "physically challenged."

(Except when they go to park, and then they are handicapped again. It says so right on the sign. Of course, if the signs said, "Reserved for the Physically Challenged" those who are reading challenged couldn't read it, and even more people would park where they weren't supposed to. Well, nobody said the system was perfect.)

Personally, I think they got it right. Referring to someone as physically challenged does help you perceive that person in a different and less biased light.

And the next thing we knew, the hard of hearing became the hearing impaired, people who had never been to a museum became culturally disadvantaged.

And the great American re-naming was underway. Once we were sensitive to the problem, we discovered there's all kinds of things that need re-naming.

But I am here to argue that we haven't carried it far enough.

We use all kinds of words that carry negative baggage with them. Words that are hurtful, words that conjure up terrible biases, words that get in the way of recognizing the humanity in all of us.

Words like: bald.

Nobody should be bald. Instead, let's call those unfortunate people "Follicly challenged." Now, isn't that better?

And to the woman in the red Honda who ran the stop sign and nearly T-boned me this morning, I didn't mean to call you stupid. (Actually, "stupid" was the modifier. I called you "a stupid ... " well, you get the idea.)

But it doesn't matter. It was a terrible thing to call another human being. You're not a bad driver, you're traffic impaired. Actually, you might be all the way to driving disadvantaged, in which case, you might want to go back and brush up on the meaning of red octagonal signs with the word "stop" in them.

See how easy this is?

If you spend more than you earn, and bounce checks all over town, are you a flake? Not any more; you're simply income impaired. It's not that you spend too much; you don't make enough. And whose fault is that? Do you know anybody who makes enough money? I sure don't.

And that's the great part about this, isn't it? The difference between being a flake and being income impaired is one of fault. When you're income impaired, there isn't any fault, because you have an affliction. It is something you can't help, and, consequently, for which you can't be blamed.

It's only a matter of time before the concept gets legit-imized in court.

"Ladies and gentlemen of the jury: the fact that my client wrote 850 checks worth $910,000 he didn't have is not in dis-pute. But I ask you to remember that we have heard testimony today from professional medical testifiers that my client is not a criminal — he is simply income impaired. And the case is made more complex because, of course, he is also honesty chal-lenged, being a congressman and all."

Now, I ask you: Would you find this person guilty?

We don't blame the hearing impaired for the fact that they have a hard time hearing — it's just a fact of life. Same thing for being income impaired. It's great! Once we get the name of everything bad changed, nobody will be held accountable for anything!

Once you've gotten your particular problem labeled as an affliction, the next step is to get legislation passed saying that it is illegal to discriminate against you based on it.

This could have serious repercussions in advertising, where about half of the agency people out there could be legally declared creatively challenged.

Imagine how that would impact agency-client relationships.

"We're firing your agency because we think your work stinks."

"Well, you're right about my work; but you can't fire me because I've been declared creatively impaired and firing me for bad work violates my civil rights."

"You mean I could only fire you if your creative product got better?"

"Exactly."

"But then, why would I want to?"

"Beats me. Looks like you're stuck with me for life. Let's talk about my fees."

Clearly, there is much work to be done in this area. And many things that need re-naming. For instance, how many of you would qualify as dishwashing impaired, cooking disadvantaged or parallel parking challenged?

You see what I mean.

It's a big job, and somone's got to do it. I'd like to help, but I can't.

I'm re-naming impaired.

I Can, Therefore, I Do

Have you ever wondered why it is that one airline charges $54 for a ticket to, say, Oakland while another charges $200?

It isn't, as you might think, because one airline makes you sit on the floor instead of in chairs, or that their airplanes are stripped-down models without wings or landing gear that they bought in some used airplane lot that had signs in the window that said, "As Is - No Guarantees," or that their pilots are minimum wage trainees from some government job corps program gone berserk.

No.

I'm sure it's all very safe. Understand, that doesn't mean I'm going to get on a plane that can get me to Oakland for $54, but that's neither here nor there.

No. It's because some smart marketer at the more expensive airline is aware that the same law that governs what you say to your child when they want to eat too much cotton candy at the carnival is the same law that governs how much they can charge for a an airline ticket. It is The First Law of Human Action, which states, "I can, therefore, I do." And it is the reason why one airline charges more for a ticket to Oakland than another airline, and why Congressmen overdraw their House bank accounts by $800,000, and why men take longer showers than women.

Because they can.

In college, you may have studied Descartes, who said, "I think, therefore, I am." (I wonder if anybody ever said to him,

"Hey, Renee: I've got an older brother who never thinks; does that mean he is not?")

Descartes was looking for proof of his existence, which was somehow not evident to him just by looking in the mirror as would be to you or me, or by the presence of hunger pangs three times a day, which I have always taken as proof-positive that I exist.

The First Law of Human Action is not as elegant or abstruse as Descartes, and it may never make the Philosophical Hall of Fame, but it goes a long way to explaining why one airline charges a hundred and fifty bucks more than another for the same service, and why a three-year-old eats mud. Because they can.

This is the law of nature that explains why college students, away from home for the first time, do such stupid things.

The collegiate version is, "I can party all night, therefore, I do." The WSU variation is, "I can party all semester, therefore I do."

One day that all changes, of course, and you become dominated by the inverse version of the law, which says, "I can't, therefore I don't."

You know you've crossed that threshold when, at about 11 p.m. at a New Year's Eve party, you turn to your wife and say, "I'm sleepy. Let's go home."

It's also the law that explains why television remote controls have turned we men into a nation of channel flippers. I can; therefore, I do. (To which our wives all reply, "I know you can, but if you want to stay married, don't.")

It's why pregnant women cut their hair and old women dye it blue; why men clog their arteries with fat and die young, and teenagers stick rings in their noses. It's why actors, football and baseball players charge millions for their services. It's why some people lie on tanning tables until they look like they're covered with shoe leather instead of skin and why some people will con you out of your money while others go to Nicaragua to build houses for the homeless.

It is also, I discovered the other night, the reason why fifth grade boys will get on a Tilt-a-Whirl at the local traveling carnival and stay on until they puke. I can, therefore, I do.

It's nice to know some things are constant in the universe.

You would think that those of us in marketing would consider all things in the context of this law, but we don't. In fact, we hardly consider it at all.

The Xerox copying machine almost didn't get made because the marketers couldn't figure out why anybody would pay huge bucks for a machine that did what carbon paper did for next to nothing. What they admit now they failed to consider or envision was that people would want to copy all kinds of documents simply because they could.

And who would have thought that anyone would look at the lowly bungee cord and conclude that if it were long enough, a) you could attach one end to your ankles and the other to a bridge and then jump off, and b) that you could turn doing that into a successful business?

I can attach this cord to may ankles and the bridge and launch myself into space; Therefore I do.

So much for market research.

Now, the problem is there's nothing in the law that says that what we can do is what we should do. Or is right to do or good for us.

That's why as parents, we spend most of our time explaining to our kids why they can't do what they want to do. What they, well, can do.

You just hope and pray that you're doing your parent thing right so that one day your daughter doesn't stand up in front of a church full of 400 of her closest friends and say "I can, therefore I do," and marry the wrong guy.

Still, one day you tell your child that she can't do something and she looks you square in the eye and corrects you. "You mean 'I may not'," she says, and you both know that your days of laying down the law are probably numbered, and her first all-nighter is closer than you thought.

Until then, you just have to remember that sometimes the quickest way to teach your child a lesson about what she shouldn't do is to let her do what she can do.

That's why when you're at the carnival and your daughter asks you to ride the Octopus with her, you fight down the nausea, smile and say, "I can't do the Octopus anymore. But you can. If you want to."

JELLO ON THE CEILING AND OTHER PARENTING TRAUMAS

My Daughter, the Appaloosa

The worst has happened.

My eight year old daughter ... I don't know how it happened.

Maybe it was my fault. Maybe I wasn't paying close enough attention. Maybe I'm just not a good parent. I just don't know.

You try so hard to raise them right, to teach them, to keep them out of harm's way, but you can't watch them <u>all</u> the time.

You can't lock your daughters away.

And yet, out there in the world, they're so exposed, so vulnerable.

It happened last week. It is every father's nightmare.

One day, she's a happy, well-adjusted second-grader; the next day, she's ... a horse. An Appaloosa, I think. Or a Palomino. It's hard for me to tell; I don't know one horse from another.

Actually, she's not all horse yet. She's kind of half horse, half rider. Her legs are definitely horse; even going out to play she gallops. But her hands are human, holding imaginary reins. The top part of her body switches between being rider to horse. Sometimes she's Dale Evans, sometimes Buttermilk.

Sometimes she a frisky colt (or is it a foal?) prancing on new, unsteady legs. It's like having Seattle Slew for a daughter.

A few weeks ago we were in North Idaho at the same time as the Budweiser Clydesdales. The horses (the real ones) were walking with that lazy, loping, knee-locking, head-bobbing walk that those horses do. The next thing I know, my daughter is walking with the same knee-locking, toe-pointing step.

A white-haired old lady passed by and said, "How sweet, she's goose-stepping."

I said, "She's not goose-stepping. She's a Clydesdale."

My experience with this phenomenon is very limited and uniformly negative.

About a year ago, friends came to spend some time with us with their 8-year-old little girl. About a month before, their daughter had seen some movie about unicorns, and had left the theater walking in a trot.

By the time they got to our house, she had progressed to the point where pawing the ground once meant "yes" and twice meant "no." If you asked her if she wanted Rice Krispies for breakfast, she whinnied and nodded her head from the waist. I asked her if she wanted sugar on her cereal, and she said, "phu-uuffft."

I should have asked if she wanted some rolled oats.

Even with a daughter that age, I was not amused.

"Aren't we lucky she didn't see <u>Godzilla</u> and become a cute little Tyrannosaurus Rex," I remember thinking.

I momentarily considered offering her an apple with an open palm, like you would to a horse, and then jamming it down her throat when she took it.

Of course, I didn't. After all, the little unicorn's parents were our friends, and her father was a policeman, and they didn't know what to do with her any more than we did.

That weekend, we established a new house rule for unicorns that kept my sanity and her face intact: no whinnying at the dinner table.

As this was happening, I thought <u>I</u> would not allow this.

And then I remembered my own childhood, and how Judy Cleghorn became a horse when we were in third grade. Judy was a knockout in third grade. (She was still a knockout thirty years later, but that's another story)

Judy really did a number on me. I was as deeply in love as a third grade boy could be. So I paid her the highest compliment I could. I'd run up to her on the playground and slug her on the arm.

Then she would run after me, crinoline skirts flying, and hit me back. She always caught me because she was the fastest runner at Crown Hill Elementary School Annex. And I was about the slowest. Especially when Judy was chasing me.

All of us who had been to Judy's house to play after school knew that she had a thing about horses. Instead of dolls, Judy had horses. Horse figurines on the window sills, horses on the dresser, horses in her closets and on the headboard of her bed. Judy was bonkers about horses.

One day out at recess, I went to find her in hopes of having a real good chase. She was sitting in the playground grass with Boo Miller and Lois and a few other friends, and they all had become horses. They knelt in the grass with their arms, which were now clearly their front legs, somehow tucked in under themselves, just like a new colt (or is it a foal?).

"You can't come in," she said., "This is our pasture." And I know I must be wrong about this, but my memory is, she leaned down and took a bite of grass.

I really wanted to join them in their pasture, even if it meant eating grass, but it just wasn't in me. I just wasn't meant to be a horse.

Maybe that's why I find my daughter's transformation into a horse disconcerting: I know I've tried, and I can't get to where her head is at. I can't share that with her.

Then again, maybe it's just that I consider kids who act like animals obnoxious.

This is a problem, but we've settled on a kind of a compromise: For my part, I'll trust that this is just a phase she'll grow out of and try not to get uptight about it.

For her part, she's agreed not to gallop in the house and not to whinny in place of English.

But when she's at play, she can be whatever she wants to be, even if it is a colt (or is it a foal?)

I just hope she doesn't eat grass.

Jello on the Ceiling

It was one of those days.

When I came home, my wife looked at me with that steady humorless gaze she gets when she's at the end of her wits. She said, "Your daughter has something to tell you."

"Oh, oh," I thought.

This was not good, because, being the liberated parents that we are, we made a pact early on that daddy was never to be made the enforcer, as in, "Just wait until your father comes home," at which time, I would be expected to beat our child to a pulp in the name of discipline once removed and a bit tardy.

No sir.

That might have worked for our parents, but that was in the fifties. This is the '90s and in our family, we decided that our roles as parents were not going to include "Father the Hitman" and "Mother the Helpless" when it came to meting out punishment. If discipline was called for it was to be doled out on the spot and at the scene of the crime, as it were, by whomever was present. This includes you, by the way.

So this was highly unusual.

"Why, what did she do?" I asked.

"I think she'd better tell you," was the dry, matter-of-fact reply.

Something was clearly amiss. This was a breach of behavior so serious that my daughter was going to have to tell me herself.

She punched a baseball through the neighbors window. She punched her fist through the neighbor's nose. She got her bike stolen. She stole a bike. She scratched our new car with her bike. She scratched the neighbor's new car with her bike.

The more I thought, the worse it got. My stomach was going into knots over the possibilities.

Now remember, I told myself, you have to listen to her side of it, whatever the little nine-year-old juvenile delinquent did.

My daughter was in her bedroom sitting on her bed, awaiting execution of sentence.

"Mommy says you have something to tell me," I said. I was trying to be strong, yet neutral. Kind of like a hip Judge Hardy from the Andy Hardy movies.

As I spoke I was thinking, "Please don't let it be the neighbors car."

She got up and, avoiding eye contact, gave me a hug. But she wouldn't look at me.

"Want to tell me about it?"

She sort of sniffled.

I tried to pull her away from me so we could look at each other. Nothing doing. She glommed onto me like a giant tree frog.

It's probably the whole right side of the neighbor's car. She was probably tearing around the neighborhood and ran the bike pedal right down the whole right side. A thousand bucks, minimum.

I was getting impatient. I couldn't play wise old young Judge Hardy forever. By this time in the movies, Micky Rooney always spilled his guts.

"Look, whatever it is, you've got to tell me. Now, please, what is it?"

She still couldn't look at me. This was serious. "Did you break something?" I asked.

"No," she replied almost inaudibly.

That still didn't eliminate the neighbor's car; not really. "Did this happen outside?"

"No. In the TV Room."

Well, hey, that was good news. I didn't have to repaint the neighbor's car. But it was also bad news. That's where the TV, the VCR, and my computer live. Besides, now we were playing twenty questions.

Time to get stern.

I pulled her away from me and put my face in front of hers and said, "Allyson, I want to know, and I want to know now. So tell me, or I'm really going to get mad."

As tears began to brim in her eyes, she said, "Well, Brookee and I were playing and we didn't mean to do it, and we, well, we, it just sort of happened, and we were just having fun and ... "

"What did you do?"

"WE GOT JELLO ON THE CEILING."

"Huh?" was my incredibly articulate and appropriate reply.

After all that, she looked at me with that injured look of someone made to confess the most heinous of crimes only to find out that the confessee, me, wasn't listening after all that, and because of that, she had to repeat it.

"I got Jello on the ceiling!"

My brain was still reeling. You got Jello on the ceiling? Instinctively I looked up at the ceiling. Was it still there, or what?

When I looked down, she went back into her tree frog position, because looking at me and bearing the news of this behavioral transgression was too much for her to bear. And there, standing in the doorway, was my wife, with a slightly smug, self-satisfied look on her face that said, "Neener, neener, neener, you figure out what to do with this one."

I gave her that look back that said, "We'll talk later."

But at least now I understood my role. I was not there to hand out punishment. My wife had done that, as was our agreement.

The punishment was that my daughter had to tell me.

My job was absolution and forgiveness — and to mix in a little guilt to see that it didn't happen again.

My wife disappeared from the door to let us work this thing out without her.

"How did you get Jello on the ceiling?" I asked. "Did you have a food fight, or something?"

"No," she sobbed. "It was, she just, Brooke took mine and I said 'give it back' and she threw it, and I threw it back and then we were laughing real hard, and then it got stuck on the ceiling."

"You were throwing Jello? That doesn't sound like you. Or Brooke, for that matter."

"It was Mommy's finger Jello," she said.

Oh, well. That explained a lot. My wife makes a finger Jello that has the shape retention qualities of a blob of hardened silicone window caulk, and the adhesive properties of Superglue.

"So you were throwing it, and you got carried away; and it got stuck on one of the little, um, whatdoyoucallum, stalagmites on the ceiling texture?"

"Stalactite," she said.

"Right."

I played Judge Hardy for a few more minutes, making sure that she knew that I was keenly disappointed in her behavior and that in the future I expected better of her. And I extracted a promise that she would never get Jello stuck on the ceiling again.

Then we both knew our little drama was over.

Without a trace of Judge Hardy, I said, "You know, I think Jello on the ceiling is a Hurd family first. I don't think even your Uncle David ever did that."

Now out of her tree frog position, she got a little glint in her eye, and checking to see if Mommy was within earshot she said, "Want to see how I did it?"

"Don't even think about it."

The Rival

I knew this would happen.

I knew it.

I knew that someday I would have to face the fact that my daughter was growing up; and that one day she would come home and, against all my advice, against all the heart-to-heart talks, against all the warnings a father can give, there would be ... a boyfriend.

I know, I know. It was bound to happen. But I didn't think it would happen in the third grade. I thought maybe she'd make ten before there were, well, boys.

Well, no such luck. It's not as if they're rushing into anything, you understand. I mean, they don't actually talk to each other. They're both too shy.

They talk through friends. You see, he has a brother who knows my daughter's best friend. So he, the brother, calls the friend and tells her what his brother wants to say but can't. Then she calls my daughter; and my daughter tells her friend what her reply is. It's kind of like talking through lawyers.

Ninety percent of the conversation consists of the words "I, he, she, they, we, 'go'." Nobody <u>says</u> anything in third grade: they <u>go</u>.

"I go: 'Is that so?' and he goes, 'well', and I go, that's not what Elissa said, and he goes, um, he goes, well he goes, 'I don't know', but he thinks he's so, um, neat."

I'll bet that nobody has actually <u>said</u> anything in the third grade in years.

Actually, I guess I shouldn't be surprised about any of this. I can recall making marriage plans in the playground of the Crown Hill Annex in the third grade.

Ricky Hart, David Grimsby, Mark Jorstad, me, and a couple of others tried to decide once and for all which of us was going to marry Margaret Bennett. Albert Lirhuis wanted to get in on it, but we told him to take a hike. Albert was not in the running, and everybody who was anybody knew it, except Albert. But he was like that, in third grade. Of course, none of us had ever actually talked to Margaret about any of this, either – that was unthinkable; she was way too perfect for that.

I hoped that this deciding who got to marry Margaret didn't turn physical, because, as much as I knew that I loved her, I also knew that in any contest of skill or daring or plain old strength, I would never win. No, I had to make sure that this remained a battle of wits and of cunning; a kind of third grade Art-Of-The-Deal kind of thing.

It was marriage poker played by third grade boys, but without cards. Or rules.

In short, it was my kind of game.

It was very complex because everyone assumed that I would marry Boo Miller, with whom I had grown up. I did, too, but with Margaret Bennett suddenly the possible prize, I was beginning to have my doubts. And there was Judy Cleghorn to consider. A winner in anyone's book.

But it was rumored that Judy liked Gary Christoffersen. But Judy had actually talked to me, and I had been invited to all of her birthday parties since kindergarten, and didn't that mean something? Of course, so had Gary; but he lived right up by her so he didn't count. Or did he?

The key to these negotiations was not to trade away a Judy or Boo until you had firmly wrapped up Margaret. It was all very tricky.

Margaret's mother taught ballet to the little girls in the neighborhood, of whom my older sister was one. I began to find ways to go along when my mom went to pick up my sister from dance lessons. Just being that close to her house made my palms sweaty.

Sometimes I would go in the house and wait in the kitchen for the ballet girls to come up from the basement.

The mothers would talk, and the older girls would come up, and I would wait and hope for a glimpse of Margaret. I knew that if Margaret and I could be seen talking on the playfield, it would lock up my deal; and it wouldn't matter how far Gary Christoffersen could smack a baseball or how fast Ricky Hart could make first base. I would win by proximity and default.

And with any luck, I wouldn't have to give up Boo. I could marry them both.

Then it happened. One day, after the girls were rehearsing their dances for an upcoming recital, Margaret emerged from the basement with the other girls. She was wearing a ballet dress of satin, her strawberry blonde hair was pulled back into a tight bun, and she was wearing makeup — lipstick and a little blush.

The effect was stunning. And as she turned to me and said, "Hi, Doug," I did what I have done ever since when I meet a woman of stunning beauty – I lost my ability to speak and I knocked something over.

Now you have to understand, Margaret and I had been in the same class for at least two years at that point. But still, there was something magic about that moment, with her smiling at me, me tongue-tied, and milk and Oreo cookies dripping onto the floor.

The whole point about who got to marry Margaret became moot the next year when Margaret's family moved away.

So given this history of my own, with its romance and third grade intrigue, I guess I shouldn't be too surprised about my daughter having a new man in her life, even though they don't actually talk to one another yet.

These things take time.

I did meet the young man once, when a group of them came over to play. He seemed very polite. Apart from saying "How do you do," he didn't say anything to me, either. Like I said, he's pretty shy.

I tried to be magnanimous to this rival for my daughter's attention. "We've got a lot in common, you and I," I muttered to him, as the kids went off and played. I don't think he heard me.

Perhaps it's just as well. It would all be so difficult to explain.

There is a post script I should add to this story. At my twenty-year high school reunion, Albert Lirhuis found me. I hadn't seen or heard or thought about Albert in the twenty years since we graduated.

Albert was an attorney now, and something quite different from the third-grader we used to dismiss from discussions about whom we were going to marry because it was already clear that Albert probably would never marry anybody.

"Margaret wants to see you," he said.

"Margaret who?" I asked as we pushed through the crowd.

"My wife," he said. Albert could still be pretty exasperating.

"Who did you marry, Albert?"

"You didn't know?" he asked. "Margaret Bennett," he said.

And there, in front of me, was the girl in the ballet dress who had taken my words away so many years before. They had re-met in college and married.

And as I reached out to give her a hug, the first, after all these years, I knocked over a glass of wine.

The First Homecoming Dance

One day about six months ago, when she was still in middle school, my daughter turned to me in the car and said, "I'm nervous about going to high school."

I knew just what she was talking about. I had gone to a large high school (2500 students in three grades — biggest in the state at the time) so I knew how scary that could be.

I also knew that this was a time to do that understanding parent thing and do a little preventive shoring up of her self-esteem, something we all know can be a problem in teenage girls, although I was pretty sure that her self esteem needed shoring up about as much as Grand Coulee needs shoring up. I slipped into my all-knowing, all-understanding, wise father role. "I know exactly what you're feeling," I said. "I had the same experience. But you won't be there two days and it won't seem any bigger than Chase."

"It's not the size I'm worried about," she said.

"Oh. Well, your classes won't be that bad. You'll have to buckle down, I'm sure, but, ... "

"It's not the classwork."

"Really? Are you nervous about playing sports?"

"No."

"Teachers?"

"No."

"Guns?"

"No."

"Well, what else is there? Lunchroom food?"

"I'm nervous about ... Homecoming," she said.

Now, while part of my brain was directing my vocal chords to say, "Homecoming?" to be sure that I heard right, another part of my brain was detached and sort of watching this from above and to the right — a sort of out-of-body experience — and it was wondering if men who have sons ever experience a parenting moment where everything seems about 180 degrees out of phase with reality — like this moment seemed to be. I was pretty sure they didn't.

"Let me see if I understand this," I said. "You're worried about a dance that's six months away at a school you don't go to yet?"

She nodded, clearly concerned.

No question about it. Men with sons did not have moments like this.

Well, that was six months ago. And I have come to learn that Homecoming is a very big deal, and that her instinctive concern about her part in this ritual was not too far off the mark.

Or, as some of you who have daughters can attest to, too early.

The problem here is gender dissonance: I still have your basic male attitude about Homecoming, which can be defined as, Yeah, I'll go, I guess. Which in tenth grade translates into, "I'll go if I get up the nerve to ask Eloise, which won't happen until her friends report back to me that if I ask Eloise, she will say yes; and without that assurance of non-humiliation, I will never have the nerve to ask her or anyone else."

Which probably accounts for why a lot of girls don't go to Homecoming dances.

There just aren't enough boys with the courage to ask someone. Or the right communication connections.

(Now, of course, some girls ask guys to Homecoming, which I think is great. I really do. First of all, it's fair. Plus, I think it's great that girls should get to live with the anxiety that comes from wondering if the person they ask to Homecoming will answer, "I'd love to go to Homecoming. But not with you. Not on the best day of your life, you little pervert." Sure. Ask the boys out. See if the stress of it doesn't make you bald at forty like it did to all of us.)

But I have been sensitized.

The first thing about Homecoming is The Dress.

Planning and shopping for The Dress starts before the actual date is secured.

I hate to break it to you guys, but we are the interchangeable component in the Homecoming equation. In fact, most guys are to a Homecoming dance what a 7-11 is to shopping: Nobody's first choice, but something that will have to do when time is short and the need great.

The dress, however, is unique. At least it begins that way.

We men can go to Homecoming in any old suit off the rack. We buy a new shirt, maybe a tie, declare ourselves spiffy and away we go.

With girls, I have come to learn, it doesn't work that way.

First they have to get in-store peer approval. (They all think the right dress is "cute.") Then they have to get parental approval. If this is not forthcoming, they argue their case before any and all judges – family, friends, parents of friends and the occasional stranger – why they should wear the dress, while the mother (usually) argues why they should not.

"I tried the dress on myself," one mother told me. "It was cut down to here."

"I don't see the problem," I said.

"Well, there are two of them," she said, "and you'll see them both when she wears that dress with her Wonderbra, which is the only thing she can wear it with," said the mom.

"Rrright," I said, convinced now beyond all doubt that men who only have sons do not share these particular parenting moments.

Now, Homecoming dance dresses are not cheap, following only wedding gowns and string bikinis when compared on a price-per-square inch of fabric basis. And they don't change all that much, style-wise, from season to season and year to year.

So it is not surprising that there is a kind of second-hand dress exchange that takes place among teenage girls. This doesn't help my daughter any, as you have to have a dress to barter with to get into the game, but in years hence, it may come in handy.

This, of course, sets up the possibility that one boy might take three different girls to three different dances all wearing the same dress.

"Nice dress. I love that color."

"Yeah, that's what I've heard."

The underground dress exchange is not without its problems, however. One must always keep in mind that turning your nose up at something in a store is one thing while denigrating a dress hanging in a friend's closet is quite another.

"I'm sure it was very cute on you, but I just don't look good in early Frederick's of Hollywood. Do you have anything a little less, um, slutty? No offense."

Still, I am told a surprising number of dresses get recycled this way which is great for everyone except perhaps, the dress buyer at Nordstom.

Is Homecoming worth all the hassle and the grief?

Sure it is.

Besides, it's great training for the Junior Prom.

The Removing of The Braces

The ritual was scheduled for Monday morning.

"You have to be there because I can't be," my wife said.

"Right," I said. That was cool. I was ready to take the day off, to do my part, do the Dad thing, play my appointed role.

"By the way," I asked, "What is my role?"

My wife looked at me like I hadn't heard these plans a thousand times before.

"What is your role in the hallowed ritual of The Removing of The Braces?" she asked incredulously. "You're the chauffeur."

"Oh, yeah," I said. "I remember now."

Like with any ritual – graduation, marriage, ordering a burger at Dicks – there is a right way and a wrong way to do it, and the ritual of The Removing of the Braces is no exception.

My job was to get her best friend, Julie, out of school so she could be the first one to see my daughter without braces (an honor Julie bestowed upon my daughter when her braces came off).

Naturally, you can't go through removal of the braces unless you go through the ritual of putting on the braces.

When I was growing up, getting braces was viewed by me and my friends with about the same enthusiasm as getting polio.

"You have to get braces?! You poor thing." We joked about getting hit by lightning and having your mouth welded shut. And we heard rumors that when two kids with braces kissed, you know, really good uvula sucker, the braces could get hooked together; and if that happened, you had to get an orthodontist to unhook you.

The girls always shuddered at the thought, and said, "Euuuu!!" while the boys who wore braces thought, "Hmmm, how bad could a ten-hour lip lock with Linda Sagstad be?" In any case, we generally moped around all day the day the condemned one went off to the orthodontist to have his or her mouth wired up.

This is not the case anymore. Today there is a kind of jailhouse, metal-mouth one upmanship that goes on.

"Two years? You can do two years standing on your head. Me, I gotta do three-to-five plus headgear. I'm telling you, Doctor Slack's tough."

Of course, for us parents, the thought of braces for our children is still a fearsome thing.

There are several reasons for this.

The first is just plain emotional. To accept braces for your child, you have to admit that your child is not perfect; and for some of us that is a problem.

"Your teeth aren't so bad," we say.

"Dad, my teeth look like yours! And no offense, but I don't want to go through life with my lower teeth looking sort of like the statues on Easter Island all bunched together and viewed from afar."

Ouch. Well, if you put it that way...

Then, of course, there is the cost.

The orthodontist takes a quick look inside your daughter's mouth and pronounces that her teeth are correctable — for about $3200. In advance.

We can do that. Assuming she only goes to college three years.

It is only then that you get to the ritual of The Putting On of the Braces.

The parent's job during this ritual is to sit outside in the reception area and wait.

This is not because you'll get in the way, but because if you hover too much, the other kids will think that your kid is some sort of wuss. And that will create a pain far worse than that of the braces.

So you deal with it. Both of you.

And together, you go through a couple of years of wire tightenings, headgear, rubber bands in her mouth, on the kitchen counters, on the floors, all over the house and all the other little traumas that go with wearing braces. ("If you come home with a boy hooked to your mouth, you're in deep trouble," I said.)

And then one day, your child develops Big Tooth Neurosis.

This is a fear passed from one braces wearer to another, sort of like a neurotic flu.

It seems that having had most of their teeth covered with metal for so long, braces wearers develop a skewed vision of what normal teeth look like; so when their braces come off, they think their teeth look huge.

"I'm going to look like a woodchuck," your child wails one day.

"No," you say. "A beaver, maybe, but not a woodchuck."

I'm just kidding. You don't say that. You don't even think it. What you think is, "I paid three grand, didn't have apples or popcorn in the house for two years, and the result is a daughter who thinks she'll look like a woodchuck?"

Like most rituals, my daughter has found that the anticipation was probably bigger than the actual event. And that a surprising number of people don't even notice that her braces were gone.

I paid three grand for your perfect teeth, and they didn't notice?

Well, so much for looking like a woodchuck.

Well, I notice. And when she smiles, she is beautiful.

Of course, I thought she was beautiful before.

I was telling a client how pretty that smile is and how nice it is to have that final ritual over with.

He looked at me incredulously and said, "But you're not done. You still have to go through the ritual of The Losing of the Retainer. Twice."

Applying For That First Job

My daughter has been applying for her first job.

Well, sort of applying. Kind of half applying.

She has to get a job because she is now driving, and with that comes some financial responsibilities. ("Insurance? You mean you have to pay for insurance? Well, that's a rip.")

Even without direct financial responsibilities, however, it is job time.

Suddenly, her friends, little girls who it seems were twelve just a month or two ago, are now sixteen and showing up bagging groceries at the neighborhood Albertsons or slinging burgers at McDonalds or Zips.

This is an aside, but what is it about getting a job that makes some kids forget they know you?

"For here or to go?"

"Christa. I've known you since you were in first grade. You can say, "Hi Doug."

"Uh, huh. For here or to go?"

Like an unseen tide, the force of work is pulling her friends from childhood into adulthood. And she is pulled along by that tide like everyone else.

Not that she isn't resisting it with heroic efforts, you understand. I mean, this is my daughter we're talking about here, a person with my genetic heritage.

And my genetic code has no direct translation for the word work.

Do you remember applying for your first job? Being told that you had to go into a business, ask for the manager, and when the manager came (inevitably a very tired, very cranky looking old man), you had to say, "I'd like to apply for a job."? And then standing there, wishing that someone would just shoot you and put you out of your misery?

Remember that?

Sure you do. We all do. (For me, those words I rehearsed so many times never quite came out like that. Usually I said, "You don't need anybody to work here, do you?") It's no wonder I was thirty before I got my first job.

So we all know how hard it is when we make our kids go out and apply for a job.

I say my daughter has been half applying because she has been coming home with job applications and filling them out.

On the one hand, this is good, because you want to be sure all the information on the application is correct.

I help her with the answers to the questions.

"Have I ever been convicted of a felony?" Ah, no. Not yet.

"What is the most weight I can lift on a regular basis?" Lift? My child?

"What is the minimum number of hours a week I will accept?" I don't know: 10, 12? "Minimum, Dad, minimum. Not the most hours I want to work each week."

And then there are the references. When you've never held a job before, who do you put down? Someone you babysat for? The parent of a friend? A teacher?

She rolled her eyes. Teachers were clearly loose cannons. There was no telling what they might say. "How important is it that this person actually show up for work? Will this person actually be asked to finish a task? Will this person have to, like, follow directions?"

I see what you mean.

"Put down Lea," I said, suggesting the parent of a friend. "She never says anything bad about anybody."

"But like, what could she say?" asked my daughter.

"Well, that she's known you for a lot of years and that you've never stolen anything that she knows of," I suggested helpfully. "Besides, she works in a Christian bookstore." That can't hurt and it's better than listing your parole officer.

Having filled out the applications correctly, I then had to explain to my daughter that having a job application posted on our refrigerator — however nicely filled out — didn't really count as having applied for a job.

"It doesn't?" she whined.

No, I said. She had to take it back. And preferably, hand it to somebody who looked like they counted. That would be the cranky looking person, I explained.

I started to explain that when she did that, it was vital that she dress nicely, because she might meet the owner or manager or somebody important; and she might get interviewed right there on the spot; and if that happened, making a good first impression was important - even crucial to being hired. But I stopped because it was clear she was going into information overload.

Besides, there are some things that you have to learn your own way.

And one of them is that finding your first job is a lot like work.

OVERPACKING DISEASE AND OTHER THINGS THAT WEREN'T COVERED IN YOUR WEDDING VOWS

How Not to Get Divorced

Okay. Let's say you're a man, and you're married. And let's say you want to stay married.

The real trick to staying married is keeping your wife convinced, over a long period of time, that she made a good choice with you, even if you know, deep in your heart, that there's evidence to the contrary and that you're not much of a prize.

So how do you do this? Well, all the books on the subject tell you to keep romancing her and buy her flowers and take her out to romantic dinners. All that is well and good, but there's a better way. It's easier, it's less expensive, and, if your marriage goes to pot, you can use it in divorce court to show how blameless you must be.

Do the laundry.

I know, I know. It's not a solution you hear on Oprah or Sally very often; and it's unlikely that any marriage counselor trying to justify 75 or a 100 bucks an hour is about to ask, "Have you thought about doing the whites?"

But I'm telling you, it works.

Now, like most things in marriage, it's not without its potential to backfire on you.

To prevent this, you have to realize that men and women do laundry very differently from one another, so you want to be careful not to let your wife actually see you doing it.

You can learn almost everything you need to know about doing the laundry by watching a Cheer commercial. Three piles, three water temperatures, nothing to it.

Your wife will tell you that it's not three piles, it's more like twelve; and you never wash the knits with the polys, and separate by color, and so on and so on. Ignore all that stuff. But do this: make a fourth pile, and call it Everything Else That Isn't White, Dark or In Between. You'll get additional points for telling your wife you didn't do her little frilly things because you didn't want to take a chance on ruining them. She'll say, "Oh, that's okay, honey. I'll do those later. Thank you."

It's amazing. She'll thank you for <u>not</u> doing her laundry and feel good about you at the same time.

So how does this help your marriage? Well, remember, I didn't say it made for a <u>happy</u> marriage. I said it was good for keeping your wife convinced that she made a good choice in you.

You see, women get together and talk about what dolts we men are. They get to crabbing about how we men don't do this, and we don't do that, and how we all seem to make the same disgusting sounds in the morning. And in the middle of that litany of woe, your wife gets to say, "My husband does the laundry."

I'm told the typical response to this little nugget of information is an admiring, "He does?"

Of course, this makes your wife feel like maybe she's luckier than everybody else in the group, and after all, that's the goal, isn't it? She actually gets to bask in a little glory. And in the long haul, that may be worth more than flowers.

If you really want her to be able to impress her friends, do the laundry and the dinner dishes. You don't have to do them all the time, just enough to give her something to talk about.

And of course, it only makes sense for you to do the dishes when company comes over. It's good PR for your wife, and if the company should happen to be boring, it gets you away from the dining room table without being out-and-out rude.

As far as the dishes are concerned, the best of all worlds is to clean up the dishes after your wife has given a baby shower or something. If you only do dishes once in your life, make it then. And be sure to start when all the women are still around to see you.

Remember – in between exclaiming about how cute all the baby gifts are, they've been talking about what inconsiderate dolts their husbands are. So when you come in and start clearing away the dishes, it's nothing short of astonishing.

And who gets the glory? Your wife! After all, she picked you! And all this for sticking your hands in some warm soapy water!

To be sure, there is a lot more to making a marriage happy than just sharing in the domestic chores; but that'll go farther than most men care to think.

The only way you can top doing dishes and the laundry is to add ironing your own shirts. Only do this if a) you really love your wife a lot, or b) you hate her and you want out of the marriage.

Because, if one day you should find yourself in front of a divorce judge, wouldn't it be nice to be able to say, "Your honor, I do the laundry, I do the dishes, I iron my shirts, and except for my attraction to 19-year-olds, which is no big deal, I don't know how I could have been a better husband."

And the judge will say, "You're right. I'm going to give you the house, the kids, both cars and the boat and make your ungrateful wife pay $1200 a month child support."

And if the judge is a woman, she'll say, "Do you really iron your own shirts?"

"Absolutely, Your Honor."

"Well, now that you're divorced, what are you doing for dinner Saturday night?"

"Learning to cook."

Overpacking Disease

There is something that honesty compels me to tell you about myself.

Something personal and quite painful.

It's a discovery I made about myself and have been keeping secret ever since. Even my wife doesn't know about it. But I feel I've got to come out of the closet with this thing, and this is as good a forum as any.

I have overpacking disease.

Now, I know what you're thinking, sitting there in your stunned silence. Overpacking disease? You can't have overpacking disease. Only women get overpacking disease the way only men become hemophiliacs.

Well, that's just not true. Men get it, too. I know. I'm one of them.

One of the reasons we don't think of men getting overpacking disease is because it used to be called "Women's overpacking disease." But that was changed several years ago when the AMA redefined and renamed all diseases and illnesses. Not many people knew it; but at the same time as the AMA in their collective wisdom dropped homosexuality from being listed as a form of mental illness and changed the name and definition of lots of other abnormalities (like idiot savant to autistic savant), they also changed women's overpacking disease to simply overpacking syndrome, and re-defined it as "the inability to travel light"; and they downgraded it from a full-blown neurosis to a syndrome. An annoyance.

Well, there went the medical benefits.

So I guess, technically, I don't have a disease. I have a syndrome.

I suspected I had overpacking syndrome when I came back from the long 4th of July weekend. As I unpacked, I realized that I had packed three pairs of socks, four pairs of running shorts, three tank tops, a sweatshirt, and tennis shoes that never even got out of the travel bag the whole weekend.

Then I went to Seattle for the weekend. And this was the telling point. It was only two days this time, but I packed the same stuff, plus a rain slicker. (I mean, in Seattle, you never can tell, can you?)

Well if that isn't overpacking, I don't know what is.

So I've been reading up on this syndrome of mine.

In their historic 1970 textbook on the problem, <u>I'm OK, You're Overpacked</u>, Feinstein and Wurzman described the disease in seven important steps, identifiable from childhood. It first manifests itself in little girls when they go to visit Grandma overnight and insist on taking eight full changes of clothes. Little boys, by contrast, want to take nothing except their He-man toys, and even they get left behind, sometimes.

The syndrome progresses through adolescence, into the late teenage years and young adulthood.

I'm quoting here: "Motherhood compounds the problem for women afflicted with overpacking disease. Babies make traveling anywhere for more than a few hours almost impossible without renting a U-Haul. Each new child compounds the problem geometrically." They note there is no cure.

Of men, they say, "Men so rarely get the disease, even to the point of forgetting to pack their toothbrush on casual overnight trips, that it's a wonder that any men over the age of forty still have any teeth left."

Men, they say, travel light. Apparently to a fault.

But that was in 1970. More recent research has indicated that a large number of men are overpackers; but they let their wives overpack for them, so they never have to face their disease head on. These are latent, or closet, overpackers.

In the 1986 best seller, <u>Overload: Women Who Overpack and the Men Who Love Them</u>, Fringle and Arpstatter cite numerous case studies that proved this point in their airport-intercept clinical testing. This where Hawaii-bound travelers were given in-depth interviews at airport check-in counters about how much extra stuff they were hauling over to the islands and were given sizable cash incentives to dump it.

In case after case, when confronted by the choice of dumping all the extra shorts, shirts, pants, jackets, and other stuff that they couldn't possibly wear in six days, 77.3 percent of the men resisted giving it up, even after their wives took the cash.

(Oddly enough, men resisted giving up their polyester slacks much more than women; and men over sixty-two wouldn't give up anything polyester at all.)

Their conclusion was the basis for the now famous Maui Test for overpacking disease, which states, "If you're going to Hawaii and you're taking more clothes than fit in carry-on luggage, you've got overpacking disease. Syndrome.

There was another study that purported to show that overpacking was a problem neither for those who did it or for those who went along and had to carry all that extra baggage. It was widely discounted, however, when it was discovered that major funding for the study came from some luggage manufacturers' association in cahoots with some California chiropractors.

I have found that there's a self-help group that meets monthly called Overpackers Anonymous, where people can vent their anxieties about traveling without something that they might want, maybe.

And of course there are the commercial organizations where you can buy help, such as The Packless Clinic and PackEnders.

Well. I feel better for having spilled my guts like this.

Maybe this public display will help me face my problem and get back to my former mottos about traveling. One was, "If

I can't carry it on, it doesn't go." The other was, "Anything I forgot, I can always buy when I get there."

In fact, on my next trip to Seattle, I'm only going to take
my shaving kit and a change of underwear.

And my rain slicker.

I mean, in Seattle, you never know, do you?

Male PMS: *Premenstrual Stupidity*

Last night was one of those nights.

It was a three never mind night.

As in, "Would you set the table? Never mind, I'll do it
myself."

I hate it when I get the "never minds."

It means I have PMS.

When you're a man, PMS stands for premenstrual stupidity,
and that means that for the next few days, I have to be really,
really conscious of not doing stupid things.

Now, I will be the first to admit that I should do that every
day (never having been described by anyone as too smart for
my own good, if you know what I mean). But boy, I tell you
what, when I am in the throes of premenstrual stupidity, I get
extra-special stupid.

And the "never minds" are the telling symptom.

Everybody knows that you can get a "never mind" at random
every now and again, and it's no big deal. A "never mind" can
come from a momentary mix up in household priorities, for
instance. Like when your wife asks you to empty the garbage and
you're carrying an armload of laundry down to the washer and
dryer.

When she says never mind then, she means, "I didn't know
you were already doing something important," with the message left unsaid that you can get to the garbage as soon as you're

done with that. That kind of "never mind" has nothing to do with being stupid, so you don't have to feel bad about that.

The "never mind" that is symptomatic of premenstrual stupidity is clearly linked to a dullness of wit, sensitivity, and action. All men I know suffer from it, except for one long-time bachelor I know. And I personally think he gets it, but he just doesn't know it. In fact, that alone is probably evidence he's got a really severe case of it.

Frankly, I'm amazed that you women put up with us when we men have PMS, because we do the dumbest things.

You wives know what I mean. Suddenly we begin...talking...real... slow. We sit around a lot more, and we never seem to see all the obvious things to do that you see. It's a wonder it doesn't drive all of you crazy.

When we do finally get moving, we move at the pace of a slug loaded up on Demerol.

When first married, couples try to pretend that male PMS is no big deal. You're in love, nobody wants to fight, and all those little lines of demarcation that frame a working relationship have yet to be established; so when a man comes down with a case of PMS, it's glossed over.

For instance, do you remember when you were first married and your husband fixed toast and left toast crumbs all over the kitchen counter, and the bread unwrapped and the butter and jam out, and had himself a little snack there in front of the TV? Did you get angry? Maybe. But being a newlywed, and unsure about why he was suddenly so insensitive to your need for a kitchen as clean as your mother's, you probably didn't say anything.

Of course, any marriage that's going to last can't go on like that, can it?

Of course not. You've got to come to grips with this thing. So after a few years, your response changed.

"You know, it really annoys me that you leave your crumbs scattered across the whole kitchen like this, and I wish you'd remember to wrap up the bread because it gets stale if you leave it open, and were you going to leave the butter and jam out here until I came along to clean up after you?"

We men know the last part is a rhetorical question, of course; and even if we did try to answer it, during premenstrual stupidity, our mouth-brain connection doesn't move fast enough to get an answer out for the one who needs to hear it – who, by that time, doesn't want to hear it anyway.

So, the PMS-afflicted husband starts to move off the couch, in slow motion, of course, suddenly trying to hide the bread crumbs and jam globs on his shirt and lap that are falling to the living room floor in plain view of his angry wife, and he's thinking, "uh, oh." And just about when he gets to a full, upright position, he hears the dreaded words: "Never mind. I'll clean it up myself."

"Dang! I gotta remember not to have toast when I've got PMS. That's stupid." But it's hard, because you don't always know when you're being stupid. I mean, that's what being stupid is all about isn't it? Not knowing?

The only good side to PMS is that it's a fleeting thing, lasting only a few days.

After that, it's gone; and while the crumbs may still show up on the kitchen counter, they're just something you haven't gotten around to cleaning up yet, not evidence of chronic, unalterable stupidity.

Now, I wonder why that is?

Never mind.

Threshold Compatibility in Marriage

One of the young ladies in our office is getting married.

"He's great looking, has a good job, I love his family, we both like to hike, he adores me, and we both like to cook," she said.

"Uh, huh," I said.

I was happy for her and all that, but I have long since come to the conclusion that none of those things really have much to do with the ongoing, daily act of being married. Not that you would ever want to start a marriage with someone you considered ugly as a stump, unemployable, from trashy stock, and with whom you had nothing in common.

Although, we all know people who have started marriages about like that, don't we? Some of you are probably thinking, "Hmmm, sounds like the guy my daughter married."

No. If you've been married long enough, you know that while finding each other attractive is nice, and having enough money to live on reduces stress, and actually being in love is certainly a bonus, what makes a marriage work is being compatible in thresholds.

Yes, thresholds. Not the door kind, the other kind.

The dictionary defines a threshold as "a point separating conditions that will produce a given effect from conditions of a higher or lower degree that will not produce the effect, as the intensity below which a stimulus is of sufficient strength to produce sensation or elicit a response."

What do thresholds have to do with being married?

Everything.

For instance, if your threshold is lower than your spouse's for cleaning the house, naturally you will always reach your housecleaning threshold first. Your partner just won't ever quite see the need. So you will <u>always</u> be the one to clean the house. (Unless you have children with a lower housecleaning threshold than yourselves. Right. Not likely.)

The first threshold you are apt to encounter in a marriage is the spending threshold, and its immediate first cousin, the debt threshold.

It's my advice to never marry someone with a higher debt threshold than you.

"Hi honey, guess what I did today? I bought a boat from that guy on TV. He's a real nice feller."

"What did you pay for it with?"

"That First City Bank of Hillyard Visa card that came in the mail yesterday. We can afford it. I'm going to get a job."

If that sort of event is a problem in your family, the problem isn't buying a boat. The problem is your husband has a higher debt threshold than you, that's all.

You know that young couple in the consumer credit counselling service commercial? They're going to stay married forever! They are in bankruptcy and they are still talking to each other, clear evidence that they both share an incredibly high debt threshold.

"Well, honey, I guess we're bankrupt."

"Cool. Let's go to dinner and celebrate. We'll put it on the Mastercard."

I have discovered I have a shopping and spending threshold. I'm not sure what triggers it. But after writing a certain number of checks, suddenly I can't shop anymore. Fortunately, my wife recognizes my glazed eyes. "You're at your spending threshold, aren't you?" she asks.

"Yes," I say.

"Try on one more pair of pants?" she asks.

"Sorry," I say. By the next day, I'll be fine, but at that moment, I'm simply over my spending threshold.

Then, of course, there is the clutter threshold.

You know you're at your clutter threshold when you suddenly feel compelled to pick up around the house.

Guys, do you remember what the kitchen looked like in the first apartment you shared with your buddies? Right. It took a grenade to clean it.

But did it bother you? No! Why? You all had the same kitchen clutter threshold!

It grossed out all your dates. But right up until one of you almost died from food poisoning, it wasn't a problem, right? Compatible thresholds.

In fact, thresholds are so important, I think there should be a universal threshold test couples must take before they are issued a marriage license.

You would go down to the courthouse and take a multiple choice test covering the major thresholds that can cause a marriage to come apart. When you were done, if you weren't threshold compatible, you wouldn't get your marriage license.

"I'm sorry. I'm sure you two kids are very much in love, but you have terribly incompatible thresholds in 47 of the 64 major threshold categories, including doing the laundry, ironing, drinking beer with your friends after work, paying bills on time, gaining weight, sports activities, doing the dishes, caring for the family car, feeding the cat, picking up after yourself, tolerating each other's families, tolerance for children, and overall life ambition. So I'm afraid I can't let you get married. I suggest you live in sin for a while until you get sick to death of each other, which, according to these test results, shouldn't take long."

I thought about explaining my theory of compatible thresholds to the newly engaged young lady, but I didn't have the time. Besides, I doubt that she wanted to hear about it, anyway.

Instead I asked her, "When you hike together, who stops first?"

"He does," she said. "But that's usually because his pack weighs more."

"Sounds like a marriage made in heaven to me," I said.

Wallpapering With Your Wife

What is it about putting up wallpaper that makes otherwise happily married couples want to get divorced?

I'm kind of surprised that there aren't more learned articles about this phenomenon in places like the New England Journal of Medicine or Psychology Today or The Wallpaper Journal.

It ought to be in the wedding vows. "And do you, Mary, take John, for better or worse, in sickness and in health, for richer and for poorer, and promise to never wallpaper together?"

Of course, most women would probably say, "Heck no; if I'm going to wallpaper, he's going to help."

In terms of marital bliss, this is a big mistake. But I can't say as I blame them. It's not a one-person job.

There are two major lessons in life when it comes to home improvement. The first is that it doesn't matter how much the drywall guy charges, it's worth it. And the second is, whatever you've heard about wallpapering together being stressful to your marriage, forget it.

It's worse.

I think it's because wallpapering crosses certain natural territorial boundaries.

For instance, how many of you men moved into your first apartment, somewhere right out of high school, and looked at the bedroom wall and thought, "This could be really cute with just the right wallpaper"?

Right. None of you.

What we thought when we saw our first, very own blank apartment wall was, "Man, wouldn't that wall look boss covered with empty beer cans? We could just stack them all right to the ceiling."

So, when you women were heading for places with stacks of wallpaper books, we were heading for the nearest 7-11 for a case of Oly. We were both getting started on our walls. We just had something different in mind.

Which is the fundamental point. It's been my experience that most women know how they want a place to look, and most men don't. It's what they call the woman's touch, and its quite real. (I suspect that most 19- and 20-year-old men could live in pens and wouldn't know the difference, so long as they could make a beer can wall.)

I find few things in life as tedious as looking through wallpaper books.

This is because you can get anything in wallpaper. Little painted flowers. Big painted flowers. ("Don't you have a dress that looks like this? Oops, sorry.") There are cartoons, patterns and geometric shapes. ("Do you like this one? It represents Bournelli's Law. It's guaranteed to make you dizzy if you look at it too long. Remember, it's for the guest room.")

Picking a paper from the thousands of choices is a talent in itself, and one that women have more than men. I know I simply can't look at a piece of paper in a book and imagine what it will look like covering a whole wall.

So all the deciding stuff is generally done by the wife.

But when it comes to putting it up, the project tends to cross over into some traditional male territory. Like moving ladders. And removing trim and otherwise destroying perfectly good woodwork.

So, if you're a man, rule number one is don't criticize your wife's choice of wallpaper if you didn't look at the books. And number two is try to have the flu that weekend – you'll have more fun. And rule number three is no matter how much you said you weren't going to help, forget it; you're going to help whether you like it or not.

I told my wife that I was positively not going to help when she announced that she was going to wallpaper the bathroom in our first house.

"Fine," she said. And she went off to the local building supply store where, in those days, they gave classes in do-it-yourself home improvements. She came home with brushes, and pans that were long and thin and two rolls of wallpaper with little tiny roses on them.

"I don't want your help," she said, standing in front of me with a crowbar, "but they said to remove the trim piece around the floor. Is this what I use?"

Just the way she held the crowbar told me that she was going to make a mess of it, so I got out my tools (wrench, screwdriver, ball peen hammer) and wrecked the trim myself. I felt much better destroying it myself, even though she kept telling me that wasn't how they said to do it in her class.

Then, after much vexation and hand wringing, she got her first strip up. This took about three hours, so she took a break. I went into the bathroom for a break of my own, so to speak, and to take a last look at the pink, high gloss walls that went so well with the ancient speckled countertops. Except for its size, this was a bathroom that Doris Day and Rock Hudson would have felt right at home in.

As I was studying her wallpaper, something didn't look right. I'm no artist, but it looked wrong, somehow, all out of rhythm and disjointed. Then I realized the little rose stems were not hanging down, as nature designed them, but pointing up.

She had hung her first strip upside down.

No wonder I was getting a kink in my neck looking at it.

Well, pulling it off was a mess and required at least four hands, so there it was. I was into this project.

We learned a lot about wallpapering that night and a lot about trying to update a fifties-vintage bathroom with wallpaper. We learned a lot about square corners and plumb walls and ceiling lines that didn't want to run straight and true.

We also learned that it was real easy to make a mess of a hard job and blame the other for it. The word "inept" kept coming up.

"You'd think you could cut a straight line with a razor; after all you shave everyday."

"Fine. I'm growing a beard starting right now."

I was proud I resisted suggesting that we cover the wall with Oly beer cans. At least we'd know which way was up.

You can get really testy wallpapering. It does that to you.

We finished that bathroom before it finished us, fortunately, which I think qualifies it as a successful wallpapering job. We like to overlook the fact that when we got all the way around, nothing matched or came out right.

Given all this, one can arrive at some basic rules for a married couple wallpapering together.

Before you begin, plan on being forgiving and patient; and be ready to cover any mistakes with pictures and wall hangings.

When you're ready to start, decide on the wall to be papered; decide on the paper to put on the wall; and finally, decide who is going to call somone else to come hang it.

Cross-Finishing Stories

Recently, my wife and I have been spending a lot of time with couples who have been married from 15 to 25 years. And what struck me for the first time about all of us was the one thing we all had in common.

Caring? No. Abiding dedication? I don't think so. Membership in multiple 12-step programs, children in therapy, tons of Jenny Craig Food in the garage? Could be, but that isn't what I was thinking about.

What struck me was that we were all cross-finishing our spouse's stories. One would start the story, the other would finish it.

I think there must be a law of nature somewhere that says a married couple will finish each other's stories in proportion to the square of the number of years they've been married.

Or something like that.

In fact, it wouldn't surprise me if a trained observer couldn't make an educated guess as to how long a couple has been married simply by listening to the way they interrupt each other as they tell about the events that make up their life.

There seem to be several distinct levels to this cross-finishing of stories.

At the newlywed level, there is little or no cross finishing. This could be because you are so in love that you are still enthralled with whatever your newly beloved says. (If you are in that state yourself right now, enjoy it, because those days end in a hurry.) More likely, you don't end each other's stories because you simply don't have many stories together yet – so you don't know what the endings are.

After a couple of years, that changes, of course; and you enter level two, where you have a certain number of experiences that you love to tell about. And you have told the stories enough times that, like actors in a long-running play, you each know the script, so to speak.

Consequently, you can correct each other. And do.

The problem here is usually one of conflicting styles. To some people, getting to the point of the story so the conversation moves on is what is important. To others, factual accuracy – who, what, when and where – is what it is all about. (Curiously, none of these people work for the newspaper.)

Some of us just meander around because we like the sound of our voice; and we're not sure why we're telling the story, except that it seemed like it related back when we started.

When a point-maker marries a meanderer, this is not good.

"Honey, get to the point, okay?"

"The point?"

It is also not good when a point-maker marries a fact-teller.

"Well, we were camping on Labor Day weekend..."

"It was Memorial Day."

"Are you sure? Anyway, We were at the lake with Steve and Kim and David and Lea and we were in this driving rain and..."

"David and Lea weren't with us – because Allyson was just one, which would have meant that Lea would have still been in the hospital with Julie."

"Do you want to tell this story?"

"No, you're doing fine."

By level three, you have progressed to the state where you each know each other's stories so well, that you tell each other's stories, which can cause some verbal territorial problems.

"We were flying back from Denver...

"Wait a minute: Are you going to tell them about the time the landing gear didn't come down? That's my story."

"No, it's not."

"It is so. You weren't even there. I'm the one it happened to."

"You were? Oh."

By the time you have progressed to level four, territoriality gives way to memory lapses. When this happens, one spouse may have to jump-start the other's story:

"Tell them about that time with the Rempings."

"What time with the Smiths? Which Smiths?"

"You know: Dale and Carol – your sister and her husband? And you and Dale got so stupid?"

"Oh, Yeah!"

At level five, stories that used to be long and detailed and colorful often become abbreviated.

"We were in Phoenix in this beater MG convertible I had and it was so hot, I changed clothes while driving the car, and when I was naked, a busload of nuns pulled up along side of us. Can we go home now?"

Abbreviated stories can mean either that it is the end of the evening or the end of the marriage. Or both.

At level six, there are no interruptions because your stories all begin, "My ex-wife and I..."

And then you meet someone new, and go back to level one.

Country Living

The quickest way to render a bathroom useless, is to give a new bride in a new house about five back issues of <u>Country Living Magazine</u>, a Visa Gold Card and say, "Go to it."

<u>Country Living</u> is the magazine that shows pictures of homes with gleaming hardwood floors, sturdy maple furniture that looks real uncomfortable, tables with red and white checkerboard table cloths with baskets of either ripe fruit or breads and rolls that look a little like they have been sprayed with Varathane Hi-Gloss finish. In fact, the breads look a lot like the hardwood floors. There is usually a wall or two of used brick somewhere and pots and pans hanging down that don't look like they get a lot of use.

The headline usually tells you what it is you're looking at. "Cozy and Bright with a Country Flair," which is good, because without that help, you'd be inclined to think it was more like, "Cluttered and Unlivable, Especially If You Have Children."

I always wonder who really lives in those homes, and whether or not they have children; and if they do, are they away at boarding school or tied up in the basement or what?

And where is the kitchen junk drawer? You know, the one that has the phone book, magic markers, assorted pens and pencils, hundreds of out-of-date coupons, keys that you can't identify but are afraid to throw away, miscellaneous batteries that you think might still be good, a couple of packages of snap-shots from Shopko you don't know what to do with, and a map of Washington. Where's that drawer?

Maybe people who live in "Cozy and Bright" country kitchens have figured out how to live without collecting all that stuff.

Maybe, but I doubt it.

The real risk behind seeing pictures of rooms like that is that you might just be tempted to have one of your very own.

You shouldn't try this unless you have a lot of space to waste in your home.

A young couple we know was showing us their brand new house, and they had really done a nice job with it. It was bright and cheery. Very clean. Very spanky. They were justifiably very proud.

The highlight of the house was the main bathroom. It was right out of Country Living Magazine. It had a skylight. It had nice oak trim. All it needed was a headline above it somewhere that read, "Snug, Light, and Lovely."

There was a basket on the floor with bath towels, hand towels, and wash cloths all rolled up and carefully placed in a gently reclining display. The basket also had several carefully arranged soap bars in different colors. They looked a little like eggs in a nest. The detergent bird had been there, apparently.

There were silk flowers and dried weeds. On the sink was a collection of round soap balls.

Round soap! And in colors! I didn't know you could buy soap in those colors. And I thought Irish Spring was colorful! Mauve soap balls. The detergent bird had been busy.

A small hand towel was draped partially over the sink, just so.

"What if I have to go to the bathroom?" I asked.

"Use the one off our bedroom," she replied.

"Do you ever use this one?"

"Mom did once," she said. "I was so mad. She came in here and washed her hands and then grabbed a towel from the basket and dried her hands off. I said, 'Mom, what are you doing?'"

"Yeah, what a stupid thing to do in a bathroom," I ventured, unsure of just what the point was, but glad that it was her mom and not me who had been so gauche.

"Yeah, so now I have to wash the towel, and after you wash them, they're never the same."

I looked at the basket of towels. Indeed, they were all new. Except for one that was behind the others. The non-virgin towel, relegated to the back row for the rest of its days because it was unlucky enough to be chosen to do what it was born to do: dry off someone's hands.

But I was beginning to get the point. Function is not what this room was about. This room was about pleasing design, blended colors, style.

Country Living with a toilet. Functionality had no place here.

Anyone with any sense at all could see this was a room to be looked at and admired but not to be used.

"What about the soap?" I asked. Did you have to throw that away after your mother touched it, too?"

Her eyes brightened, and she disappeared for a moment, returning with a small bag.

"I almost forgot," she said. Then she pulled out more round soap eggs, these carefully wrapped in colored tissue, tied off with a bright ribbon. They looked sort of like the fruitcake you get at weddings that nobody eats. She arranged the fruitcake-looking soap by the sink and took the other soap balls, and put them in the towel basket.

"There," she said. Then she added, "You don't think anyone would unwrap one, do you?"

I said I didn't think so because I was sure I wouldn't, and I was a pretty good test for the lowest common denominator of human behavior.

I suggested that she put a big, wide ribbon across the door, like they do in the home shows. That would let people know the room was for looking, not using.

"That's an idea," she said.

Later in the day came the news that they were going to have a baby.

"I guess that means we'll have to turn the guest bedroom into the baby's room," said her husband.

"You lose a guest room, but you gain a bathroom," I ventured, knowing how a baby was going to crowd out baskets of soap eggs and rolled up towels. "But it's a bargain."

"And when the baby gets a little older, I can turn the bathroom back into the way it is now," she said.

"Sure you can," I said. "Just as soon as your child leaves for college."

Checkbook Adjustments

My newly wedded friend was telling us that she and her husband had their first fight since they got married.

She was feeling bad because he called her stupid.

"It was over the checkbook, wasn't it?" I asked.

"How did you know?" she asked.

"The first place 'stupid' usually shows up in a marriage is in a discussion centering around the checkbook," I told her.

The checkbook is the traditional site of the first fight of a marriage.

I asked her what happened.

"I don't always write down the exact amount of the checks I write," she said. "But that doesn't give him the right to call me stupid."

"Right," I said.

I told her the good news is that the adjusting of two people to one checkbook is not really a fight. It's more of a navigational course correction.

The bad news, which I didn't bother to tell her, is that a lot of people can't decide upon what the course should be.

The problem is everybody handles their checkbook, not to mention their personal finances, differently; so the first time you have to balance your joint account checkbook, you have to do more than reconcile your bank balance. You and your spouse may have to reconcile your spending patterns.

In a young marriage, this is where the male bumps up against the reality of the cost of women's clothing.

"What did you buy at Lamont's for $35.00?"

"Nylons."

It starts to make the way a man buys socks, which is usually an impulse buy at the checkout counter at the supermarket, look like a pretty good deal.

And it doesn't make you feel much better to hear what she didn't buy that would have cost a lot more.

Eventually most wives learn how to get around their husband's price gag reflex by bringing home three things and letting their husband reject one of them. That way when he sees the check amount, he will feel he has had some control over it.

It's a shameless manipulation, but it sure works in our household.

Another area of dispute is the discovery of a left out check. You suddenly realize that someone has forgotten to register a check somewhere. If you live and die on the float (that time between when you actually make your deposit and when you expect a check to clear) and what newly married couple doesn't – this can cause a lot of stress.

Trying to remember who you wrote a check to a week ago and forgot to register is like trying to remember the names of all your co-workers' spouses at the company picnic. Just about impossible. I have learned that it's best not to be too accusatory about this sort of thing, because, as likely as not, I'm the one who forgot to register the check.

The occasional unregistered check is a lifelong phenomenon. In our household, we eventually solved the problem by going to the checks with the copies underneath.

Another area of contentiousness is the check that has an amount registered, but not to whom. For years, my checkbook had long lists of numbers with no accounting of whom they were to. This would occur when I was paying the bills and got lazy.

It drove my wife nuts.

It drove me nuts a month later when I would be wondering whether I actually got around to paying the Penney's bill or not and couldn't tell.

Which brings up another key point about the checkbook fight. The outcome of the fight must determine who is going to be in charge of paying the family bills. It's a part of the course correction you have to make together. Somebody has to be designated navigator.

When you aren't married, it's your business whether you pay your bills the day they arrive, the day you get paid, or in some more esoteric method, such as some particular alignment of the planets and the stars. But when you're first married, unless you both happen to like to pay your bills the same way, you're going to have to find some happy ground you can both live with. Or you're going to have the checkbook fight over and over again.

It's been my observation that, generally speaking, sooner or later, one person gets the bill paying job. And that person becomes the de-facto controller of the household finances. Sort of the Arnold Greenspan of the marriage.

It's a real power position.

When you're out shopping, the bill payer has absolute veto power over all purchases. "What do you think about this $40 blouse for my mother?"

"Can't afford it."

"What about this $85 bikini? I really need a new swimsuit this summer."

"Get it."

You see what I mean.

Of course, this doesn't mean that when you come home with a 16-foot ski boat with a hundred and ten horse Merc on the back, that you won't have a fight on your hands. But if you're in the bill paying seat, you can always say, "Hey, I pay the bills. We can afford this." What goes unsaid is, "As long as you get that promotion and I don't get laid off."

Settling how you're going to handle the checkbook is one of those minor passages that takes a couple into true adulthood. It's one of those things that lets you give a little and take a little and compromise on for the greater good and happiness of all. It's also a good indicator of whether or not everybody in the marriage is rational when it comes to money, which has a lot to do with the long-term viability of the marriage.

Having heard all this, my friend said she felt better.

A day or two later, she told me they had decided that he would take care of the bills; and they were working out a household budget.

Besides, she said, she had figured out a way to avoid some of the checkbook problems. She was using her Visa card more.

"Did I tell you what the second fight in a marriage is usually about?" I asked.

Holding Garage Sales

When you have a garage sale, do you report the income on your income tax or collect the state sales tax the way you're supposed to?

Yeah, I didn't think so.

You're under arrest.

Just a little joke.

Around our house, spring used to be garage sale time for us because it coincided with our annual Post-Winter Clutter Toss. During this annual event, which usually takes place about the end of March, my wife and I used to look at each other like Mickey Rooney and Judy Garland and say, "Hey, instead of throwing this stuff away, let's have a garage sale!"

Yeah! What a great idea. Let's take all our stuff that is broken or ugly beyond description and let's sell it to someone with less taste than us. We've got tons of stuff like that! We'll be rich!

But garage sales never work out the way you hope, do they?

I think part of the reason is that we, as a society, are over garage-saled. The government tried to help us with this by putting a limit of one sale per household per year on us.

They said it was to protect us from buying stolen goods in permanent moving outdoor stolen merchandise bazaars, but I think that's a smoke screen. I think the government knew that, left to our own devices, we Americans can't help but overindulge in anything, so they put a limit on garage sales like they do on catching fish or shooting deer or injesting alcohol or drugs or anything fun. But now I think that even one garage sale per household per year is too many. So our government has failed us again.

Because we live on a cul-de-sac, my wife would always call the neighbors, and we would arrange to have all of our garage sales on the same day. I mean, there's no sense in having a bunch of strangers poking around week after week, is there?

Besides, the kids get cranky if too many cars keep roaming through their baseball diamond out in the street.

The thing about a garage sale that's easy to forget is they aren't any fun.

And they can be really brutal on your ego.

And if I'm going to get my ego brutalized, I'd rather be playing volleyball or something.

The other thing is they're tough on your sleep patterns on Saturday morning, because the Early Guy always gets there well before the announced starting time.

Start at eight, the Early Guy arrives at 7:30. Start at 7:30, he's there a little before the paper boy.

Next come the Glass Ladies. Doris and Thelma. Doris and Thelma hit garage sales the way kids hit houses on Halloween. But they only want glass. And if you don't have any, they aren't interested.

"I've got some great records over here. Remember Iron Butterfly?"

"No thank you. But do you have any old milk bottles, medicine bottles, or funny looking glass with the name 'Steuben' on it?"

"No ... "

"Thank you so much. Yo! Thelma! This is a dry hole. Who's next?"

Next come the antique ladies. I don't mean the ladies are antiques, I mean they're looking for antiques. Actually, now that I think about it, the ladies are antiques, but that's neither here nor there.

The antique ladies take a quick look around and if they don't see what they want, they won't hesitate to ask if there's any antiques inside you might want to sell. We invited them in one time, to look at our piano. That was a mistake. They took one look around and identified our furniture as, "Early American Married Eclectic." They told us that the piano that I inherited from my great Uncle Billy that was the first piano ever in Reardan, wasn't worth a lot but never to sell it and that it really should be on an inside wall and be dusted more often.

I wanted to ask, who do you think you are, my mother? But I didn't.

They didn't want my Iron Butterfly album, either.

After the antique ladies come the expanding families. Some look like they might expand right there in front of you.

"I need a car seat for a baby. Oooph."

"Are you Okay?"

"I think I'm in labor. Now, I need a car seat, do you have one or not? Oooph."

We did sell our car seat, but it was a struggle. "Five bucks? That's a Strolle. Top of the line. My daughter lived in that car seat. With her little shoulder straps and lap belt, she looked like Parnelli Jones with a binky. How about $7.50?"

One couple came in and marvelled at a table lamp we had for sale. She said to her husband, "Uncle Harry bought a lamp like this."

"Which one is uncle Harry?" her husband asked.

"The blind one. I didn't believe anyone with sight would have bought such an ugly lamp."

About this time, all the neighbor kids begin rummaging around and trading toys.

"What's that?" I asked my daughter, who was dragging home a new prize.

"Devon's drum set. His mom said I could have it."

"Wonderful. Why don't you give Devon your light toy? The one with the ten thousand pieces of glass that we keep stepping on?"

Somewhere in here you begin comparing the take with your neighbors. $74.50. $90. One neighbor claimed to have made over a hundred.

"A hundred bucks? What did you sell?"

"My husband's complete collection of Playboy. Won't he be surprised?"

Indeed, he will. In fact, I'm a little surprised myself. If I'd have known the Reverend had those, I'd have made an offer myself.

Then they would ask me how much I made. "You mean, not counting what I owe Devon for the drums? About 19 dollars."

They would shake their heads sadly, more of a comment on the nature of my junk than of my lack of success on the day, and head back to their customers.

So, we aren't going to have garage sales anymore. They're just not worth it.

Besides, it may just be rationalization, but I'm getting to the age where I'm not sure that parts of my past should be for sale. Given away, perhaps, but for sale? Something doesn't seem quite right about that.

But, the good thing about garage sales is that they put you face-to-face with your past. And they allow you to ponder the larger questions in life, like what is the meaning of material things, are we really owned by our possessions, and why did I ever buy an Iron Butterfly album?

Old Married Couples

One of the young ladies at work was berating her fiance for not wanting to go out and party on Saturday night. "It's like we're an old married couple," she said. Then she looked around and realized that most of the people in the room were old and married and probably hadn't seen eleven o'clock on Saturday night for years.

"No offense," she said. "I was thinking of my parents."

That didn't make it any better, knowing that we were all a little older than her parents. That's getting to be a fairly common thing where I work. But we were gracious.

"No offense taken," we all agreed.

We all knew that getting to the rank of old married couple is no easy thing. In the first place, to qualify, you have to successfully pass the critical years in a marriage: 0.8, 3, 7, 11, and 15 through 18.5.

Furthermore, if you last that long, you will also have to get past three career changes, two thirtieth birthdays, one fortieth birthday, and a rancorous discussion about birth control pills, any one of which has enough tension in it to snap all but the strongest of marriages.

I'm here to tell you that any two people who get that far have earned the right to hit the sack early on Saturday night.

Qualifying for old married couple is an odd thing. It's not like you aspire to it. But on the other hand, when you agree to stay married for the rest of your life, where else do you expect such a promise to lead? To a lifetime of discos?

But maybe she's right. Maybe we need a chapter of Old Married Couples Anonymous. Every Friday night when you want to go to bed early, another member will call you up and say, "Get out there and boogie! You're turning into an old geezer!"

Well, not for me.

It seems to me there is a natural aging process that takes place in a marriage – sort of like the aging process of wine.

Mostly it makes for a better product. Occasionally, of course, one goes bad on you, and there is nothing to be done but toss it out.

This aging process might be called the "Old Married Couple Automatic Boogie Shutdown Syndrome" because it is marked by the realization that if you never see the inside of bar with a loud band again, it will be okay with you. Your boogying days are over.

This is difficult to understand from the vantage point of someone who has only recently been let in to such places, and who still thinks that nine-thirty is a good time to get a Saturday night party rolling.

When you're an old married couple, that's just about the time you start planning your exit, and calculating how much you're going to owe the babysitter.

Now it may be entirely possible that this transformation from rock and roll party animal to sloth takes place whether one is married or not. Maybe it's a natural part of aging to suddenly gravitate to places where they play a lot of Creedence Clearwater Revival, and to realize that the time you like best in a bar is 5:00 p.m., when they put out the free chicken wings and beer is two-for-one.

You certainly don't need your wife along to feel out of place in a singles bar. That happens sooner or later, married or not. There's something about sitting in a bar with a bunch of twenty-year-olds, sniffing around each other like they are covered with meat scent, that makes you feel like you don't belong there.

The other thing that may be hard to see from the perspective a young married couple is that just because you don't boogy your brains out on Saturday night doesn't mean your life is stupifyingly boring.

It's difficult, if not impossible, to explain to someone that if you just stay married long enough, the the day will come when sitting around with friends and sharing kid stories will sound like a lot more fun than watching Bruce Willis shoot bad guys in Die Hard 7. Or that sitting home alone with the other half of your old married couple until 10:30 or 11:00 p.m., when you have to go retrieve the kids from somewhere, will look like a perfect way to spend the evening.

And how do you explain that the day will come when you'll look forward to going grocery shopping together on Saturday night? "Yeah, we've got a big weekend planned – we're going to Safeway."

Well, I'm not sure you do.

With about half the marriages ending in divorce, it's probably not worth it. Half the people you'd tell won't get there anyway. Or maybe they'll get there, but not with their current spouse.

So I don't try. I tell young couples to party as long as they can. There's plenty of time for acting old later.

And if they ever make it to the status of old married couple, maybe they could join my wife and I on our walks around the neighborhood, or our early morning coffee on the porch.

Or, maybe we could meet some Saturday night and do the meat department at Safeway.

Selective Deafness in Men

I think the traditional wedding vows need to be revised.

We need some sort of protection against the time in a marriage, that inevitably comes, when we become selectively deaf.

We need the vows to say, "Through sickness and health, for richer and poorer, when you listen and when you don't ... " Or words to that effect.

This was pointed out to me the other day when I walked into the room right when my wife was saying to my daughter, "Sometimes, you listen just about as well as your father."

To which my daughter replied, "What?"

I was so proud of her.

Even as I saw problems for her twenty years hence, the genetic linkage was clear. And I had one of those parental moments where you realize that you have passed along a family trait, a heritage, so to speak, and it makes you proud, even if it is a trait that someone else might describe as a major personality flaw.

My wife, who was already frustrated at not being listened to, turned to me. "What are you beaming at?" she wanted to know.

I thought about giving her my blank-eyed-idiot stare and saying, "Huh?" But I wasn't sure just what had precipitated her earlier remark, and I've learned the hard way that sometimes such wonderful moments of family levity like that aren't appreciated if she's too close to the end of her proverbial rope.

So instead I said, "I'm not beaming. This is not a beam. If I were proud of the insensitivity my daughter displayed by tuning out whatever it was you were asking her, I would have looked like this."

I then tried to approximate what beaming looked like. I don't think I did it right, though. It's hard to beam on demand.

"Dinner's ready," she said, dropping the subject.

I have always been selectively deaf. It's just one of those things. It's like being short. I can't help it.

The problem isn't in the ears, it's in the brain. I'm simply no good at splitting my attention.

Put another way, you could say that I can't do two things at once – listen and read, think and talk, see and hear, listen and remember.

(Listening and remembering is a whole different cognitive problem that also should be addressed in the marriage vows, but I don't want to go into that here.)

I really admire people who can read the paper and stay involved in a conversation at the same time. But it just doesn't work that way for me.

It's like my brain has these little toggle switches that limit my sensory input to only one system. When one system is engaged, everything else goes into the equivalent of sensory shutdown.

So, in it's simplest form, which means when I'm watching television or reading a magazine, I won't hear someone (usually my wife, unfortunately) talking to me. It probably doesn't help any that she's usually asking me to empty the dryer.

(My wife used to come out and ask me who I thought she was talking to, but she doesn't do that anymore. I usually didn't hear that, either.)

I have found there is a direct correlation between the intensity of the diverting stimulus and the shutdown of the other senses. A Victoria's Secret catalog might impair my auditory input, while Penthouse magazine, for instance, can practically shutdown my whole autonomic system. Of course, it fires up other systems, so nature stays in balance and harmony.

The problem is compounded by the synaptic switching mechanism which determines what is going to get my attention and what is going to get shut out. This prioritizing mechanism is, by and large, outside of my immediate control.

So what happens is, in the middle of a conversation, I can be instantly diverted. I can be looking right at someone, and without changing my attentive look, suddenly be listening to the radio across the room or reading the magazine cover on the coffee table.

Click. I'm out of there.

This is real embarrassing if it happens when they are asking you a question. There's nothing like toggling back into a conversation and realizing that everyone is waiting for you to give them an answer, and you don't know what the question is because you weren't there for a few seconds.

And I don't know about you, but I find it real hard to say, "I'm sorry, I know I was looking right at you and nodding and saying, 'uh-huh, uh-huh' and all that, but I really wasn't listening. I was reading that *Cosmopolitan Magazine* cover and wondering what was in that article titled, "Which Men Make The Best Lovers." Now, what were you asking?"

I know I'm not the only one who suffers from this affliction. Men confess it to each other when their wives aren't around, which leads me to believe that maybe more men have it than women; but I know some women who tune out their husbands at least once in a while. For all that, I know some who tune them out altogether.

So I think we need a little upfront tolerance for this listening deficiency, and I think the wedding vows are the perfect place to make the point.

Of course, if a listening clause had been inserted into my wedding vows, I don't think I could have resisted saying something like, "I'm sorry, Reverend, I wasn't listening for a moment, there. What was it you asked me to say?"

Wife School

Okay, tell the truth: there is a place called Wife School, isn't there?

That's where every wife that ever there was learns to use the "Were you going to...," phrase.

You know. Were you going to hang up your coat? Were you going to fix the leaky faucet? Were you going to be pleasant to my mother this Christmas?

Since every wife uses "Were you going to ...," I figure there's got to be a place called Wife School where they all learn it.

A "were you going to" question, is really a nice way of saying, "I'm going to rearrange your life for a while by resetting some of your priorities to match my priorities."

You see, depending upon how the question is framed, the answer to a "were you going to" question is usually "no" in it's most honest and basic form.

Sometimes it's "I hadn't thought about it." Rarely is it, "Yes."

Let me give you an example. Something we've all heard. "Were you going to leave your socks there in the middle of the living room floor?"

That's one of my favorites.

And, what is the answer to this question? The honest answer is, "Socks? What Socks?"

Then you say to yourself, "No, I wasn't going to move them, at least not until next Wednesday, at which time there will be enough stuff around them to make the effort worthwhile."

Of course, you don't say that.

(If you want to know how healthy a marriage is, listen to the answer to a 'were you going to' question. If the answer is, "Oh, gee, no. Here, let me heave them into the dirty clothes," this is a marriage where the husband, probably still new at the game, wants to accommodate. Husbands who have been around the block for a couple of years are apt to answer neutrally, if at all. They say "mmmmmm." If he picks up the socks, the marriage is basically sound, even if the honeymoon is long since over. If he doesn't pick up the socks, this is a marriage in trouble. If the husband goes eyeball to eyeball with a challenge like, "If my socks offend your delicate sensibilities, I suggest you move them yourself," I wouldn't move the socks, I'd move out. If you get a sarcastic answer like, "I prefer my socks right where they are because socks on the living room floor are the essence of American family life and symbolize all that Carl Sandburg was striving to express when he said, 'Home is the place you come to die', or whatever it was," I'd say at least one of you needs counseling.)

What else is learned in Wife School? The no-help/there's-a-moral-here answer.

One of our account executives regularly loses his nice, gold-plated Cross pen. He asks a single woman for help finding it, and the reply is apt to be something like, "Sure," or, "Did you look in the conference room?"

He asks a married woman, and the inevitable reply is: "Where did you leave it last?"

Well, if he knew that, it wouldn't be lost, would it?

That's a no-help answer, with the implicit moral: if you put it back where it belonged, you wouldn't lose it so often. Dummy.

I know some men who would rather walk to work than ask their wives for help in finding lost car keys and have to endure the no-help/there's-a-moral-here answer.

I think my mother was a Magna Cum Laude graduate of Wife School. There she learned that you always, always give the reason for a request.

She told me a zillion times that you put water <u>in</u> your milk glass SO IT DOESN'T LEAVE A RING ON THE BOTTOM!

The theory here is if children and mental defectives like husbands understand the reasons for doing something a particular way, sooner or later they'll do it right. Meaning the mother-approved way.

But it doesn't work that way, does it?

At least not for me. I know lots of reasons why I should do things I don't do. Like leaving milk in my glass when I put it in the sink. (I figure I should get partial credit. At least I'm putting it in the sink.)

I've wondered if Wife School is where women get training for "The Company's Coming Panic Attack."

It goes like this: You're sitting around your home, surrounded by your normal clutter, with no one feeling particularly in need of doing any actual cleaning, when your mother-in-law or someone calls to say she thought she'd drop in for a few minutes.

All of a sudden, an okay, livable kind of place instantly becomes a pig sty; and everybody has to drop what they're doing and clean this place up!

I've found it's not good for your marriage to keep playing Nintendo while your wife is sweeping your empty beer cans into every available trash basket.

And then, just when you think you've got the panic under control, and everything is stashed away, what do you hear?

 "Were you going to leave your socks there in the living room for mother to admire?"

Socks? What Socks? Hmmmm.

You might think I'm complaining about all this, but I'm not. I'm just making an observation.

Actually, given the alternative, the "were you going to … " question probably strikes the right balance between nothing ever getting done and clubbing one another.

Certainly we were never taught a better way in Husband School.

9 TO 5: THE INVERSE LAW OF SIMPLE EXPLANATIONS AND OTHER WORK RULES

The Inverse Law of Simple Explanations

We were sitting in a meeting at work, hearing a sales pitch from a potential new Internet provider. He was talking a lot about bandwidth and modem rates and ISDN lines and dropped calls and init strings and unlimited time and generally explaining how hooking each of us up at home was going to be so easy that we would all be surfing the Internet in no time flat.

And then he said those two words that told me that this trip onto the Internet was going to be bumpy.

He said, "You just."

"We give you a disk with all the software, and you just load it up. Then you just put in your entry code and password, and you just enter the type of modem you have and the right init string, and it's done. Once in a while there is an extension conflict, but you just run the extension clean-up program – which we give you – and then you just restart your computer. That's all there is to it."

"You just ... ?" I thought. "You just ... ?"

Right then, I knew I was in trouble.

Not because I didn't understand what he said, which I didn't. For all I understood, he could have been speaking Swedish. But because in a couple of sentences, he had said the words "you just" five times, and that meant the inverse law of simple explanations was bound to be a factor.

The inverse law of simple explanations postulates that tasks are difficult to learn in direct inverse proportion to how simple they are explained to be. And the law is usually invoked when the person doing the teaching uses the words "you just" to explain this supposedly simple task you are supposed to learn.

I first became acutely aware of the inverse law of simple explanations while trying to windsurf on vacation.

"You just balance the mast against the wind like this," my instructor said, balancing the mast upright with two fingers. "And then you just swing your feet up on the board; and as the wind picks up the sail, you just stand up."

Right.

Thought I was going to drown.

By the end of the second day of hanging upside down in salt-water and listening to my instructor explain again and again what I was "just" supposed to do, and facing the prospect of returning from vacation a total windsurfing failure, not to mention all pruny instead of tan because I was spending so much time in the water, I was seriously considering "just" shooting him.

It wouldn't have made me a successful windsurfer, but I'd have felt better.

The problem is, of course, the simpler a task is made to seem, the more of an idiot you have to be not to get it. And the more you don't get it, the simpler it is explained to be, making you an even bigger idiot.

This is very bad on your self-esteem. Assuming you have any to begin with.

If you have ever had anyone explain how a computer program works, you probably know how this feels.

"Let me show you: You just highlight the column you want to move, then press command C. Then you just go over here and hit command V, making sure that the regression analysis button, which is shift/alt/R, is off and that the record function is off, and bingo! There it is."

Huh?

When people do this sort of thing, they generally hit all the keystrokes at the speed of light, so even if you could see the keys, which you can't because their hands are covering the keyboard, you still wouldn't have a chance of remembering the exact sequence of keystrokes, which is what you have to learn to make the computer do what you want it to do.

And there is a family corollary to the rule that says that when the people involved are family members, the magnitude and immediacy of the difficult/simple dichotomy is exponentially increased.

This is why you should never try to teach your husband – or wife – to ski.

"No, look. You just shift your weight from the down hill ski to the uphill ski, and you turn, see? It's easy." Idiot.

"I think I'll just shift my weight to the lodge, and you can ski alone."

For those of you who may be contemplating a ski weekend with a little inter-spousal ski lesson planned, you may want to remember that ski instructors cost a lot less than divorce attorneys.

It doesn't have to be a husband or wife to invoke the family corollary. It can also be a child.

If you have ever tried to teach your child how to parallel park, you know what I mean.

So, faced with the daunting prospect of installing their software for my Internet hookup, and knowing that the inverse law of simple explanations would assert itself, I immediately threw myself on the mercy of the court.

"How about if I bring in my computer, and you install it?" I pleaded. "I mean, if it's so simple and all."

"Sure, we can do that," he said, hesitating. "But I'm telling you, you just follow the instructions and it's idiot-proof."

That was three days ago. He's thinking that today, maybe, he's going to get it to work. Which shows that sometimes, the law works both ways.

In the meantime, I resist the urge to say, "When you're done, you just tell me."

Casual Fridays

Men: It's seven-thirty on Friday.

Do you know what you're going to wear today, on casual Friday?

Ladies: Have you ever wondered what your husband is actually thinking when, in the morning, he stands there, catatonic, and stares into his closet with such a completely blank look on his face that you think maybe he's had a stroke and just hasn't fallen down yet?

What he's doing is praying.

He's saying, "Oh, please Lord, don't let me pick something out that will make me look dorky. Please don't let me wear something that will expose me as fashion-challenged." And he's hoping for some sort of divine message that will guide his hand to this shirt with those pants.

Not getting such a message, of course, he falls back to what he knows, to a particular shirt and pants combination that he has worn before. (Hopefully, not the day before.) A combination that hasn't made you stop and stare and ask the dreaded wife/mother/protector question, "Were you going to wear that ... to work?"

Or worse, actually get to work and have people there saying, "Good morning! Picked out your own clothes today, huh?"

Oh, ouch! I hate it when they say that.

Now, I know what you ladies are thinking. "What? Men only have to put together a shirt and pants and the occasional sweater, and it sartorially hobbles them? We have to deal with blouses and pants and sweaters, and skirts, and dresses, and shorts, and shoes, not to mention undergarments that may show that are part of the total look, plus the accessories, the hose, the hair and the makeup and the jewelry."

Right. Well, nobody said life was going to be fair.

And now it's worse. This casual Friday thing is spreading like a virus.

I recently saw a news report saying that the Japanese are doing it, and they are so regimented in their business look – dark suits, white shirts, subdued tie – that it is causing havoc over there. Even the Men's Warehouse guy, the "I guarantee it" guy, is talking about it.

Five years ago when my bosses announced that henceforth and forever wearing jeans on Friday would be acceptable business attire, we felt like we were breaking new fashion ground.

"We'll show the world that we are creative, loose, forward-thinking and adaptive – all the things you want an ad agency to be," they said.

That was news to me. Based on my experience, I thought most everybody wanted an ad agency to be cheap and quick.

This was both good and bad news. On one hand, I was getting used to wearing suits to work. I was getting to like it. I felt like a success in the business world. More importantly, I knew which ties went with which shirts and which suits. I had reduced my catatonic time in front of the closet to practically nothing. Five minutes, max.

On the other hand, deep down inside, I've never had much use for a tie. If the clothes make the man, I'm made out of more casual stuff.

Well, it didn't take long before casual Friday free-fell past casual, past "dress down," all the way to grubby Friday. I'm not sure that when my bosses announced that jeans were acceptable on Fridays, they also meant to include the grody sweatshirt you painted the bathroom in last weekend.

I mean, we're not a public radio station, after all.

And it also didn't take long before casual Friday expanded to include Thursdays, and then Wednesdays, and then all the rest of the week.

Pretty soon, the dress code, as we knew it, was gone.

Well, not gone, actually; replaced would be more like it. (Understand, of course, that I'm talking about the account executive types. The artists never had a dress code to begin with. Artists and teenagers share the same dress code, which is to say, beyond covering the body to meet certain legal requirements, none. That's why we don't let them out too often.)

Now we only wear suits and ties when we are going to meet with a new client or a visiting CEO or someone else presumed to have a business-look fixation, or whom we want to, um, impress, I believe is the polite word for it.

It's the business version of a first date mentality. "We're all going to dress up, and impress you with how we look so you will hire us so we can come back and show you what we really look like."

So is all this better?

There is an old adage that says, "Be careful what you call because it just might come."

Well, I was all for the new relaxed dress code.

But I must admit that sometimes, early in the morning when I don't know what to wear, I look at the suits hanging in the closet, and the dress shirts and the ties, and I realize how easy it was when we were more restricted. And I think, "Oh take the easy way out. Put on a suit and tie and be done with it."

And then I put on my jeans and the same shirt I wore the day before yesterday and go to work.

Soap Operas

I have been banned from the company lunchroom.

Not because my table manners are so terrible, although that might be reason enough. Nor because, as your basic male with no culinary sense and less taste, I eat most anything in Tupperware, which leads to lunches of re-heated frozen pizza, mixed with peanut butter and pickle sandwiches and leftover fruit cocktail complemented by a half eaten yogurt of undefinable flavor and all washed down with milk that is about two days past its expiration date. All of which both astonishes and nauseates other lunchers, but also which has nothing to do with being banned.

No.

It is not for these reasons I have been asked not to return.

It is because, in our lunchroom, there is a TV, and on the TV are the noon soap operas. And I find it impossible to watch the soaps without adding a running social commentary.

And I confess – it is not especially complimentary.

I've never been drawn into those stories. Not even in college when it was considered hip to watch the soaps because watching soaps was considered a viable alternative to studying.

I'm not sure what it is. Maybe it's that the people all talk so slow. I don't think God meant for people to talk that slow.

"Miranda! What ... are ... you ... doing ... here?"

"I, ... Derek said, ... Kuriarkis, ... he wanted .... to .... see me ... "

"To .... see You?"

"I.......................................   was   afraid, ... so ... "

By this time, I'm going nuts. What's the matter with these people? Are they all on Quaaludes or something? Maybe we're supposed to be on Quaaludes to watch them.

So I start answering for them. You should try it some time. There's plenty of time in between lines.

"Miranda, what are you doing here?"

"Hey, I was just on my way to Safeway and thought I'd pop over to get my daily dose of your after-shave and see who you're having an affair with this week."

If you do that, though, be ready to be very unpopular. Soap opera fans don't like people adding unauthorized dialogue to their shows.

Another thing about the soaps that I've wondered is, why is everybody so beautiful?

Except for some weaselly looking bad guys, who sometimes turn out to be good guys, I've noticed that everybody in the soaps is pretty good-looking.

The bad guys are good-looking, although they don't seem to be able to get a close shave; the manipulative business man is always – and I believe this is the right word – dashing. And the women! Whoa! These women must live on a steady diet of Ultra-Slim Fast or something because there isn't a tubby one anywhere.

Even the occasional granny-type looks great. They don't let a lot of old bitties on daytime TV, but when they do, even they look pretty terrific. I figure that a) they're not really as old as the characters they're playing, or b) they've had blepharoplasties and face-lifts until when their nose itches they have to scratch their eyebrows, or c) they sleep in a tub of Oil of Olay every night.

The point is, the people on the soaps don't look at all like the people who catch the bus down at First and Pike at five every night.

They don't even look like the people I work with, and I work in an office with a lot of pretty good-looking people.

The other thing about the soaps is these have got to be the stupidest best-looking people on earth. I sure hope that in a thousand years, when everything known about our society is obliterated, tapes of the soaps aren't the only remaining evidence of how we lived.

If that's the case, future historians will have no choice but to conclude that we were on drugs, we had a myriad of problems, and we were stupid.

Plus, we never went shopping in K-Mart, we never went to the bathroom, and we got caught in compromising situations with alarming regularity.

I used to ask questions about those things, questions like: why doesn't Nick get his hair cut, or why doesn't Chad get his eye fixed, or why don't they just call the police, or why are we watching people with no visible means of support and more problems than everybody put together in a mental institution?

The answer you get is a very perturbed look and a very articulate frown, which is soap opera lover-ese for "Why don't you eat your lunch where we can't see you?"

Remember when you were in literature class, and your teacher asked you what you thought Hamlet really meant when he told Ophelia to go to the nunnery? Or what Biff in <u>Death of a Salesman</u> was trying to say when he stole the pen? And you said, "Whatdaya mean what does it mean?" because to you, all those people were just figments of some nutty writer's imagination, so the question made no sense? Remember that?

Well, you should have paid more attention, because the people who get into soaps are asking and answering questions like that all the time. Plot analysis is big part of watching the soaps.

"I think Carmen is the illegitimate daughter of Victor; and Samantha knows it and has told Eric, who is setting up Stephen to break up the thing between Cynthia and Donald, except Donald and Samantha have some secret that Victor wants to know that I can't figure out what it is. Yet. It might be that Cynthia and Donald are both Victor's children that he lost when the Vietnamese overran his plantation. I think we'll find out tomorrow. Something's up, that's for sure."

Wow! Where were you in English Literature when I needed you?

When I hear something like that, I want to lean over and say, "I know this is changing the subject a bit, but why do you think Hamlet didn't just go kill his stepfather, the King, when the ghost of his father told him to?"

I don't though. Partly because I work around people who might just lean back and say, "Because if he did that, there wouldn't have been any play, would there?"

Now, I don't mean to cast aspersions on those who like the soaps or draw any deep sociological meanings from their harmless addiction to this mindless drivel, such as they like this stuff because their lives are stupifyingly boring, barren of romance, excitement or meaningful human contact or anything like that.

That's somebody else's job.

Maybe they just like looking at pretty people who are preoccupied with money, sex and intrigue and have problems that don't get resolved for years. That would certainly make any problems of their own, like figuring out what to have for tonight's dinner, seem trivial, wouldn't it?

And maybe that's the attraction and the whole point. Maybe the main attraction is seeing all these beautiful people have bigger problems than you.

Maybe it's better that I've been banned from watching the soaps. After all, it allows me time to wonder about more important things during lunch, like what was this stuff I'm about to eat when it first went into the Tupperware, and why didn't Hamlet just go kill the king?

Maybe the answer to that is on Jeopardy. Now, that's a TV show worth watching.

Technology I Can Do Without

Today's subject is, "Technology We Can Do Without."

Normally, I like technology.

I like being able to take videos of my family, to have the gee-whiz convenience of laser disks, laptop computers and microwave ovens. ("Wow! Look what that does to the cat!"

Just kidding. I would never put our cat in the microwave. I might put the neighbor's cat in there, but never ours.)

But occasionally, the technodweebs go too far.

A case in point: Voice mail.

I used to work where we had an early and very crude version of voice mail. My partner would scream from his office.

It was quite effective, but admittedly, had a very short range, and you couldn't save the messages. Not that you'd want to. When we finally got a phone system with an intercom on it, he screamed at that, believing, I think, that every telephone is born slightly deaf.

But that's a different kind of voice mail.

The kind the phone company is selling these days is the illegitimate offspring of answering machines and the audio tones telephones use for routing and switching.

On paper, voice mail looks like a good deal. I mean, who wants to lose a customer call?

"You'll never again lose a customer because you don't have enough lines," says the telephone company Customer Account Executive Service Consultant Representative (formerly called a salesman).

Wrong.

That theory presumes that all of us just love talking to a tape recorder instead of a person.

Some of us will hang up on voice mail faster than a garden variety answering machine.

My accountant's firm put in voice mail this year as a part of their major remodeling project (the logic of which completely escapes me since they have about the best receptionist in the business). So, during tax time, when I have numerous anxiety attacks, and I need to be soothed by the reassuring voice of my accountant ("It's okay, Doug. They are not going to come and take you away. I don't think."), I would call.

And the receptionist, who knows my voice, would say, "Just a moment, I'll ring Tom."

And Tom would say, "Hi, this is Tom."

And I'd say something like, "I can't find that lunch receipt, Tom!"

And because he wasn't there (but I couldn't tell because the audio fidelity of voice mail is so good that, until they tell you, you don't know you are talking to a machine), Tom would go on to say, "I'm either away from my desk right now, or I'm in conference, or I just don't want to be bothered by anxious clients this close to April 15th. But if you will leave your name and number, I'll return your call as soon as possible. Like in July."

Now, on the other end of the line, what I say is, "Well, shoot."

At that point, the voice mail lady comes on, with further instructions, which you have to have an IQ of a sheep not to understand. You know the voice: soothing, deliberate, unruffled, calm. Valium in the form of a female voice.

"If you'd like to leave a message and you know what you want to say, press 1. To check your message when you are done, press 2. If you would like to reach another department, you may press 3, then dial that extension. If you don't know the extension of the department you are trying to reach, press 4. If you need to talk to an operator, press 5. If you need to go to the bathroom, press 6. If you are having a dissecting aortic aneurysm and you need emergency treatment, press 7. If you're having a dissecting aortic aneurysm and you need a priest, press 8. If you are being audited by the IRS and you're already handcuffed, press 1 through 9 at the same time, using your forehead. If none of these options seem appropriate, stay on the line and an operator, trained to deal with the mentally impaired, will assist you."

Just what I need.

Once I've been through that drill about once, at the first sign of voice mail, I hang up, punch automatic redial, call back and leave my message with the receptionist before she can transfer me.

If I am calling somewhere new and I'm a customer and I get voice mail, I just hang up. So much for not losing any customers.

Depending upon the kind of voice mail system you get, you can transfer calls automatically to another phone. This sounds like a good idea, but isn't.

When you call into a system like that, you call one person, but you get someone else. The risk here is that you get routed from Bob, whom you wanted but who tells you he's sending you to John, who tells you he's out and is sending his calls to Eric, who's away from his desk for a moment, to Cindy, who says she'll be back at three, to Fred, who tells you he's out for the day. But it's okay, because Bob is taking his calls, and he'll transfer you now.

Or worse, this starts to happen but then you actually get somebody.

"Who are you?"

"Doug Hurd"

"Uh, huh. Who are you calling for?"

"Bob. In marketing."

"That dilwad still working here? Hey, what do you guys do in marketing, anyway?"

"I'm not in marketing. I'm trying to talk to Bob, who is in marketing."

"Oh yeah. Is that Bob Peters?"

"No, Bob MacClean."

"Oh, I don't know him. He's not the dilwad I was thinking of. I wonder how you got me?"

"Voice mail sent me to you."

"Lucky break for both of us, I guess."

"Isn't that the truth."

So before you decide that voice mail is going to make the difference between your success and failure, remember, I'm your customer, and given a choice, I'd prefer a real human being on the other end of my phone.

Or a nice, old fashioned busy signal.

Getting Home From Vacation

There ought to be a line painted on the airport floor by the baggage claim area that says, "Your vacation ends here. Begin reality NOW."

That's because while you are lugging three suitcases of dirty clothes plus forty pounds of souvenirs, T-shirts and macadamia nuts out to the parking garage, you have your first non-vacation thought, which probably is, "Hey! There's nothing to eat in the house."

This poses the dilemma of whether or not it's appropriate to do some grocery shopping on your way home from, say, Puerto Vallarta. Personally, I'm against it. I'd rather get all the way home before my vacation ends. This is influenced by the fact that I have the culinary discretion of a goat and will eat almost anything that can be thawed, reheated, or put between two pieces of bread. So I figure I can survive a while without food, if I have to.

My wife, being much more practical and discriminating about what she will and will not eat, is apt to conclude that a quick stop to pick up some bread, milk, chicken, potatoes, maybe some fruit, and some cereal for tomorrow morning will look like a real good idea about three hours from now. And of course, she's always right.

Your second non-vacation thought is, "I have to go back to work tomorrow."

Depending upon how you feel about work, this can be a good thing or a bad thing.

Once back at work, we all can extend the joys of our vacation for a little while by playing the social game of Back From Vacation. The object of the game is to position your vacation as a grander experience than it actually was, thereby inspiring envy and awe among your co-workers.

You can do this because of the unwritten rule that states that when you come back to work from vacation, everyone must ask how your vacation was. Not asking about vacation is a clear breach of social work ethics, unless, during vacation, the company has decided to fire you, in which case everyone will avoid you like you have Drug Resistant Tuberculosis.

The game of Back From Vacation is played by a few simple rules:

Rule 1: It was either the best vacation in the whole world or the worst. In between just bores everybody and reflects badly on you. Understand, of course, that telling people it was the best or worst should not be influenced by what really happened on your vacation.

Remember, what is taking place here is social positioning. If you're talking to a client, for instance, you should tell them it was great, because you don't want your clients to think that you're not smart enough to figure out how to have a good vacation. While if it's your bosses you are talking to, you might take an opposite approach because you certainly don't want them to think you like being away from work all that much.

Rule 2: Don't tell too much about your vacation all at one time. In the first place, nobody cares. But that's beside the point. The point is if you tell all the stories about your vacation at the coffee maker before eight o'clock, what are you going to tell them at noon?

Rule 3: The "sun rule." This rule has changed in the last few years because of the heightened awareness we have to skin cancer. It used to be that the sun rule stated that you had to complain about getting real sunburned the first few days and being just miserable thereafter, so you could explain why you weren't as tan as you should be. Now however, you want to complain about getting real sunburned and being just miserable so you can explain why you're tanner than you should be. If you are very tan, which is absolutely not cool, just deny it. When someone says, "Wow, you're really tan!" say, "No, I'm not."

Rule 4: Complain about the food. I've always found this best done at lunch, when you can bring the subject up without appearing to ram yet another reference to your vacation down everybody's throat, so to speak. People love to hear that you spent $5,000 going somewhere exotic and couldn't get a decent hamburger.

Rule 5: Rave about the food. I realize this sounds like a contradiction to Rule 4, but look at it this way; you ate more than one meal, didn't you? Of course you did. Besides, both complaining and raving about your meals makes you look like you know what you're talking about. Discussing a great dinner is how we decide who ranks above whom in the civilized pecking order, so you can't lose; unless, of course, everyone present knows that you usually eat from a feed bag – in which case, I just wouldn't mention food at all.

Rule 6: Complain about someone else's children. Vacation stories and horrible children just go together, don't you think? How many times have you heard someone tell about being stuck on an all-night flight with a screaming child? (I have a friend with a story like that. What makes it really funny is it was his child who was screaming. He spent all night in the bathroom of a 747 trying to muffle his two-year-old's wailing. When they finally landed, he said 400 very angry, sleepless people gave him dirty looks as they left the plane.)

Rule 7: Always mention how expensive everything was.

Rule 8: Talk about all the great bargains you found. This is like the food rules. You win both ways.

Rule 9: The corollary to Rules 7 and 8: Never explain how you are going to pay for your vacation. Remember: What it cost and how you are going to pay for it are two entirely different things. If you don't explain that you had to plead with the VISA people to extend your credit limit so they would let you get a ticket to get on the airplane to get home, you may just leave the impression that you can actually afford the vacation you just took.

That alone may make the whole trip worthwhile.

Finally, there is Rule 10: "When asked if it was easy (or hard) to come back to work, you answer with a smile and a far-away look in your eyes.

How to do Business Meetings

If you had to pick tomorrow's corporate leaders, what would you look for? Drive? Ambition? Greed? Ruthlessness?

I don't think so.

I think I'd find the most boring afternoon college class and look for the ones who stay awake. Because if you can stay awake in, say, an afternoon Econ 355 class, the chances are you have what it takes to be successful in today's business world.

Which is a high tolerance for meetings.

The Japanese think American workers are lazy. Well, I beg to differ. We are not lazy. We just like to meet. And meet. And meet.

Corporate success is measured by how well you survive meetings.

Meetings have become so prevalent and important to business that there are actually seminars for how to put on successful meetings, making the meeting, I guess, the business equivalent of the dinner party.

("Let's see, we'll put the boss over here, and the boss's sycophant over here. We'll serve the agenda with a touch of history first, and then we'll dim the lights and bring on the graphics ... ") But these seminars are always are filled with mundane rules like: have an agenda, start on time, end on time, get something done, have someone take notes, that sort of thing.

Get real. What has any of that got to do with anything? What does "starting on time" tell you about how to maneuver yourself up the corporate food chain?

Right. Nothing.

Why do you call a meeting? I think there are three main reasons. First, you don't know what to do; second, you know what to do but you want someone else to do it; or third, you've done something or you're about to do something, and you think someone else should know about it.

There is also the simple reason that it sounds important to say, "Let's have a meeting and talk about that."

Subversive, anti-meeting types nip that in the bud saying, "No, we are meeting now, so let's talk about it now and get something decided." What a party pooper attitude that is.

Personally, I like to call meetings when I don't know what to do. I usually have some sort of general idea of where I'm supposed to go, but it helps me focus if I can get a room full of people talking about what I'm supposed to do.

The benefit of having other people figure out for you what you should be doing is when all is said and done, you get to take credit for it all, as if the meeting never took place.

There are certain rules for meetings. The first thing you have to do is establish pecking order. One good way to do this is to ask the I'm-smarter-than-you irrelevant question.

Quoting something from the stock market is always a pretty safe bet for this: "Tele-Mex is really going through the ceiling, isn't it?" When they look at you blankly, you can dismiss them all with, "Oh, I'm sorry, it's a Mexican phone company stock. I thought you had a position in it. Where were we?"

Another pecking order ploy is to change the subject, as in, "I know it's off the subject, but did anybody see the Simpson's last night?" The higher up you are on the corporate ladder, the more you can change the subject with impunity.

In fact, it's never a good idea to start a meeting without having first done your homework; which is knowing what was on Letterman last night and in the paper this morning and what was the latest thing the County Commissioners said about each other. And never, ever start a meeting without first covering all of these.

The earlier the meeting time, the more important the coffee is. If you are going to meet before 8:00, you should plan to meet no further than 15 feet from fresh coffee.

Donuts are also a good idea at this time of the morning.

If kissing up is a major reason for meeting, I'd recommend leapfrogging donuts and going all the way to Cinnabon. The rule of thumb here is you just can't feed them too much sugar in the morning.

I like to schedule morning meetings for another very important reason. I have a real tendency to fall asleep in afternoon meetings. This is very embarrassing. It's not that I'm not interested. Usually, it's just that with a belly full of food and sunshine pouring through a window, my brain is announcing it's nap time and throwing the "off switch" to various part of my body, like my eyes.

Almost as bad as actually falling asleep is simply wandering away mentally. This can happen anytime. You're watching someone intently, but you're really wondering if his wife is concerned about all the weight he's gained recently; and he turns to you and says, "Don't you think so, Doug?"

"Huh?"

Not wanting to appear totally out to lunch, I usually reply, "I don't have any major problems with that, but I'm not sure there isn't another answer," and hope and pray that I'm not asked to repeat what was just said.

The question inevitably arises, if everybody is always in meetings, who is doing the actual work?

Darned if I know, but I do know this: if you're always in meetings, it isn't you.

To avoid work coming out of meetings, you want to take control of the meeting at the end. Effect a little bloodless coup d'etat, as it were. Understand, it doesn't matter whose meeting it is. Your job is to pull a Corporate Alexander Haig, "I'm in charge here," because at the end of the meeting is where they dole out the work. And if you are in charge, you can assure yourself of not getting any.

What you do is, at the exact point where tired butt combines with information overload, you want to say, "It seems to me that what we need to do next, then, is ... " and then you hand out work assignments. "Jill should gather the data we need, Ed should write some sample copy ideas and creative platforms, and Bob should run the financials. I'll call the client and let them know what we're doing. Can we meet again next week?"

If someone actually sees what you are up to and suggests that maybe you should do some of the work, just pull out your daytimer and say, "Gee, I'd like to, but I don't see when I can. Between now and next week I'm all booked up with meetings."

HOLIDAYS, HIGH AND LOW

My Zermatt Christmas

Did your family gather around the Christmas tree on Christmas Eve, and listen to the adults tell family Christmas stories and read "A Christmas Carol" by Charles Dickens?

Neither did mine.

This is the only Christmas Story I know. The only reason I know this one is because it happened to me.

After I graduated from high school, I went to Europe and bummed around for about a year. At Christmas I was skiing in Zermatt, Switzerland, under the Matterhorn.

I spent about a month in Zermatt, and because I was traveling cheap, I was staying at the cheapest hotel in town. It was down by the train station.

In the days before Christmas, the hotel began to fill up with American teachers. These were Americans who taught in military installations, private schools, embassies, that sort of thing. Talking to one or two of them, I found out they got together every year at this hotel and spent a week or so partying. They, too, were there because it was cheap.

On Christmas Eve day, it was clear and sunny; and in honor of the holiday, I decided to splurge and have a hot chocolate in the ski lodge at the top of the hill. It cost about 50 cents, which, on my budget, constituted reckless spending.

I was sitting out on the sun deck, sipping my chocolate, when a mother and daughter came by, looking for a place to sit with their lunches. All the tables were taken. I was alone at my table.

The mother said, "Maybe we could sit here, with this young man." They were American, but they didn't know I was. The mother said to me, "May we join you?" sort of indicating the empty chairs and using the slow deliberate speech you tend to use in foreign countries when you think English isn't going to be understood.

I said, "Yes."

As they sat, she said, "Oh, you speak English!"

I said, "Yes."

She said, "Did you learn English in School?"

I thought about that for a moment, and, recalling all the English classes I had in school, I said, "Yes."

Then she asked, slowly and deliberately so I would understand her, "Where did you go to school?"

I said, "Seattle."

Well, they had lunch, and I had cocoa, we shared some conversation, and when it was all over, they asked me if I would join them for Christmas dinner.

Now, understand the socio-economic gulf here: These people were fairly well-off New Yorkers who were going to spend on dinner just about what my total living allowance was for three months. Obviously, I couldn't afford anything even like Dutch treat; I couldn't even afford to get caught having to pick up the tip. Like I said, I was traveling cheap. So, I stammered around about how I was traveling on a shoestring, and that I really couldn't afford to eat in a place like that, and ... when she interrupted me and said, "Douglas, we are asking you to be our guest."

I said, "Oh. In that case, I would like that. Very much. Yes. I accept."

Well, I went home, and, as Kris Kristoffersen said, put on my cleanest dirty shirt (I only had two) and, at the appointed hour, went off to meet my new friends in their hotel room where they were gathering with a few other friends.

They had a nice Christmas tree, and when I got there, they were opening presents. It was nice to watch, and even though it was my first Christmas away from home, I wasn't homesick. I was quite happy to watch and be a part of their Christmas.

After a while, the young girl who was passing out gifts handed one to me. "This is for you," she said.

I was stunned.

You see, being a fairly typical 18-year-old male, my manners, at least in the area of thoughtfulness, were not what you would call fully developed. (They're still not, my wife would argue.)

They gave me a present – a bar of Swiss chocolate, as I recall – just because I was there, and it was Christmas.

As I unwrapped this gift, which must have been intended for someone else but was rerouted to me – a virtual stranger – so I would feel included, I realized that it never even occurred to me to go buy this family that was literally taking me in for Christmas – a present.

I remember doing some fast rationalizing to myself. It went along the lines of why didn't I think to get them something, but what could I get them? They were rich, I was poor, et cetera, et cetera, and as usual, I missed the point.

When it got right down to it, it just never dawned on me that they would buy me anything, and worse, that I should buy them something.

And that made their kindness all the more evident to me.

Well, after gifts, we all went off to a magnificent turkey dinner, served at an elegant hotel, with silverware running off in all directions from the plates, and fine French wine was served by several hovering waiters. Given that I hadn't thought to bring anything else, I tried to give them the best of what I did bring, which was me.

I tried to be charming. It wasn't much, I admit, but it was all I had.

By the end of dinner, fast friendships were forming; and we all agreed to meet again the next day and ski together.

Happy and full of good food and wine, I crunched on back through the snow toward the train station and my cheap hotel full of poverty-stricken teachers. As I walked back, I remember thinking what a wonderful Christmas Eve it had been, and how I looked forward to telling my parents about it.

When I got to the hotel, there was a Christmas Eve celebration going full swing in the basement. The basement of this hotel looked like the basement of an old church where spaghetti feeds and pancake breakfasts took place, if you know what I mean.

Well, I was feeling pretty Christmassy, so, even though I wasn't invited, I went down anyway. Trying hard to be inconspicuous, I took a place along the wall and watched, as these teachers and their families had their Christmas Eve away from home.

One of them was playing Santa in the middle of the room. He had on red long johns and a red sleeping cap, and was pulling presents out of a bag.

"Kevin!" he'd say, and one of the children would come running over to receive his present. "Eric!" and an adult would go out and get a present. It was obvious that they all knew each other and shared this event year after year.

Santa was almost at the end of his bag of presents.

"Doug!" he called.

But this time, nobody came out. He looked around. "Doug?" he said again. I began to feel uneasy. It was my name, but it couldn't be me, because I didn't know these people. My only connection with them was that we were all Americans and we happened to be in the same hotel.

"Is Doug here?" asked Santa.

The man standing next to me leaned over to me and said, "Your name is Doug, isn't it?" I said, "Yes, but, it can't be me because ..."

"Here's Doug," he said to Santa.

By this time, the search for Doug had made the room pretty quiet. Santa came over and handed me a small present. As he did, he looked at me, and with a little smile said, "Merry Christmas, Doug."

Well.

I don't think I actually said thank you, because if I had spoken, I would have cried. And at 18, I was still trying to live up to the code that said men didn't cry and all that stuff, so I just sort of nodded, blinking back tears and trying to ignore the fact that my nose was suddenly running real bad and I didn't know whether to wipe it on my sleeve or just ignore it and hope my face wasn't covered with snot.

Then Santa went back to giving away his last presents, and attention focused away from me.

I opened the present. It was a little Swiss cow bell with the name Zermatt engraved in it.

It was a long time before I could talk without fear of tears and outright blubbering. And when I could talk, I didn't know who to thank.

Not only that, but I probably couldn't have expressed very well what I was feeling at the time, even if I did know who to thank.

Because, you see, I'm sure that these very generous people, my new friends from New York and these teachers – these strangers to me – thought they were giving me, an 18-year-old kid, alone and a long way from home on Christmas Eve, a couple of little knick knacks to make Christmas more pleasant.

But that really wasn't what they gave me.

What they gave me was a little gift of love, neither asked for, nor required, but given just the same.

They gave me what I had somehow missed up 'til then: What the meaning of Christmas giving is all about.

That was their gift to me.

And my story about that Christmas Eve is my Christmas gift to you.

Merry Christmas, everybody.

Mission Control Christmas 96

You know how NASA scrubs the space shuttle flights at the last minute because some computer chip in some backup of a backup of a backup system malfunctions? You know how, even though they know years in advance the exact moment they are supposed to light those rockets and blast billions of our dollars off into space, they regularly get to within minutes of that moment and then announce that because of some part failure, they are going to have to simply delay the whole event?

Well, I think we need that capability for Christmas.

I think we need a mission control that can delay Christmas.

There are two reasons for this: First, because Christmas has gotten very complex, and we need the systematic approach of a rocket launch to get everything done. And second, because I'm not ready.

"Uh, Houston, we have a problem."

"What kind of problem?"

"I think I'm experiencing a malfunction of my biological calendar."

Your biological calendar is your internal timing system that tells you in the spring when the snow should be gone, and in the summer when it's time for your vacation. When it's off a bit at the end of the summer, you say stuff like, "Labor Day? Can it be Labor Day already?" When it's off later in the fall, Halloween sort of sneaks up on you.

But somewhere around Thanksgiving, our biological calendars are supposed to reset themselves so Christmas and New Years always happen on time, as it were.

But this year, that isn't happening to me. We had Thanksgiving, but it's like my body and mind didn't register the event. So Christmas can't be happening.

"Ladies and gentlemen, this is Christmas Mission Control. Out in the Hurd unit, we have a failure in the internal timing system that controls Christmas activities. Can we run the checklist? Christmas Cards?"

"Sent."

"Christmas lights?"

"Up."

"Christmas tree?"

"Up."

"Christmas list?"

"Negative on the Christmas list, Houston."

"Oh, boy. Four days to go and the Christmas list isn't done. Will someone check the Scrooge circuit and make sure it's not on manual override?"

"Scrooge circuit is off, Houston. We're just getting no response."

Personally, I blame the ice storm we had in November for this failure of my biological calendar.

Somehow, when the lights went off, so did my internal timing mechanism. Even though I was not personally inconvenienced a great deal, the rest of the world sort of stopped for about two weeks there, and apparently, so did my biological calendar.

I suspect I'm not alone. According to the paper, gifts to the Salvation Army are way off, too. Probably because like me, people are walking into stores and looking at the bell ringers and thinking, "What are you doing here?"

Now, I know what you wives are thinking. You're thinking, wait a minute. Men are never ready for Christmas! It's a family tradition that two days before Christmas, we ask you if you are done shopping; and you say, "Shopping? Uhhhh, almost." Which is husband-speak for, "You mean, I have to get the kids something for Christmas?"

All too true. But the difference is usually about this time, we know Christmas is coming and we're simply behind schedule. That's okay. Being behind schedule is what being a man is all about.

But this is different. This is like my Christmas gland has been anesthetized with a megadose of zylocane.

"This is Christmas Mission Control. Have you tried manually starting the timing unit?"

Have I ever. I've even played the Carpenter's Christmas album back-to-back with the Judd's Christmas Album. And I've even sung the Salad Shooter commercial to myself when I've been home alone.

Nothing. My body just refuses to acknowledge that Christmas is really going to happen – launch, as it were – in 5 days. Whether I'm ready or not.

Oh, well.

I suppose if there were a mission control for Christmas and we could delay the entire event, I might not be any more ready in two weeks than I am now. Plus that would put my Christmas ski vacation two weeks behind, not to mention New Years. And certainly that won't do.

So there won't be any scrubbing of the Christmas launch this year, no matter how bad my biological calendar is malfunctioning. And this weekend, I'll join the rest of you for some final Christmas shopping.

You'll know who I am: I'll be the guy muttering, "Houston, we have a problem."

Valentine's Day

Next Thursday is Valentine's Day.

I love Valentine's Day. I can count on my wife and my daughter giving me wonderful, thoughtful cards. And sometimes a little present.

What I don't love is Valentine's Day Eve, when I suddenly sit bolt upright in bed at 10:00 p.m. and realize that I haven't bought them anything, yet.

Yikes!

So I get out of bed, throw on some jeans, and make my way to one of the big grocery stores that's open all night, and stand there with about fifty other middle-aged men, and look at the cards that are left, and try to find one that is just right. It's not uncommon for one of these men to ask a complete stranger, "Do you think my wife would like this card?"

"Well, I don't know you or your wife, but in as much as it starts, 'To my favorite nephew ... ' I'd keep looking. But it's a nice card."

"Yeah, maybe you're right. I was thinking I'd cross that part out."

"Trust me. She'd notice."

What you do about Valentine's Day has a lot to do with where you are in life, and who you are there with.

For instance, if you aren't married, and you aren't going with anybody or anything, this is a non-holiday. This doesn't mean you can't buy yourself a box of bon-bons if you want to.

If you are dating casually, this is an opportunity to let Hallmark say some romantic stuff that you may find difficult to put into words and to score big points on the romantic/sensitivity scale upon which you are being measured, whether you know it or not.

For daters, Valentine's Day is a good time to ratchet up the seriousness of the relationship. A nice Valentine card along with some candy can, depending upon the size and mushiness of both, say "You are special," small s; "You are Special," capital S; or

"You are SPECIAL," all caps. Or you can ignore Valentine's Day, which communicates very clearly, "You aren't <u>that</u> special."

If you are engaged, a present is mandatory.

Chocolate is the traditional gift of choice, but don't let yourself be bound by that. We're talking romance here, so let your heart be your guide.

Or the Avon Catalog. Or, better still, Victoria's Secret. Perhaps a romantic dinner. (If you are planning a romantic dinner, though, don't make her cook it. That's considered bad form. Maybe later, when you're married, but not when you're engaged. Just a little hint to you men who don't think these things all the way through.)

If you've been married less than three years, a present along with a card is required for you, too. By this time, you should have some idea of what she would consider romantic in the way of a gift. Flowers are a nice touch for the traditional; but for all I know, your wife considers a case of Bud exceedingly romantic. Hey, if that's it, that's what you get her.

Women, on the other hand, can give their husbands anything they want because their husbands won't expect anything, so anything will be more than what they thought they were going to get. For most men, a case of Bud is just about as romantic as anything.

Now, after about three years of marriage, you're kind of on your own out there for Valentine's Day. This is because everybody is different. I know some couples who ignore it altogether and some who are terribly romantic.

Most ebb and flow from one extreme to another, depending upon the state of their marriage on or about February 14th.

For instance, it may be real difficult to get all worked up and romantic when your hubby has just come home with an $8,000 stereo you don't need and can't afford.

"Honey, it's a great buy. And it's only $420 a month until we die or go deaf, whichever comes first."

At that point, it's understandable that you don't want to be his Valentine. You want to be his widow.

On the other hand, if fortune has smiled on you both, and he just gave you a nice little red BMW, you might be feeling real good about him. It all just depends.

If you don't know if you should get something or not, the rule of thumb is: get something.

They say that the world would be a better place if we kept the spirit of Christmas alive all year long. And for couples, the same can be said of Valentine's Day. What a great opportunity to say again, "I love you, and I want you to be my sweetheart."

And I suspect that if we men could just remember to do that much, it would be okay.

Just remember that whatever you do, whatever you give, be sure it comes from the heart, and not because it is something you have to do.

Remind me of that, will you, when you see me at the card counter on the evening of the 13th?

Christmas Giving

Just about any day now, you can pick up your local newspaper, and see which groups and individuals have contributed to the newspaper's Christmas fund for the needy. Like you, I tend to scan through it, looking for a familiar name. I recognize some of the company names in there, but not many of the individuals.

Most of the people I know don't give to the needy. We're still in the acquisition stage of life; maybe next year there will be something left over.

When I see that list and read the names of the people who have contributed a small amount of money to help someone less fortunate, I think about the one time I was involved in such a program, sponsored by the Seattle Times.

And that makes me think about one of the best teachers I ever had, an old maid school teacher named Miss Erickson.

Miss Erickson was my homeroom and English Literature teacher. In memory, she resembles no one so much as Eleanor Roosevelt, buck teeth, 1940s dresses and all. She seemed ancient when I first met her as a high school sophomore, but that probably had more to do with a fifteen-year-old's perspective of age than reality.

By the time I met Miss Erickson, she was almost completely hobbled up by rheumatoid arthritis, a disease that came on quite suddenly and put her in crutches and leg braces within a few years of its onset.

She moved to the blackboard only rarely and with great difficulty. Mostly she stayed behind her desk, but it didn't matter. She was a great teacher, and her immobility didn't change that. She had a way of getting the most recalcitrant of students to perform. I know – I was one of them. She was one of those teachers who didn't teach you subject matter so much as how to think.

But like I said, I had her for homeroom first, a fifteen-minute waste of time during which the daily bulletin was read, forms passed out and returned, attendance taken and about 11 more minutes wasted.

Not being the type to waste time, Miss Erickson used the homeroom time to teach us a little daily lesson in democracy and Robert's Rules of Order.

Each semester we elected a homeroom president, vice president and secretary. Each day the president called the homeroom to order, had the secretary read the daily bulletin, and asked if there was any new business to conduct.

There never was any, of course, so the president would turn the classroom over to Miss Erickson, who would get on with the business of the school, like passing out report cards, poor work slips, hall passes and stuff.

One day early in December, the vice-president had some new business.

He had this great idea. If we all chipped in, we could come up with some money, five bucks being the target, and we could contribute to the Seattle Times Christmas Fund.

I would like to report that I supported this worthy idea because I was among the most civic-minded and altruistic of young men that Ballard High School had ever produced, and I was driven by my need to help those less fortunate. Unfortunately, this was not the case.

I was after ink. I suddenly saw the Christmas fund as a way to almost get my name into the paper. The fact that we would have to be listed communally as "Miss Erickson's Homeroom," instead of "Doug Hurd and others" didn't seem to matter. I would know who they were talking about, and that was enough.

I immediately saw the potential great personal glory. Count me in, here's my fifty cents.

In accordance with how Robert said the Rules were to be Ordered, a motion was made and carried, money collected, the five dollar target eventually reached, and sent off.

When it finally ran, I read it and re-read it. It said, "Frances Erickson's Homeroom #206, Ballard High School, five dollars." Everyone was quite proud, including me. My name was in the paper, almost. What a heady moment.

It was then that Miss Erickson put a twist on the event that turned it from being just another high school moment, soon to be lumped with all the others and forgotten, to one of those things that stays with you for life.

She hobbled up to the front of the class on her crutches and, looking like Eleanor Roosevelt up from the coal mines, looked us over with a kind of parental pride I had not seen before.

Then she said, "What you have done makes me very proud of all of you, that you would do this on your own. And what makes it very special and personal to me is that some of the money collected in this fund goes to the arthritis foundation to help find a cure for this terrible disease that has twisted my body so. And the other is the day you decided to do this, to take up this collection, was my birthday. And no one has ever given me such a wonderful birthday present."

An awkward silence followed, where no one knew what to say. The vice-president, whose idea it was, looked at me as if to say, "That settles it. As soon as I'm old enough, I'm running for the United States Senate."

I had rather mixed feelings.

In that short moment, my ego-driven elation had been replaced by a kind of warm glowy feeling, the feeling, perhaps, I should have had all along.

Quite accidentally, I had been swept up in a small act of kindness, and had done some small good for a lot of people I didn't know, and a larger good for a couple of people I did: Miss Erickson and myself. The fact that it all kind of came about through an accident of timing and because the VP and I were motivated by the crassest of personal reasons didn't really matter.

It was another lesson learned, and one that would stay with me.

So today, when I read the names of contributors, I also look for a class listing, thinking maybe a high school homeroom got together and donated a few bucks to some people less fortunate – maybe for all the wrong reasons – and in the process, gave their teacher and themselves a very special Christmas present.

Taking Those Holiday Family Pictures

I hate to bring up a bad subject, but have you taken your Christmas family picture yet?

I know what you're thinking: "Oh, man. Why did you have to mention that? Now my wife will want to take a big chunk out of next Saturday and make us all dress up and go sit in a photographer's place to get family pictures that nobody is going to like."

Sorry.

We just got our pictures taken.

For years, we have tried to get by with either random snap-shots of us taken sometime during the year preceding Christmas or pictures we took of ourselves especially for Christmas cards. On those years where I promised that we would take a picture up skiing, we got rained, snowed or fogged out and didn't send anything.

This year my wife decided we were going to take a family picture and informed my daughter and me in such a way that we both knew arguing about it was useless.

This was good, however.

It had been years since we had a family portrait taken.

I had forgotten what a drag it could be.

And I had forgotten all about family picture paradoxes.

The first paradox is, with the possible exception of surgery, there are few things in life that we want to have turn out better but resist more than the family portrait.

Every year, I scan the professional photos we receive in our Christmas cards and I think, "We should do that," but when it comes to actually doing it, I hesitate.

I think it's because of the pressure.

This is, we must presume, the picture that will outlive all the other snapshots that chronicle our lives. This is the photograph that will live on the refrigerator doors of friends and relatives for years, and the eight-by-ten will hang in the in-law's front hallway until their house burns down.

It is the one that you want most of all to capture the real you in each of you, because it is the one that will say: this is what you looked like then.

So the pressure is on. So you go to a professional photographer.

The second paradox is the "Look natural" paradox.

By definition, you want the picture to capture the real you. So what do you do?

You dress up in a way that probably isn't natural for a Saturday unless you're going to a wedding or funeral, you go to a place of business you don't naturally frequent, you sit in front of sets and lights and on stools and benches and who knows what else in positions that are anything but natural ("Sit up straight and twist your shoulders around this way. Good. How does that feel?" "It feels like I'll be seeing my chiropractor on Monday, why?") and then we are asked to look at the camera and smile and act like we are happy about the whole thing.

Naturally.

There is also the "good child/bad child" paradox. This states that angelic children will turn into bad children on the entire day of the shoot, putting the whole venture at risk; while bad children become angelic, which can be a good thing, if not altogether photographically truthful.

A variation of this paradox is that a bad child suddenly becomes a good child under the lights or vise versa. In either case, you look awful because of the stress of the whole thing.

And there is the hair paradox. You can have perfect hair every day for years, but on picture day, it will be a bad hair day. The more you count on your hair to tell the world who you are, the worse it will be and the more it will resist fixing.

When I get my picture taken, my hair tends to want to stick up like Alfalfa's in the Our Gang Comedies. It doesn't help my confidence any when the photographer looks at me and says, "Do you want your hair like that, like you're plugged into a light socket?"

Finally you get the proofs back and must choose the one you want to represent you for all time. In our family, this is done more by rejecting than accepting. Everyone has veto power over their own image.

"Nope. Nope. Nope. Nope. Nope. Nope. Okay. Nope. Nope. Nope. I like this one; it doesn't look like us at all."

Which brings you to the final paradox, which is that the picture you finally choose probably flatters everyone just enough that it more closely resembles a reality you want than the reality you are.

And it looks almost as good as that snapshot your mom took a month ago.

Post-Holiday Shoulda's

It comes every year, just like clockwork.

Christmas is gone, New Year's Day bowl games are over with, and I get a severe case of the Post-Holiday Shoulda's.

The Journal of the American Psychiatric Association recognizes Post-Holiday Shoulda's as a mostly a male disease. Women tend to get its more virulent cousin, Post-Holiday Depression. If you are in the military, you get Post-Holiday Stress Syndrome.

The Post-Holiday Shoulda's is the Christmas equivalent for men to what post-partum blues are for women who have just had babies.

It is a kind of mild depression about how you did during the holidays and a general let down now that they are over.

I knew I had a case of the Post-Holiday Shoulda's when I went into the local auto parts store and saw a 64-piece standard and metric socket set and thought, "That's what I shoulda got my father-in-law for Christmas." And then in the next moment thought, "Father-in-law? That's what I shoulda got _me_ for Christmas."

(This in spite of the fact that my father-in-law, being a retired farmer, has every socket in every size ever made, up to and including the sizes you would need to unbolt the Space Needle. Not to mention the fact that being retired, he has no use for the ones he's got anymore, much less a new set.)

I confirmed my Post-Holiday Shoulda's diagnosis when I saw a riding mower advertised on television and thought, "I shoulda got one of those for my wife for Christmas." The reason a riding mower looked like something I shoulda got for my wife is because it looks like it would take a blade or a snow blower attachment. And right now, anything that looks like it could clear Biblical amounts of snow looks like something I maybe shoulda got.

The problem with having a case of the shoulda's is they aren't confined to just what you bought or didn't buy, got or didn't get for Christmas.

Very quickly they spread to other parts of your life. And that can be terribly depressing.

Like your body. Who doesn't sit through sixteen bowl games on television and think, "I shoulda exercised more last year"? Or look at his teenager's flaming pink hair and think, "Maybe I shoulda spent more time with my kids – Susie, Bill Junior, and Whatshisname."

If your shoulda family list is long enough, it is probably a pretty good bet your wife is thinking that she shoulda found a new husband last year.

I look at the stock pages and get such a severe case of the financial shoulda's, I need antidepressants. "I shoulda bought IBM when it bottomed at 40. I shoulda bought Boeing. I shoulda shot my stockbroker when I could have pleaded temporary insanity."

This year, the Post-Holiday Shoulda's are geographical and weather-related. If you live in St. Maries, Idaho, where it is flooding for instance, it is likely your Post-Holiday shoulda's have to do with not buying flood insurance. Or moving.

If you live elsewhere in North Idaho, they have to do with shoveling snow off your roof. "I shoulda got that snow off the gym roof last week."

If you are nursing low back pain like I have been for a week, you may also be thinking that maybe you shoulda paid some teenager with a younger back to clear your driveway of the snow the snowplow guy left there.

Of course, there is not much you can do about last year now, besides being glad it's over.

Which is why the Post-Holiday Shoulda's tend to beget New Year's Resolutions.

And it doesn't take too long before you are looking forward instead of looking back, and with all your New Year's resolutions, you leave behind all your last year's shoulda's and move into the new year with all your good intentions.

And your Post-Holiday Shoulda's fade away.

All except for one short relapse which we have in a month or so.

That's when we realize that we haven't managed to keep any of our New Year's resolutions, and we think: I shoulda seen that coming.

Mother's Day

I have some startling news for you men out there: Sunday is Mother's Day.

I know what you're thinking: AAAAGGGHHHHHHH!

Why do we men have such a hard time remembering things like Mother's Day? And Valentine's Day? And our anniversaries? Even our wive's birthdays? What a bunch of clods we are.

Let me ask you men a question: Do you know your parents' wedding anniversary? Do you know your own? Those of you who have divorced parents and have had multiple marriages, I realize you're at a disadvantage here, but you get my point, right?

You don't know, do you?

What's more, I'll bet your wife does. Not only does she probably know her own parents' birthdays and anniversaries, but she probably knows your parents' birthdays and anniversaries, too.

I can practically hear men saying "Yeah, yeah, yeah" while they're fumbling for their Daytimers to make themselves a note that reads, "Buy Mother's Day card. Get wife something."

If you are newly married and without children, this is the year you want to have your wife take responsibility for making up for your gross insensitivity to birthdays, holidays and anniversaries by buying all the necessary Mother's Day Cards.

You may be surprised that she will not only buy one for her mother (and your mother, if you're lucky), but also for assorted grandmothers and favorite aunts, her sisters with children, your sisters with children, and all sorts of people to whom you would never think of sending a card.

So now is the time to make sure your mother is included on that list, because in America, here's the rule: If she buys your mother a Mother's Day card once, your abdication of responsibility is complete and her assumption of card-buying duties instantly becomes a hallowed family tradition, and you never have to buy your mother a card again as long as she (your wife – or your mother, for that matter) lives.

Of course, you still have to sign the card. There's no getting out of that.

If your wife ever asks after this year, "Have you bought a card for your mother for Mother's Day?" you can reply, "No fair! No fair! That's your job. I keep track of the Seahawks and UW football passing statistics and when the cars need a tune up; you keep track of minor holidays and other card-buying occasions. That's the rule."

I'd make sure there weren't any sharp objects in her hands when I said it, of course.

If the woman in your life _is_ a mother and this is your first Mother's Day with her as a mother (still following me?), you must determine if she wants you to get her something for Mother's Day, because, after all, she is not your mother, unless you are very strange, or if she is content to wait for her children to grow up enough to get her something.

If you have boy children, she probably knows this could take forever.

So take my advice. Get her something.

It's your job to take all of her children to the local card shop and pick out a suitably gushy card.

The rule here is you can't get too sentimental.

The reason for this has to do with being a mother, which, whatever else you may have been told, is not the same as being a father. Being a mother has to do with being pregnant and uncomfortable, labor pains, giving birth, and just a whole host of things I don't want to get into here, but which come down to this: It's different than anything a man can experience.

And this is true, even if all her children are adopted.

And if you don't get her at least a card to acknowledge that difference and praise that difference on the one day set aside for that difference, then you're nothing but an insensitive, unfeeling, self-centered, pathetic excuse for a father and a husband.

I don't know about you, but I can be comfortable with that.

That was all most of us ever aspired to in the first place.

Now, I don't want to add complexity to your misery, but there's something else you first-time husbands should know. If your wife has been buying all the cards for your mother for several years now but this year she's a mother herself, she's not going to buy her own card.

I realize that may come as a shock to some of you, and you're thinking, "Why not? She's there at the card rack, isn't she?"

Try to understand, it just doesn't work that way. She's just not going to come up to you and hand you her Mother's Day card and say, "Here, sign this. It's to me, from you."

This is one of the fundamental differences between men and women. You would be at the card rack before Father's Day and decide you didn't need a card. But then, you've got the sensitivity of a bolt.

She, on the other hand, will look at the cards and wistfully wonder which one you will pick out for her that will express whatever it is you feel about her on Mother's Day, and "None of the Above" is not a choice.

That's why I said earlier that the notes that husbands all over town were scribbling down said, "Buy Mother's Day Card. Get wife something."

It's times like this that I wish I had more of whatever it is that my wife has that keeps her on top of birthdays, anniversaries and things like Mother's Day.

She cares, and because she remembers those things, it shows. I care, but because I forget, it doesn't show. She's really good at that sort of thing.

She's good at being a mother, too.

The evidence is nine years old now and getting better every day.

So sometime between now and Sunday morning , I'll take my daughter to the local card rack, and we'll look for something that says, "You're a very special mother, and we love you," and then my daughter will insist that we buy her a present of some sort, and I'll say, "Hey, that's a great idea," and wish that I'd thought of it first. But then, she's a girl, and she's already better at this Mother's Day thing than I am.

And maybe I'll even buy a Mother's Day card for my mother.

Or maybe I'll just sign the one my wife has already bought.

Thanksgiving

Next week is Thanksgiving.

Now you women are saying, so?

While most of the men are probably saying, "Thanksgiving! Next week? Are you sure?"

I'm sure.

This is because last week I had the Universal Male Thanksgiving Reality Check Moment. That is the moment when it dawns on men that Thanksgiving is suddenly here. No longer is it some vague week off in the future that one must remember to schedule work schedules around – it is now.

Next week.

It is time to answer the question our wives have been asking for a month. Will you be able to get off a little early on Wednesday?

Sometimes the Universal Male Thanksgiving Reality Check Moment has the decency to occur in the privacy of your home, where it is usually precipitated by your wife, and you can feel stupid in the bosom of your family. "Thanksgiving is next week? Are you sure?"

Unfortunately for me, my moment came this year at work, so I got to feel stupid in the bosom of my co-workers – not an altogether unfamiliar experience, but one that I can do without, just the same.

While I was feeling stupid and we were contemplating the passage of time and wondering just where another year of our lives had gone, I took the opportunity to ask the Great Thanksgiving Day question of my co-workers: "Where are you going for Thanksgiving this year?"

Now, when women hear that question, they hear a validation question that goes like, "At this stage of your adult life, have you been entrusted with the baton of responsibility for creating for your extended family a lovingly prepared, sit-down turkey dinner in the tradition followed by your mother, grandmother and great-grandmothers for untold generations, with all the emotional trappings that go with it?"

In other words, have you validated your adulthood, marriage and ability to be a quality parent by proving you can cook a turkey?

In contrast, when a man hears the question, he's more apt to hear, "Where do you have to spend four days against your will?"

When you are in your early twenties and newly married, the answer to that question is fairly easy. You go home. It is assumed by all concerned parents that young people and couples in particular can go anywhere, and that no drive is too far, and there is no reason why you can't be home for the holiday, except that you may not want to, which is not acceptable.

But as you get older, the question gets more complex.

Because at some point, every couple wants to have their own Thanksgiving, which puts them in conflict with the existing family tradition, whatever that may be.

In fact, how a family chooses a site for Thanksgiving is not unlike how a city gets selected for, say, the Olympics. And in some families, the negotiations can start early.

"Okay, we'll go Aunt Selma's this year, and Gramma's next year, but we get the '98 Thanksgiving, right?"

"Well, that depends. We have a bid in here from your brother, and he says that by 1998, he'll have his family room remodeled with one of those big TV's with stadium sound. What can we expect from you?"

"Okay, okay. We'll see his surround sound TV, and raise with a TV for the kids, two VCRs, Gameboys for all the kids and a Windows 95-equipped home computer with Internet connections for the family techno-dweebs. Now, do we get the '98 Thanksgiving or not?"

For a lot of reasons, parents may be reluctant to give up holding Thanksgiving at their house.

But then an interesting thing happens: you have children, and the entire balance of power shifts.

All through your twenties, your parents use guilt to keep you coming home for Thanksgiving. After you have children, the tables turn, and you get to use guilt.

"We thought we'd have Thanksgiving here, Mom. We'd love to have you, unless of course, you don't want to see your grandchildren ... "

That only works for a while, of course, until your brothers and sisters start using that same ploy; and then it falls apart. And it never works on your brothers or sisters, who are having enough trouble trying to balance their own Thanksgiving dinners with all of their in-laws.

What's curious is just about the time you have come to the conclusion that what is important is not who has the Thanksgiving dinner, but simply that one exists so everyone can get together, and that attending a Thanksgiving is much less stress than hosting one, your parents may have concluded the same thing, leaving you obligated to have it whether you want to or not.

Unless you've got a brother with a big screen TV – in which case, he gets it.

Christmas Presents You Should Not Buy

Right now, right this moment, men all over the world are saying to themselves, "Today, I've really <u>got</u> to do some Christmas shopping."

Of course, deep down inside, down where they really live, men know that with tomorrow being Saturday, and Christmas Eve day being Sunday – traditionally the really and truly last shopping day before Christmas – (assuming they haven't fallen to the totally degrading level of issuing Christmas present IOUs to family members), there is still lot's of time left to shop.

Still, there is pressure this close to Christmas to stop *thinking* about what to get and to take the action step of actually *making* some purchases.

And with this pressure comes the risk that you will inadvertently buy something you shouldn't.

Because – and nobody tells you this – there are certain gifts that are not Christmas approved.

Gifts you shouldn't buy come in three pretty distinct categories. Gifts that are misguided, gifts that are politically incorrect and gifts that are just plain stupid.

You know how the government makes certain products carry warning labels? Like tobacco? "Caution: The surgeon general has determined that smoking makes you a social reject."

Well, there is a whole class of Christmas gifts that tend to misguide you into buying them for the people you love. Or for yourself. Which might be the same thing.

Like Revlon make-up. I think that there ought to be a warning that says, "Caution: The surgeon general has determined that unless you look like Cindy Crawford to begin with, the use of this make-up will not make you look like her and will not make people of all ages lavish their affection on you, making you the love center of the entire universe, just because your make-up doesn't smear."

There are thousands of products that need warnings. Just about everything in Victoria's Secret catalog, for instance. Warning: Wearing a Wonderbra will not make you look like Tyra Banks."

Every razor and after-shave commercial seems to promise me that if I just use their product (which, presumably, my wife buys for me). I will become incredibly handsome, tall and sexy because of my smooth skin that covers my strong, granite-like, Italian looking chin. I think a warning label might be in order here, because, frankly, I don't think that any amount of shaving or after-shave lotion is going to make me look like that.

Still, gifts that come from a misguided view of reality don't hurt anything.

A step up from the misguided category are the gifts that are politically incorrect. You give one of these, and you're in a damage control situation.

And I'm not talking about globally politically incorrect like whale blubber lamp oil or endangered species fur coats, but politically incorrect within the confines of your own family.

Like getting your worthless son-in-law a subscription to the Employment Weekly.

"Merry Christmas, Jason."

"This is weird. There's nothing in here but job listings, Dad."

"Yes. I know. Perhaps you'd like to start reading it now."

Another gift that is politically incorrect, even though it may seem like a good idea, is Rogaine. Now, I know that the TV ads imply that we men are okay with talking about our balding heads, but the fact is, we're not. In fact, most of us are deep in denial.

You know how you ladies would feel about getting a tub of industrial strength Oil of Olay? Rogaine is our Oil of Olay, if you know what I mean.

The problem with politically incorrect gifts is that a gift that might be perfect at one time in your life might be all wrong later. And when you're up against a shopping deadline, like Christmas Eve day, you might fail to recognize that, which can have a bad effect on Christmas morning.

"Oh, look," your wife says, "a cute aerobics outfit the size I wore when we got married. And a gift certificate to Jenny Craig. Aren't you the subtle one. Are you trying to tell me something, you little dead man, you?"

The last category of gifts you have to avoid is the really stupid ones. This is where I spend most of my money. Usually, these are gifts you want to give to your spouse or family member because you want them yourself.

And the later we men Christmas shop, the greater the tendency to buy really stupid gifts. Looking for a gift for our wives, we walk through the department store saying, "Sweaters? Nah. Luggage? Nah. Candles? Tree ornaments? A diamond ring? Nah. She wouldn't like any of those. Wow! A workbench! Oooo, I think she'd really like this."

Of course, knowing that there are problem gifts out there should help you avoid them.

Right. That's why this year, I'm giving my daughter a Black and Decker detail sander and one of those snake lights.

They'll be a perfect complement to my wife's new workbench.

Christmas Cards

December 23rd:

My wife has laid down the law: I <u>have</u> to write my Christmas cards tonight. No going out to play, no television, I can't even have my customary Henry Weinhard's until I finish at least one Christmas card.

Cheez. It's not like time is running short or anything.

I don't know about you, but I have a kind of love/hate thing with Christmas cards. I love getting them, and I hate writing them.

In my book, writing Christmas cards is right down there with writing thank you cards. I still have a few of those left to write from my wedding, and I was married twenty years ago.

I make a solemn pledge every Christmas to get my thank you notes out by Easter.

In my family, we never wrote thank you notes to each other. Or anybody else, that I can recall. It was a real void in my social training. My parents sent Christmas cards out, of course, but I never had anything to do with it.

My wife, on the other hand, came from a family that sent so many cards, Hallmark stock spiked every time even a minor holiday rolled around.

They send cards to everybody for everything. Christmas. Easter. Wheat harvest. The Advent of the Walla Walla Irrigation Festival.

So when we got married, one of the things we had to sort out was who had card duty during which holiday. Being a real believer in the '60's philosophy of "If it makes you feel good, do it," I thought she should do it.

This, however, did not make her feel good. It seems that even though <u>she</u> was the one who came from the card sending environment, <u>we</u> were now sending out cards, and we could share in the effort.

We had been married less than a month when it was time to consolidate our individual Christmas card lists. That was easy. The only one on my Christmas card list was my mother, who, coincidentally enough, was also on my wife's list.

"What about your brother and sister," my wife asked. "Don't you send them cards?"

"I never have," I said. "Should I? We?" They've been on the list ever since.

That was the year we sent Christmas cards to almost everybody I worked with and everybody she worked with and all of our known living relatives.

For the next couple of years, the list grew exponentially, what with changing jobs and people moving in and out of our lives and all. After a while, we didn't know most of the people on our own Christmas list. And we kept getting cards from them, too.

"Who are Craig and Cindy?" I would ask my wife.

"I don't know," she would reply. "Give me a hint."

"Well, their little Kevin is in the second grade and his sister Melinda has new glasses and they all wish us a Merry Christmas. Are you sure you don't know these people?" We began to wonder how many of our cards were being received the same way.

It was time to purge the list.

For me it was no problem. I could cut the list back to my mother and be happy. (I could even cut my mother out, if I had to, because I figured I'd see her at Christmas.) But for someone raised on cards, like my wife was, it was not so easy.

For my wife, Christmas cards are the frail communication webs that keep us connected with each other. They are the wiring through which an annual burst of communication is sent. Cut the Christmas Card web and something is irretrievably lost.

"You're right," I said. "We should talk about that with John and Cindy and Kevin and Melinda with her new glasses, the next time we all get together," I said.

But there are people you want to stay in touch with. People you don't see, but don't want to lose. People out on the end of that web who are too important to just let go of. These are the people I send Christmas cards to, although, I must admit, sometimes they don't get them until mid-July.

For these people, though, the Christmas greeting is probably the least of the message.

So our Christmas list has evolved over the years. We no longer automatically send cards to the people I work with. They get my Christmas greeting in person.

And we don't send cards to our neighbors either, preferring instead to drop in unannounced and spread our Christmas wishes like demented, disruptive children. When you move out of the neighborhood is when you're most likely to get a card from us.

And I'm here to tell you, getting a card from me isn't nearly as much fun as having me show up on your doorstep with a smile, a Christmas wish, and an '87 Latah Creek Merlot under my arm.

The paradox of all this is just because I don't send a card doesn't mean I don't wish you a Merry Christmas and a Happy and Prosperous New Year.

I do.

And it doesn't mean I don't enjoy it when someone makes the effort to send a card and a family picture and make sure the thread we share is still connected. I do.

I even like hearing from John and Cindy, especially now that Kevin is a Navy fighter jock and Melissa wears contacts and is in nursing school.

I just wish I knew who they were.

So tonight, I'll be writing out my Christmas cards and sending my little communication burst that says, "I'm in Spokane. We're all well and happier than any one family has a right to be. I hope you're happy and well, and I hope you have a very Merry Christmas, and a very Happy New Year."

I just hope I get them mailed before Easter.

Making New Year's Resolutions

Here we are, three days into the new year, and I want it to be known that I have not yet abandoned all my new year's resolutions.

Of course, I should also tell you, in the interest of honesty, that I didn't make any this year.

Well, I made one.

The older I get, the less inclined I am to make new year's resolutions. That's because I know I won't keep them.

I mean, let's face it: New year's resolutions are like chores your parents used to give you when you were a child, except bigger. These are chores for your whole life.

Your parents made you weed the garden and carry out the garbage. A new year's resolution is like weeding your personality and carrying out the garbage of your life.

That's a lot tougher than just weeding a garden, plus it never ends.

I used to make new year's resolutions. Actually write them down. In fact, when I first heard about new year's resolutions at about the age of ten, I got very excited about them.

Clearly, this was the road to self-improvement and perfection. This was the way to get everything I wanted and become all that I wasn't. About the only thing I can equate it to today is buying one of those self-improvement seminars you see advertised on television late at night that promise you wealth, good looks, a slim body, happy marriage and – this is the part I like best – passion – for just three hundred dollars. Sounds like a deal to me.

Then it was as simple as making a list. Now you have to send some guy with big teeth 300 bucks. But it's the same thing: Carry out that garbage, yank out those weeds! Let's be better people out there.

My list of resolutions as a ten-year-old was pretty predictable:

1. Grow.

2. Do 100 freethrows and 200 layups a day. Do this until you make one.

3. Stay up late every night, especially New Year's Eve.

4. Beat up David.

Well, you can imagine what happened. The first thing was my older brother David would find the list and beat me up just to let me know that was never going to happen. (After that, I added a fifth resolution: "Hide this list from David.") The next thing was my parents sent me to bed at the regular time, and because we lived in Seattle where it rains all of January and February, and I wasn't dedicated enough to the concept of playing basketball to risk hypothermia for it, I never practiced my basketball. Growing turned out to be more of a prayer than anything I could do much about. A prayer that God, in His curious benign way, has chosen to ignore.

As the years went by, my resolutions changed in predictable ways. I turned twelve, my hormones took a squirt, and I added "Kiss a lot of girls" to my list of things to do more of next year.

If that didn't work, I had plan B, which was, if you can't kiss a lot of girls, kiss one girl a lot. That, too, was more of a prayer than anything else, I found out.

As I moved into my twenties, I stopped writing down my resolutions. I still made a list, but I kept it in my head.

1. Grow.

2. Kiss a lot of girls.

3. Get more exercise.

4. Shoot David.

5. Make a lot of money.

I didn't keep these either.

Actually, it took twenty-five years, but I did do a couple of them: I don't kiss a lot of girls, but I do kiss my daughter and wife a lot, so that counts. I now exercise pretty regularly, and I took my older brother down the steepest ski run I could find last time we skied together, which he said was about the same thing as trying to kill him.

It was certainly every bit as satisfying.

Now if I could just figure out how to make more money and grow.

The thing about making up a list of resolutions is to do it, you have to admit that you're not perfect. Now, most of us know we're not perfect, but that doesn't mean we like admitting it. Even to ourselves.

Because of this, New Year's resolutions are a very singular activity. I mean, if you want to ruminate on the size of your thighs and whether or not it's time to spend four hours a day on an exercise bike, that's fine. But don't bring it up for a family vote. There's no telling what else they might come up with.

"Daddy: Mommy and I came up with a list of new years' resolutions."

"Good."

"They're for you."

"Oh. Not so good."

"1. Stop going bald. 2. Make more money. 3. Take us to Hawaii more often. 4. Lose weight. 5. Learn how to dress. And 6, um, grow. We're tired of you being so short."

You aren't the only one.

But, you see what I mean. Much of that and you could find yourself resolving to get yourself a new family.

Still, the end of the year being what it is and all, it is a time for closing old chapters and opening new ones; and taking a look at the garden of your life and deciding whether or not a little weeding is in order.

So I used to take a few contemplative moments before the end of the year, and do just that. And I would come up with a short weeding list: Stop going bald, make more money, go to Hawaii more often, lose weight, learn how to dress, and please, God, is five-foot-ten too much to ask for?

But three days into the new year, I knew I wasn't going to do any them.

And I'm probably not going to grow any, either. Like that great American philosopher Popeye said, "I yam what I yam."

So finally, somewhere in my forties, I resolved to stop making new year's resolutions altogether.

Because that's the new year's resolution I can keep.

MAINTAINING A HOUSEHOLD BY HUNTING, GATHERING, AND BECOMING RAMBO OF THE NIGHT

Adopting Cats

There is a sign out in front of a veterinary office on my way to work that declares this to be "Adopt a Cat Month."

That's nice, but it's been my experience that the cats have always been the ones doing the adopting.

The first time I was adopted by a cat was about ten years ago. We had a hot tub; and one day in the middle of winter, a cat took up residence on it.

Not wanting a cat for a pet, but not especially concerned if it stayed, we watched it for a while. During this time, we didn't feed it because everybody, especially itinerant cats, knows that feeding a stray animal is the non-verbal and moral equivalent of accepting life-long responsibility.

So we watched. And we waited.

What the heck, it drifted in; maybe it would drift away.

Well, it didn't. It stayed.

We came to call it "Kitty." Had I known how big it would get, I would have called it "Cat."

Before too long, and against what we considered our better judgment, we started to feed it. "Just a little," my wife explained.

Kitty accepted our food with what is best described as equanimity. After a while, we let it into the house – but only the laundry room and only when it was really cold out.

This drove our dog crazy. He would look at me and look at the cat and look back at me and with his eyes say, "How could you do this? I thought we were happy here." And then, because he was just a young pup and really stupid, he would turn back to the cat and wag his tail as if to say, "Wanna play?" And Kitty would look at him with chin down and back up and say right back, "You come near me, dog, I'm going to rip your eyeballs out."

Since the dog was having a hard enough time understanding the meaning of sit and stay, I decided not to try to explain what the cat was doing there and let them work it out for themselves, which they did.

Eventually some neighbor kids had told us that the people on the next block thought they had been adopted by Kitty, too. It would split its day between our place and theirs, knocking down double rations, which accounted for it's enormous size. This cat must have been the envy of all its peers on East 17th.

We sold that house and the cat with it. It was the way everybody, including the cat, wanted it.

Last winter we were adopted by another cat.

(At the time, it made me wonder if perhaps cats identify people the way people do animals. Maybe in the same way we know certain breeds make good hunting dogs or watch dogs, maybe cats have the same knowledge about us; maybe they say to each other, this breed of human is an easy touch, or you can tell by the set of his eyes this human's a real cat-hater.)

We looked in the paper for lost cat want ads that might have been this cat and even called a few; but we never got a match.

As before, we resisted feeding it until our basic humanity outweighed our good sense.

This time, however, we had a child. So we laid down the rules for the cat in advance. This was my job, being the daddy and all.

"The cat doesn't come inside the house," I said.

""Right," said my daughter. "What else?"

"Ummmm," I said. "I don't know. I think that's all."

"Great," she said. "Can I bring her in now, please?"

"Sure, why not?"

That was six months and a hundred bucks ago.

You never want to take a cat to a veterinarian, I have found out.

This is because after the vet takes you through the cat diseases you have heard of, like rabies and worms, they hit you with things like, "Has she had her Dipto-feline mortoleukoid shot?"

I mean, how should I know? This is a stray. But a halfway competent vet will run right over you on that one.

"We'd better give her one. It's only $7.50 for the serum." Of course, it's another twelve bucks for his assistant to load the syringe, $3.50 for her to hand it to him, and $25 for him to inject the cat with it. And a fifty cent syringe disposal fee.

"There," he said with a smug smile, "no dipto-feline-mortoleucolia for you."

I know this sounds cruel, but after an experience like that, I tend to turn to the cat and say, "You understand, cat, that from now on, you get sick or hurt, you're on your own. You just bankrupted the Hurd Animal Medical Health Care Delivery System."

The cat and I both know that I'm probably bluffing. Cats probably have marked me for that, too. "He bluffs. Go ahead and get run over by a car. You'll get all the care you need." I'd like to think I'm keeping the cat guessing.

What's weird about this cat is, and I know this is going to sound egotistical, but I think this cat has a crush on me.

When I walk up, she stretches out her front legs, sticking her rear end way up in the air; and then plops down and sort of rolls over and looks at me like she just woke up on a Sunday morning after a terrific sleep, with a look that resembles no one so much as Kathleen Turner in Body Heat.

"You've been watching too much Walt Disney, cat," I tell her.

She also brings me things. Dead birds, mice, that sort of thing. Understand, these are not things I want; but the cat doesn't know that.

I've been told that a mouse on the porch is the cat equivalent of a dinner invitation to a fancy restaurant.

So I'm flattered, even as I'm a little nauseated.

She plunks down her kill, sticks her hind end up, walks and stretches; and if she could talk, I'm sure she'd sound like Mae West. "That's for you, big boy."

So, we've got a cat. Or rather, it's got us.

Now, I know that having a pet has its drawbacks. But when I'm sitting there with the cat in my lap, with its purr engine running on high, it's hard for me to remember what those drawbacks are.

Besides, nobody else ever brought me a dead mouse.

Gardening

Okay, I'm going to say a word, and you say the first word that pops into your head.

The word is ... gardening.

Gee, I sure hope I didn't ruin your day.

Some of you may think of lush vegetable gardens overflowing with red tomatoes and sweet corn, and, of course, zucchini. Thousands of zucchini. Zucchini growing up the side of the house. Enough zucchini to feed everybody in Ethiopia, if only they would eat it. (Actually, when I see a zucchini, I see a tasteless botanical joke played by a perverse God, but that's kind of a different subject.)

When I hear the word gardening, the word that comes to my mind is "weeding."

Are there any adults alive today who did not spend their entire childhood hating the phrase "weed the garden"? There were no words that could ruin a Saturday morning (or a whole weekend, if your parents were feeling particularly ambitious) faster than the announcement that "this morning we're going to weed the garden."

"Dad! Do we have to? How about if I carry out the garbage for the rest of my life? How about if I do all the laundry, whites and everything? How about if I rebuild the transmission on the car? I hate weeding!"

Now in my case, my parents' idea of a flower garden was a place where most of the square footage was occupied by big rocks, so there was less room for weeds to grow, and I still hated weeding.

The thing about weeding was it was futile.

(Curiously, it was also feudal. Weeding always made me feel like an indentured servant or some wretch out of a Dickens' plot. All this before I knew who Dickens was, you understand.)

(I could feel very put upon as a little boy.)

What got me most, though, was the futility. I don't know why it is that mowing the lawn once a week was not an exercise in futility, but weeding the garden twice a summer was.

Today, with urban agriculture being what it is, if you have a lawn fertilizing service, you have to mow twice a week or more. Right after they come, you have to mow about every fifteen minutes. What's really amazing is, we pay for this service. "Let me see if I've got this. I'll pay you forty bucks, you spray my lawn, and I'll get a hernia mowing three times as much." I don't get it.

I do it, but I still don't get it.

But back to weeding.

One of the side benefits of getting your own first apartment (besides being able to stay up late, play your rock and roll loud, and eat all the junk food you want is when you live in an apartment, there's no garden to weed.

Actually, there usually is, but you don't have to do it.

But then you get married and the urge to own a home asserts itself, and there you are, back in the weeding business again.

Except this time, your parents aren't there to tell you when it's time to weed the garden.

So the first thing you do is nothing. Hey! You're an adult! Nobody tells you what to do! So at the end of your first summer, your house is so overgrown with weeds it looks like Boo Radley's in "To Kill A Mockingbird" and you half expect Gregory Peck to come up and ask if he could mow your lawn.

Well, that clearly won't do.

So you have the "rock conversation" with your wife. "You see, honey, what we do is, we lay down thick black plastic that nothing will grow through, and then we cover it with rocks."

"Rocks?"

"Yeah. River rocks or the red ones they make."

"You want a yard made of rocks?"

"You don't have to weed it."

"But I want a garden and some flowers."

Deja Vu. A voice echoes out of your past: "I want you to weed the garden ... for the rest of your life."

At this point, every man has a choice. You can go get rock and a new wife. ("Hi. I need ten yards of river rock and a new wife. Something in a size five, please.") Or you can go to Eagle and start buying Triox in 55 gallon drums.

Personally, I went the chemical route.

So when Weeding Day comes, I roam my garden armed with spray bottles of vegetation killer. I have farm connections so I've graduated from Triox to farm-strength Roundup.

And it kills everything.

I act like a brain damaged Clint Eastwood in The Good, The Bad and The Ugly," shooting down odd looking plants like they're evil gunslingers. "Sorry, Perennial Rye Grass, but the price for growing in my garden is death."

Occasionally, a tulip or pine tree gets caught in the cross-fire, but I figure, what the heck, every war has its innocent casualties.

After that, I scorch the earth with an array of powdered soil sterilizers.

I use everything except Agent Orange. You're probably thinking the garden isn't the only thing I'm sterilizing. But I don't care. I'm caught in a cycle of weeding that is bigger than me – a throwback to a feudal, agrarian society – and I can't escape.

Finally when I've sterilized everything in sight, I cover it all with bark.

Now, what's especially curious about all of this is, when we're done with Weeding Day, our flower beds look pretty good. They don't look great, you understand, but they don't look like the jungles outside of Saigon, either.

And there's a satisfaction in that.

But then in a few weeks the weeds reappear, and secretly I wonder: Could I be happy living in an apartment again?

Depends on how much weeding I could avoid.

Gathering Wood

Can you smell it?

If you're a man, you can.

It's something in the air.

The hint of fall, of cold weather to come.

For the same reason geese suddenly pick up and head south, all real men get the call from somewhere deep in their genetic code: Go to the forest and gather wood for the winter.

And I'm here to tell you, it's a really stupid thing to do.

I know. I used to heat with wood.

I used to think my wood heating experience was economically driven. We lived in a house that, like everybody's first house, was old and built with inadequate insulation and poor heating equipment, and it cost a fortune to heat. This was in the seventies, remember, when oil prices were going through the ceiling. It didn't help that money was scarce, primarily because I was at that age where I was still wondering what I wanted to be when I grew up so it was hard to hold a job. (If you're a woman, and you're wondering what that age for men is, specifically, I'll tell you: It is above 12.)

So one day, I decided that I would just show them. I'd heat my house with wood.

When I told my wife that I was going to save us a ton of money by buying a fireplace insert and heating with wood, she asked if I had really thought this wood heat thing through.

I was ready for that wifely logic approach: I showed her a brochure of a fireplace insert. "See?" I said, triumphantly showing her a picture of the masterpiece of welding technology that was going to take up residence in our living room.

She was not as impressed with the huge metallic blob that would plug up our fireplace as I had hoped.

"We'll never have to pay for heat again as long as we live," I said.

"What are you going to haul this wood in?" she asked.

"Well, I've got to buy a pickup truck, but we needed one anyway," I replied.

"Why?"

"To carry the free wood," I explained patiently. Sometimes women just don't get it.

"I need to take some money out of savings," I said. "I need to buy a chain saw." I had been studying chain saws, too.

"You have a chain saw," she said.

Well, technically. I had this dinky thing with a 12-inch bar that was okay for cutting branches in your back yard that went, 'yingyingyingyingying' but if I was going to heat with wood, I needed a chain saw that I could barely lift that went 'romm-rommmromom'. $360. On sale. I showed her the brochure.

"Do you have to buy the plaid shirt and red suspenders, too?" she asked, looking at the guy in the picture.

As I was wondering if I should ignore that remark, she proposed a compromise. Why don't we stick with the little chain saw until we see how this wood heat thing went. She thought this made more sense, partly because we had no money in savings.

And so it began, the end-of-summer ritual of going into the forest to gather wood.

I loved it. We were out in the woods, out in the big timber, stocking up for the winter like our pioneer forefathers, with the smell of chain saw smoke in the air and bar oil under our fingernails. We were together as a family, meeting the challenge of insane heating costs while surrounded by the greatness of nature. It was an equal mix of Hansel and Gretle, Paul Bunyan and Milton Friedman. It was great.

My wife had a slightly different opinion.

I don't know what it is, but women just don't get the same thrill out of seeing a pickup truck loaded so far down with stacked wood that the suspension breaks, as men do. To men, it's a thing of beauty; to women, it looks like a good way to permanently screw up your back.

We would get back, and I would split the wood and stack it, and all winter, morning and night, I would carry it inside and stoke up the fire and smoke up the house and the neighborhood, while simultaneously ruining the carpet.

"It's smoking," my wife would say.

"No it's not," I would reply, coughing. "Besides, wood smoke is good for you." Like most wood-heating macho-type guys, I lived with the mistaken impression that wood smoke was somehow different than cigarette smoke – that it was "clean".

It's not, but I didn't know that then.

I don't heat with wood anymore. Three significant events altered my perception of how much fun I was having.

The first was I had a crisis of conscience one day watching huge billows of smoke go up out of my chimney and settle directly over our neighbor's house. The second was a basement flood that got us a new furnace (the old one being, probably, thirty-five years old). With the new furnace, the house got warm, fast, just by turning up the thermostat. The last, and most significant reason was while unloading wood from the truck one fall day, I dropped a chuck of it directly onto my big toe.

You may have heard me scream.

I lived in Spokane, and I have no doubt that people in Seattle turned to each other and said, "Did you just hear somebody swear?"

As the chunk of wood (in this case, Black Locust, which has the specific gravity of lead) was headed for my sneaker-covered big toe, two things happened. The first was my brain, which had already calculated the trajectory and time-to-impact, was telling other parts of my body that it could not get my foot out of the way fast enough and to prepare for about the same amount of pain as blowing your foot off with a shotgun. The second was another part of my brain was saying, "I don't think I want to do this wood heat thing anymore. This isn't fun."

It's a curious thing. I don't want to heat with wood anymore, and haven't for years. But as summer fades into fall, I still get the urge to go out into the forest during the last week in August and return with a manly load of cord wood.

The urge passes, though.

Probably has something to do with the curious throbbing I get in my big toe this time of year.

Cleaning the Garage

In January, I hear it: "Clean Me."

In March, I hear it. "Clean Me."

In May, I hear it. "You snivelling little waste of time: CLEAN ME!"

It is a ritual of Spring in America, and I have been putting it off.

This is a ritual that, to the best of my knowledge, only men take part in; but that might be changing. Like all rituals, I'm sure that this one has deep socio-cultural roots and extends back to our tribal past, perhaps back to the Savannahs of Africa. By performing this ritual, we men are affirming, in some unspoken way, our brotherhood and manhood. By taking part in this springtime ritual, we are making a gesture of asserting control over our own destinies, even though the forces that control the universe are clearly unimpressed and ignore our efforts at control, making this ritual, like all rituals, a bonding experience within humanity, even if futile and inconsequential in any practical sense.

By now, the men know what I'm talking about: The Cleaning of the Garage.

I don't know about you, but to be done right, the cleaning of the garage must take place on a sunny Sunday, and actually pre-empt lots of other things that were planned for that day and also need doing. It takes a minimum of four hours.

In my garage, there is a flat surface I euphemistically refer to as my work bench. (It's euphemistic because almost no work ever takes place there. It would be more appropriate to call it "a flat, junk-collecting surface," but that just doesn't have the ring to it that "workbench" has.)

This is where I begin my ritual.

I generally move the accumulated clutter on my workbench clockwise around the room.

This includes bottles of Pennsoil, Windex, car-washing mittens, toys my daughter has left behind, newspapers and pots that plants once lived in, now empty. There are screwdrivers and metal files, frisbees, and hammers and bubble-blowing stuff that all needs to find a home.

What I don't know what to do with gets moved to the right.

I have a table saw, something I convinced my wife I had to have one day when we were newly married and I was discovering how magnificent the tool department at Sears was.

It inspired visions of my making fine wood cabinets in which our fine china and handcrafted rifles would be beautifully displayed. Of course, we didn't have any fine China, having bought all our dishes on sale during various specials at Safeway, and the last rifle I ever had was the M14 I gave back to the Army at the end of basic training 25 years ago. But this didn't seem especially pertinent at the time. So I got a table saw.

On time.

At 18 percent.

When I got it home, an odd thing happened. Its character changed. It went from being my partner in crafting wood to a finger-eating monster that seemed better left un-messed with. So, like my workbench, it, too, became a junk collecting surface.

A table saw, I have discovered, is a great place to collect and stack old newspapers, which during the Cleaning of the Garage, need to be bundled for recycling. Time must be allowed for reading the headlines of these old papers during the bundling, because old newspapers represent fleeting moments of events passing and are linked, therefore, to your own memories and past.

While one must discard them, they must be discarded with care.

On shelving above my workbench are enough garden chemicals to make Muhammar Khadafi proud. I'm probably at risk of a pre-emptive surgical bombing strike from the Air Force. When I see them, I wish I had bought stock in Ortho and Lilly Miller. Many have labels that are gone or unreadable.

I don't know what to do with those, but I know I don't want to throw them away because they might come in handy someday. So I leave them alone.

During the winter, leaves and grass clippings come into a garage to rest and die. In spring, it's time for them to go.

You can do this with a broom, but the disposal instrument of choice is the shop vacuum. I bought a shop vac precisely for spring garage cleaning and I've used it now, let's see, I bought it three years ago ... three times.   It's also good for cleaning up dried winter road muck remnants - the residual that is left when the gunk of winter falls off your car and the water evaporates.

During the cleaning, you have to put away the sleds and other toys of winter. These are best hung up on the wall.

If you don't have wall space, they tend to move to the right.

I have lots of things I don't know what to do with; an ancient clock radio ("Solid State," it proudly declares) that only plays AM. I take it down from its freezer-top perch and toss it around a little bit, and then, not knowing what to do with it, I put it back where it was. "I might play this someday," I think.

In my garage, the area between the wall studs is filled with garden stakes, poles, and hand tools for gardening – some of which I know the names of, and some of which I don't.

I don't know what any of them do, but I don't throw any of them out either. I'm not getting any younger, and maybe one of these days I'll take up gardening and need these things. So they don't move.

When I've gotten all the way around the garage, I sort through those things that I didn't know what to do with.

Some go into the trash, some go to the garage sale pile, and some are arranged carefully and neatly on various available flat surfaces.

Like my workbench.

It is the moment of triumph. Dirt has been banished, clutter cleared away.

It is the moment for a wife to come out and speak the words that end the Cleaning of the Garage ritual. Words which every man knows so well.

"I thought you were going to clean the garage. What have you been doing out here?"

Rambo of the Night

Remember how Clark Kent used to boogie off to find a phone booth at the first sign of stress, only to emerge as Superman a few moments later?

From nerd to super-hero just by getting undressed. Sounds like the perfect male fantasy to me. Something I can sure relate to.

I think I know what inspired all those writers to turn those geeks into The Hulk, Spiderman, Superman, and all the others.

I think it was a dog barking on a hot summer night.

I think that because that's when I, in my imagination, turn into The Silencer, a kind cross between Bruce Lee and Rambo.

Let me set the scene for you. It is a hot summer night, and I'm in bed. It is late. When you're my age, that means it's after nine-thirty.

There is no wind, and the house is not cooling down. All the bedroom windows and doors are propped open to take advantage of any cross breeze that might develop, but none does. It's hot.

I turn to my wife. "Hi," I say as pleasant as can be.

"Go away," she says. "You're all sticky."

In the silence that follows, I hear our neighbor's TV: I can just make out the McDonalds commercial and the <u>Mac The Knife</u> tune. With nothing better to do, my mind wanders.

Hmmmm. Ray Charles with a Crescent Moon for a head. Sure would have liked to have been in the meeting where the agency sold that one to the client. "You see, we create this character who's in a tuxedo, who's head is a crescent moon, and he sings like Ray Charles, and he plays a grand piano on these rooftops ... "

Yeah, that must have been something to listen to. I wonder, idly, in my sweaty state, if Kurt Weil and Bertolt Brecht, a couple of good German communists who wrote the original tune in the thirties, would have not written it if they had known that, almost sixty years later, it would be used by those capitalists at McDonalds to hawk Big Mac Hamburgers.

It's late, it's hot, time is passing slowly, and I'm not sleeping.

Pretty soon I hear the familiar TV announcer: "From the newsleader ... " then the voice goes dead. Apparently the neighbors aren't going to stay up to see what's happening in the world. It's now eleven o'clock. Way past my bedtime.

My child comes in complaining that she can't sleep.

"Try," I tell her.

"Daddy," she says, with just a little snootyness in her voice, "how do you try to go to sleep? I thought it was just supposed to happen."

Good point, I think, but I'm not about to lose this nocturnal debate to an eight-year-old on a semantic TKO. I say, "Make your mind an abyss, a chasm of blackness and white noise."

She stands there for a moment, wondering what I've said, while I wonder if she has a dictionary in her room.

Finally she concedes the point. "I'm all sweaty," she says.

"I know, so am I, apparently," I say. Gee, we're all getting a little testy, aren't we? "Go to bed and lie real still, and you won't notice it as much," I tell her.

She leaves, taking her parting shot. "Some help you are."

That's when I hear it: A dog barking in the distance.

Not tonight, I think. Please doggy, go to sleep.

But it doesn't. It barks. And barks. And barks. There's a rhythm to it.

I wonder where its owners are.

After an indeterminate amount of time has passed, that changes to I wonder <u>who</u> its owners are.

I try to place the sound. It's coming from over there. No, it's the other way. Maybe it's the whatstheirname's dog. No, it's farther away than that. At night it's hard to tell. Sound carries.

The LED on my clock radio blinks out the time: 1:42. The dog has been barking for two hours now. My patience is long gone. My love of animals is long gone. All the Sunday school lessons about brotherly love, all decency and humanity, all sense of fair play, all the love and peace sit-ins of the sixties, even my concern over saving the whales has all been shredded on the altar of lack of sleep.

I want to kill that dog.

That's when it happens. That's when I fantasize changing from nice guy to the cold-blooded killer all noisy household pets fear in the darkness; when I envision becoming Rambo of the Night, The Bruce Lee of the Suburbia: The Silencer – Avenger of the Sleepless, Defender of the Nighttime Silence.

At one-thirty, my Rambo fantasy has me barefoot and clad in dark pajamas, looking like some yuppie VC, vaulting over fences, traversing a backyard course that brings me to the offending animal. I am so silent that it never hears or even senses my approach. That's the Bruce Lee part.

Scooping the animal up, I duct tape its mouth closed. Nothing too violent. Then I make my way silently home, knowing all the other sleepless people in the neighborhood know The Silencer has struck on their behalf.

At two-thirty, lack of sleep has made the fantasy uglier. Now when I meet the dog, I kill it, usually by ripping out its throat with my bare hands.

"Sorry pooch," I say. "But the price for keeping me awake all night is death."

By three-thirty, my hatred for the dog now includes its owners. This is war.

No more Bruce Lee. Now I'm Rambo. This time, when I get to their backyard, I lob a couple of grenades at their back door, taking out the dog, the hot tub and the family room. I imagine meeting the detective who comes around the next day. "Gee officer, I didn't see a thing, but it doesn't surprise me. Their dog was barking pretty late last night."

By four-thirty my fantasy doesn't even take me out of my bedroom. In true Rambo fashion, I load up the anti-tank rocket launcher I keep around for just this sort of thing and fire it at the offending dog right from my bedroom window, blowing away all the houses in that general direction.

But of course, I don't do any of those things I fantasize about while lying sleepless and tormented. I know that a) sneaking around through people's backyard is a good way to get arrested, and b) if I ever did meet the dog, it would probably be so glad to see someone that it would wag its tail and lick me half to death, and who can hurt a dog like that?

So I just live with it. Sleeplessly.

We all do.

Sometimes I ask my wife if that barking dog kept her awake.

And the answer is, "No, what dog?"

Oh well. So much for The Silencer, Avenger of the Sleepless.

So I say, "Never mind. By the way, have you seen our anti-tank gun anywhere?"

Refrigerators

I have come to the conclusion that the primary purpose of a refrigerator, apart from being a place to store Tupperware and to keep your beer cold, is to provide a large, flat, magnetic space, upon which you can spread the important things of your life.

It is one of the curiosities of our culture that you can learn just about everything that's important to someone simply by studying their refrigerator door.

In most homes, the refrigerator door is the family scrapbook, appointment calendar and message center all in one. It's a metallic snapshot in time of what's important to the people who use the kitchen.

It wasn't always this way.

For years, the refrigerator door's main job was to give you something to hang onto while you wondered what it was you were looking for when you opened it.

This is kind of an aside, but for me, at least, opening the fridge door has the effect of canceling out my extreme short-term memory. Do other husbands do this? I stand there, transfixed by all the choices (or none of the choices) arrayed before me in various stages of decomposition, and I go completely blank.

"What are you looking for?" asks my wife.

"I don't know," I answer, wondering if the little light really does go off when you shut the door.

"Then shut the door," she says. "You're letting all the cold air out."

"But if I do that, how will I find what I'm looking for?" I reply, looking really hard now and hoping that the sight of something will trigger my memory into remembering what it was that I wanted in the first place, and wondering why it isn't there or I can't see it. At this point, I usually start rummaging through things like a pig rooting around for truffles until my wife asks again, "Well, what are you hungry for?" and we're back where we began.

At that point, I usually just pull out a beer. It may not be what I wanted, but it'll almost always do.

I think what changed the nature of the refrigerator door was the invention of the lowly refrigerator door magnet.

Now, in the grand cosmic scheme of things, the refrigerator door magnet is way down the technological food chain, being somewhere below, say, velcro shoelaces and above giant push pins; but it's an important part of the social glue that holds our families together.

What you put on your fridge door depends completely on what is important to you.

You can tell how you rank among your friends' friends by noting whether or not the picture of your family you sent them in your Christmas card still adorns their refrigerator door in August.

Generally speaking, you can't tell much from positioning – all positions on the door being more or less equal. For instance, if you were to find your picture right next to a note about your friend's liposuction appointment, you shouldn't make too much of it.

Unless of course, it's a picture of your thighs.

When my daughter was a pre-schooler, we bought her one of those toy blackboard things with the magnetic letters and numbers. They went directly from the box to the fridge. Perhaps that is one of the reasons why she learned the alphabet in random order.

"What letter is this?" I would ask her.

"C," she would say.

"Close. It's a 'W'."

To this day, some of them still are on duty holding up notes and recipes.

The refrigerator door also doubles as a sort of pre-school art museum.

For a while, my daughter's works of art took up a lot of space – pictures of rainbows and mountains and horses and sub-atomic particles during nuclear fission and killer amoebas. Some of the amoeba's had the word "Dad" under them.

We kept those high, so as not to scare the cat.

Some people put up newspaper clippings of things they find inspirational: pictures of friends, their niece's wedding picture, obituaries, a Dear Abby column they want their family to take particular note of.

"Dear Abby: My husband stands at the refrigerator door for hours without getting anything. What do you suggest?"

"A feed bag with beer and potato chips in it. If that doesn't help, get him professional counseling. Let me know what happens. I really care."

I like rummaging through people's refrigerator doors, so to speak. It's a good way to get in sync with where they are and what's happening in their life that I should know about.

I always want to know the story behind the picture of everybody at the campfire in the rain at Crater Lake and why they all look mad at each other.

"Why does Craig look so grumpy?"

"Kelsy had the flu and he had diarrhea that weekend."

"Gee, what a shame we weren't with you guys."

We keep emergency numbers up there: 911, Heidi's Cleaning Service, Domino's Pizza.

We also keep various receipts and things we suspect we might need to know the whereabouts of if family birthday gifts need to go back. You can tell which gifts have been accepted into the family by when the receipts come down.

It's been my observation that grandparents tend to have the most cluttered refrigerator doors because of all the grandchildren's school pictures. These can stay up for decades.

If you blur your eyes and scan quickly, it almost looks like those kids are growing up right before your eyes. Which, the grandparents will tell you, is exactly what's happening.

I'm not sure what happens to the pictures and notes and things that get replaced by newer pictures and notes and things.

A lot of ours make an interim stop in the kitchen junk drawer before making their way to the scrapbook.

I'm sure that some of them find their way into the shoeboxes full of pictures that live in the backs of closets, prizes for future family archaeologists to discover.

And if everything that goes around comes around, someday someone will pull out those pictures and say, "Look: It's a picture of that camping trip we took at Crater Lake when I had the flu. I'm going to put this up on the fridge door. I wonder why Dad looked so grumpy?"

A Most Respectful Letter to the IRS

Dear Internal Revenue Service, Sir.

This year, I thought I would just add this little note along with my tax return and check.

You'll notice that the check brings the total I've sent you to one-third of every dime I made last year. Not that I'm complaining, Sir.

I know that it costs money to run the government, to do all those things that we ask the government to do, like protect us from the bad guys who used to be the communists but, now that Mao and Uncle Ho and the evil empire are gone, they don't seem so bad anymore.

So I have a suggestion. Protect me from the Crips who live mostly in L.A. because they scare me a whole lot more than the commies.

Which gets me to the point of my letter, along with my return and a check that represents a full, ever-loving third of every last dollar I earned last year.

First of all, don't waste any of the government's money by having one of your functionaries audit this return. I mean, I wouldn't cheat on my taxes, because right after getting gunned down by a bunch of Crips armed with AK-47s, I'm afraid of you guys most.

This is because my experiences with your people have not been uniformly positive, if you know what I mean.

For instance, last year one of your people sent me a form say-ing that I owed an additional $800 in taxes. The next day, the lady who sent it sent a handwritten note saying it was all a big mistake and to disregard that form and that she was sorry if that form caused me any "inconvenience."

Inconvenience? No. Incontinence? Yes. And in as much as that was inconvenient, well ...

I did, however, have a few sleepless nights wondering if she wrote that note right there at 4:30 when it was quitting time and didn't quite have time to get down the hall to tell the big old Cray computer you have that it was her mistake and not mine, like she said.

Because that Cray never sleeps. And when it sends out a form, it wants to see a check. And when you don't feed it a check, it gets ugly and sends out guys who are always real cranky and who will tell you that it isn't their job to sort out mistakes – they just have a job to do and that is to impound.

("Theirs was not to reason why,

Theirs was to impound, and fly.

Into the jaws of hell rode the tax impounders.")

Which brings me to my first question. Can I write off the Grecian Formula 16 I needed to return my hair to its natural color so my child would recognize me the day after I got that $800 notice?

I didn't think so.

Second, if you want to spend my money, which represents all the money I made for every day of work from January first right on through to April 30th, with no vacations or anything, do this: First of all, don't give any of it to Newt Gingrich. Pay him out of Jesse Helm's taxes. If he pays any.

And can we talk about this one-third thing? I know you don't make the rules and I know that the tax rate has come down and all that, and I sure don't want to seem like an ingrate, espe-cially to you, with the power and the glory to impound and all, but in Sunday school, which I admit was a long time ago, we learned to give up ten percent, which seemed like a reasonable amount, especially when you considered that God, who set the amount, is supposed to be omnipotent. Difficult to understand, at times, but all-knowing and all-seeing, just the same.

Well, your tax majesty, I've got to tell you: if God who knows everything thinks 10 percent is about right, you can imagine what 33 percent – one full day out of every three – arrived at through the collective wisdom of a government that has gotten us a trillion dollars in debt – feels like.

I'll tell you what it feels like. It feels like getting kicked in the solar plexus. When I saw how much I was going to have to pay, here's what I said: Ooophfff!

I get my taxes done by a very big firm right downtown, and from about April first on, if you stand outside the doors of all those big accounting firms, this is what you hear:

"Here is your tax return John."

"Oofff!"

"John? Are you all right? Someone call 911."

Even now, on this night before taxes are due, you can hear solar plexuses caving in all around us. It's like every taxpayer in the country getting the dry heaves at the same time. And for what? A trillion dollars of debt?

Sorry. I didn't mean to get emotional.

It's just that if that one-third of my life is going to be wasted, I'd just much rather waste it myself.

Well, I know you're busy. You can just put my return on that big pile marked, "No audit; not worth it."

And just think. In two more weeks, a third of this year will be gone, and the money I make will all belong to me.

Sincerely,

Doug Hurd

Doing the Wine Thing

OK. How many of you really know what you're looking for when you look over a wine list in a restaurant? Let's see a show of hands.

Right. That's what I thought. Two of you. And one of you owns a winery, so you don't really count.

Not only do I not know what I'm ordering, I don't know what I've got when it gets there. And since I have no idea what the wine I ordered was supposed to taste like, naturally I can't tell if the wine I got tastes like it's supposed to.

So I do what you do. I swill it around like Listerine, and then, unless it tastes like turpentine, pronounce it okay. It is all a complete crapshoot with a heavy dose of social theater thrown in.

It didn't used to be this way. I seem to recall that back in the late 1960s, wine was a fairly simple matter. It was Chablis, which I thought was white, pink Chablis which was pink, or it was rose, which was dark pink Chablis.

Everything else was French, which I couldn't afford.

There was also something called Burgundy which left stains on your skin if you spilled it and left your mouth feeling like it was full of cotton when you drank it, which I never did, because I couldn't drink that much cotton. As I recall, nobody paid any attention to brands in those days.

Back then, I knew what I liked, which was beer. But if I had to drink wine, it was pink Chablis.

The trouble with wine was it made me thirsty. So after a couple of glasses of pink Chablis, some witty conversation, and on those rare occasions when I could afford it, food, I'd have to guzzle down a beer or two to keep from dying of thirst.

Well, there went the witty conversation. With both wine and beer in me, just listening was a chore. Still is. I've got to be careful because with a couple of ounces of alcohol in me, I get stupid real quick.

Anyway, somewhere between then and now, a thousand wineries have sprung up, each putting out about three hundred different types of wines, all of which have names and labels that look the same.

And if that isn't enough, the weather each year changes the quality of the grapes that go into each of those thousand wineries' three hundred wines, and besides that, they ship around the basic wine juice to one another the same way refineries exchange gasoline. They actually ship it in great big tank trucks.

So who really knows what's in that bottle? I sure don't. I don't think the waiter does either, or else why would he stand there waiting for you to say it's okay? And what do you do with the cork? Sniff it? Feel it? Check it for fungal growth?

The one thing I do appreciate is being shown the label of the wine I ordered, because in the interval between ordering the wine and getting it, I can never remember what I ordered, so I'm always pleasantly surprised.

I have learned that some wines are better than others. You can tell because they have won a gold medal. You may have noticed that almost every wine that doesn't come in a box has won a gold medal somewhere. ("Gee, here's one that won a gold at the East Elbow Jerk Wine Competition.")

I'm just insecure enough to figure a gold medal winner is a safer bet, even though I suspect that such competitions may give out lots of gold medals. Like one to everyone who shows up.

But, like I said, there is a difference. Several years ago, my wife and I received a Christmas present of a Latah Creek Chenin Blanc. Latah Creek was a new winery then, and it took a while to get around to drinking it. When we did, we were amazed at how good it was. I made a point of memorizing the name and the year and all that. Of course, by the time I went looking for more, it was all gone.

This was very disappointing. Not because I couldn't drink anymore of it, but because it blew my one chance to talk all that wine talk – you know, about its character, bouquet, and legs (whatever they are).

There are a few wines I stay away from. I avoid anything that tastes like it's got 7-Up mixed in it, all Burgundies and any wine with "MD" in the name.

So, I don't know about you, but I admit I'm faking it when I order wine. No, not faking it. "Winging it" is a better term.

So here's what I do. I usually start with the prices. I hate to say it, but I think we've all discovered that some dinner company isn't worth a $12.95 bottle of wine regardless of how the wine tastes.

Of course, you could argue that the worse the company, the better the wine ought to be.

Anyway, then I look for names that look familiar. Like "Chardonnay." I always ask what people are ordering for dinner; but this is pure social theater, since I don't know what food goes with what wine. I may be wine ignorant, but I try not to be impolite about it.

Finally, I settle on something about midway down the page and the price range, check to see if it is okay with everybody, and after everybody nods all around, I ask the waiter to bring me a Henry Weinhards.

So, if we have dinner sometime, you bring the wine.

Dealing with Life Insurance Agents

A lot of the younger people I work with are confused about when they really become adults.

They are confused because here they are, out of college, holding down a real job (well, as real as a job in advertising can be, which, take my word for it, isn't very real); some of them are getting married, some are buying a house, and they still don't feel like adults.

Of course, they don't look like adults, either, but that's neither here nor there.

The problem is they haven't acquired the one thing that identifies you as a card-carrying member of the adult community.

And that is having your very own life insurance agent.

Now, I don't mean just having bought a measly term policy by accident, which happens to everyone at some time during their adult apprenticeship, nor do I mean having automobile insurance. Those agents are about as closely related to a true, acquirable life insurance agent as the orangutan is to your Aunt Flossie. They're just not the same species, regardless of what the biologists tell you.

I like having a life insurance agent for two reasons.

One is lunch. Every year, my life insurance agent takes me out to lunch. Now, this would normally not be any big deal, but my agent is a car nut – he actually reads, on a regular basis, Road and Track magazine; and he's bought 17 cars in the last 18 years, or 22 cars in the last 21 years or something.

The point is he always picks me up in a new car with that new car smell. It's not like actually owning the cars myself, you understand, but it's as close as I'll ever get to it, and I like it.

By the end of lunch, we have brought each other up to date on our kids and wives and why he bought another new car – "Well, the girls are growing up, and now we're into soccer and hauling kids in a big way ..." and blah blah blah.

It's the same reason as last year. I think he's just addicted to the smell of new cars; and when that goes away, he has a Pavlovian reaction. And one day he wakes up and says, "Whoops, gotta haul more soccer players – better go get a new car."

Then he tells me how much more insurance I need, the premium for which is suspiciously close to what his new car payment is.

The other reason I like having my very own life insurance agent is for when other life insurance agents call me. Lunch notwithstanding, this is the reason you should have one.

They introduce themselves and say, "Mr. Hurd, I'm from Mutual of Mossy Rock; and I'd like to sit down with you some time and take a few minutes to review your financial goals and show you how we at Mutual of Mossy Rock can help you attain those goals, while at the same time giving your family a measure of protection against the financial hardship that would come with the loss of your income. Would next Tuesday morning be good for you, or is Wednesday afternoon better?"

Ah. The dreaded, "yes-yes" question.

Well, I'm not a complete fool, I know how to sink one of those.

Depending upon how much time I've got at that moment and how much coffee I've had and how cranky I feel, I say, "You're not going to try to sell me any life insurance, are you?"

This is like pushing their reset button. "Well, what we at Mutual of Mossy Rock do is, we, um, we look at all of your financial goals and tailor a program that will help you attain these goals and give your family and loved ones a measure of protection in case of loss of income, and, um ... "

"But you won't ask me to buy life insurance, will you?" I interrupt, trying hard to make life insurance sound like something you step in.

Or, if I'm feeling really perverse, I'll wheeze a bit and say, "Nah. Wednesday is no good for me; that's the day I'm having a lung removed. How about Tuesday?"

There's usually a long silence here. Nobody wants to sell insurance to somebody who needs their lungs removed. After a silence, they say, "Gee, actually, I see here that I'm tied up Tuesday. How about I call you back later?" and they hang up.

Sometimes I just tell them up front whom I've got all my insurance with and say, "Now, if you think he doesn't know what he's doing or that he's professionally incompetent or something, just say so, and we'll get together. Wait a minute, let me start my tape recorder first."

I realize that this isn't very nice; but hey, nobody ever said cold calling was going to be fun.

If they call and they're from my agent's company, I listen to them and say, uh huh, uh huh, uh huh; and when they get to the end and ask for an appointment, I tell them to walk down the hall to my agent's office and tell him you've got me on the phone and you want to have lunch with me to review all my policies and if it's okay with him, it's okay with me.

Of course, as soon as they realize they are on the turf of one of their brethren, they send all engines into full reverse. Suddenly they're the captain of the Northwestern Mutual Valdez and they're carrying 20 million gallons of Alaskan crude life insurance, and the career equivalent of Bligh Reef is dead ahead.

And that's the moment when having my very own life insurance agent is worth every penny I pay in his new car payments.

Now, you might ask, "What about having all that insurance and attaining your financial goals and protecting your family from the tragic loss of your income (not you, you understand, just your income), and all that? Isn't that worth having a life insurance agent for?"

To which I answer, "No. I don't think so."

I just hope he never decides he needs a Ferrari.

Finding The Right Housesitters

Do you ever wonder if back in ancient times, back when Ulysses made his odyssey or when Marco Polo went to China or the average Roman senator just took the wife and kids down to Pompeii for a few days of fun on the beach and a little mountain climbing – do you ever wonder if before they left, they got housesitters?

"Got the chariot loaded? Great. Oh, by the way, I got Octavius Disgustus and his younger brother Vomitus to housesit while we're gone. Honey? What are you looking at me like that for?"

I sort of doubt it.

Of all the decisions you have to make about going on vacation – where to go, where to stay, whether or not to go with other family members or good friends or to go with just your family and hope for the best – perhaps the most crucial decision, the one upon which your total overall vacation anxiety level will hinge, is who did you get to housesit?

"Good news, Hon. You know SueAnn, at work? Her brother is going to housesit for us."

"Isn't SueAnn's brother the one who is doing three to five for burglary and vandalism?"

"No! He got out. Some sort of early release program!"

"And isn't he a cross-dresser?"

"Well, yeah. But I didn't want anybody who would be wearing my clothes."

The first time my wife and I had housesitters, it was at the suggestion of the housesitters themselves. We were in our first house and some of the single gals my wife worked with volunteered to housesit while we took a ski vacation.

Now, it could have been that they were just extremely nice, generous, warm, loving friends who wanted us to have a good time skiing and not worry about the house.

Or it could have been the fact that we had a hot tub, this being 23 years ago when hot tubs were still kind of a novelty.

There's nothing like having someone you don't know roll a keg up to your home exactly a week before you are scheduled to leave on vacation to put your mind to rest. "Is, uh, Diane or Jodi around?"

"No. They don't start housesitting until <u>next</u> weekend at this time."

"Oh. Well, in that case, would it be okay to store this keg in your garage for a week?"

If I'd have known how much fun they were going to have, I'd have passed on the skiing and stayed and partied with them.

When we came home, they passed along some interesting information I never thought we'd know about our house. Like how many wine bottles it takes to make a trail from the back door to the hot tub (77); and the fact that if you put 12 people in the hot tub all at once, you'll displace enough water to run the pump dry when you get out.

And how much a new pump costs.

The key to having a good housesitting experience, of course, is having all parties understand what is expected of them. And what isn't. Which boils down to are they expected to be you or not?

"We vacuum the carpet everyday."

"Yeah? So? I guess the carpet is going to get a vacation too, huh?"

I mean, are housesitters ersatz renters, where they get to make their own rules, or are they more like your children, where they are expected to obey your house rules?

"No food in the living room, glasses must have coasters under them, no loud music, no sleepovers and all puking must be done in the toilet."

Until she was in her seventies, my mother used to do some house and pet sitting; and frankly, I think she carried her responsibilities way too far.

At times I felt like the guy in the Unisom commercial who tells his mom it's okay to take a sleeping pill. "Mom, it's okay to leave the house for food. Or if it's on fire, Mom. Yeah. You can leave the house if it's burning. Well, if the dog doesn't get out, that's not your fault. Yeah. Love you, too. Now leave the house, Mom."

I suppose it all depends upon what you want from your housesitter. When we get a housesitter, my wife wants someone to make sure that if a natural disaster strikes, like a pipe bursts, someone is there to do something about it. I want a human presence to make the house look lived in and ward off burglars.

Or if the house is going to be burgled, to be there instead of me, if the truth be known.

And I'm willing to accept some partying in the hot tub to get that.

I just hope I don't come home to a note from my housesitter that starts, "Did you know that if you put twelve people in the hot tub, you'll displace enough water to run the pump dry? Oh, and by the way, the guy from Pool World called to say 'Thanks'."

Why Saying Goodbye Takes So Long

What is it about standing in a doorway, saying goodbye to dinner company, that makes people want to bring up new subjects?

What is there in packing a kid into a car seat that makes you want to ask a question like, "Whatever happened to that uncle of yours who went to Australia with his secretary?" Especially when you've had all night to ask, if you cared, which you don't.

It's odd: your kid's lips may be turning blue from the cold, and suddenly, in the middle of saying thanks for the wonderful evening, you feel compelled to explain the intricate keystrokes that took you from one area of Windows 95 to another.

As if anybody will remember. Or care.

You know what I mean – you've been sitting around enjoying a nice evening with your friends, some dinner, some wine, some good conversation – usually about parts falling off airplanes and what you would do if you saw forty feet of the roof rip off above you, and all of a sudden it's eleven o'clock and time to go.

You would think that as you gather up the coats and the kids, a few profuse thank yous would get you out of there. But it doesn't work that way, does it?

What should take four or five minutes starts dragging into fifteen and twenty. There is something in an entryway that doesn't like a goodbye and won't tolerate a silence.

If it's been a family visit, the goodbye process can take upwards of an hour, depending upon how long you've been there, which high holiday you've been celebrating, and how much food is left over.

Mothers hate to send off their children without food. Even their adult children.

You're sitting in the car, everybody has hugged, seat belts are snapping down all around you, and your mother says, "Oh, I meant to give you kids some turkey."

"No, Mom, please. We don't want any. We ... "

"Don't be silly; it'll just take a second. We had some extra rolls, too. And the gravy is already in the Tupperware."

So you sit there, trying not to appear ungrateful or impatient to leave, which of course, you are.

I think the inability of our parents to send us off without food is rooted in their experiences during the Great Depression. Or maybe it's a Skinnerean reaction. Maybe we accidentally trained them to load us up when we came home from college and never left without cleaning out the fridge as we headed back to the dorm.

In any case, there is something almost Pavlovian in the way opening the front door triggers an urge in parents to load up their children with leftovers.

Of course, all this presumes that you know when it is time to leave in the first place. With family, it's easy. You leave just before nap time, or just after the bowl game, whichever comes first.

With dinner company, it's a little trickier.

I'm still not sure exactly how you tell when it's time to go – and I've had a lot of practice leaving places. Sometimes it's a real fine line between eating and running and overstaying your welcome. It's sort of the social equivalent of the number Pi; you can get close but never right on.

One way you can tell it's time to go is when everybody is yawning with their mouth closed. (That's the moment you pray nobody asks you a question, so you don't have to look like you're in the first stages of lockjaw trying to answer.)

Another good sign that it's time to leave is when your child comes up to you in the living room, grabs you by the hand, and says, "Can we leave now?" and starts tugging you off to the car. And your hosts don't protest. Or protest too much.

Plus, a breech of manners like that is a good sign that your child is about to self-destruct. And it's always better not to inflict that on people who have just fed you and laughed politely at your jokes.

You can tell whether you've picked the right moment to leave by the response of the host or hostess. If they seem genuinely surprised and beg you to stay, you've probably timed it a little early. My rule is, unless the coffee is actually percolating, it's a good idea not to take their invitation to stay too seriously. There's always a chance they're just excessively polite, and generally it's better to leave too early than too late.

If they don't beg you to stay but don't protest your leaving, that's a good sign. If they enthusiastically agree with you that, yep, it is really late, and start heading for the coat closet ahead of you, you probably missed your moment.

But you really haven't blown it until they actually nod off during one of your stories. If that happens, go get a book on body language before you venture out to dinner again.

Curiously, being tireder and more eager to end the evening doesn't make the actual leaving happen any sooner or go any faster.

And once in the entryway, opening the door doesn't help much, either. About all that does is let the bugs in and the heat out.

Opening the door for company is the polite thing to do, but it seems a little pushy at the same time. I only do it when it becomes apparent that new subjects are coming up like The College Bowl, and if we don't move out to the car, we might all still be there at dawn.

Not wanting to say goodbye at the end of an evening is probably deeply buried in our genetic code from the days when our ancestors didn't want to leave a friend's cave and venture back to their own because there were things that could eat you out in the dark. And everyone knew it.

Or maybe it was started by Adam and Eve when they had to leave the Garden. Maybe in their reluctance to leave, they stalled, and we've been stalling since.

Or maybe it's easier than that. Maybe it's hard to say good-bye because we like each others' company so much.

Yeah. That's it.

Remember that the next time I overstay my welcome.

Thatch Me

There comes a time in the spring when every male home-owner walks outside and somewhere deep in his inner self hears the plaintiff call of the domesticated Kentucky Bluegri. (The Bluegri is the singular of the ususally plural "Kentucky Bluegrass," known to you botanical types as Domesticus Blue Grassius).

When my lawn calls to me this time of year, it always says the same thing.

"Thatch me."

And I think, do I have to?

And the answer is, yes, I do.

I do, because I am part of the specie Ameripithicus subur-bii, and, along with a receding hairline and a house we can't quite afford, one of the key identifiers of my particular subspecies is the need to answer the call to thatch.

I live in a whole neighborhood of Ameripithicus suburbii. You can tell because, like swallows returning to Capistrano or the Monarch butterflies all arriving at some small patch of Mexican real estate, we all fire up our lawn mowers and thatch our lawns on the same spring weekend.

We all hear the call of the bluegrass: "Thatch me."

This year, after hearing the call, I decided to have a heart-to-heart talk with my lawn.

I cut right to the chase. "You look like hell," I said to my lawn. "You look like you need plugging, you've got something that looks like the lawn equivalent of mange and ringworm, and except for a couple of shoots that didn't get the word, you look dead."

"Thatch me, " came the reply.

"You're just like my wife. You just want your back scratched."

I tried to reason with my lawn. "Remember last year when I thatched you? Was that fun for either of us?"

Last year, I had a new lawn mower, and I went at thatching with an uncharacteristic zeal that a new mower will give a guy. I thatched like there was no tomorrow.

For my lawn, that was almost the case.

For weeks, my lawn looked like some berserk Army barber got a hold of it. It looked like it had radiation sickness. I mean, it was bald. But not a nice clean bald, but a patchy bald, like when your cat comes back from the vet after being treated for a skin infection.

This is not the way a lawn is supposed to look.

I kept wanting to cover it with a hat.

I checked the covenants of the neighborhood where I live. You can't park boats or RV's permanently on the street, and you can't keep goats or pigs or other farm critters, but it didn't say you couldn't have a lawn that looked like it was on chemotherapy.

Still, I felt awful.

I wasn't sure this was better than the year before when I set the mower too low, and every time I stopped, I dug these perfect little circles into the turf.

That year, my lawn looked like a thousand Roundup-soaked frisbees had landed on my lawn in perfect formation around the edges.

Did you know those circles last until August? You thatch your lawn in April, and on Labor Day weekend, there's still a circle of death burned into your lawn where you paused to catch your breath as you turned the lawnmover/thatcher around to head the other way.

When you see that on Labor day, when you're seeing the end of actually mowing your lawn for a season, you think, "I'm not going to thatch next year."

Then you come to spring, and your lawn says, "Thatch me."

And against that call, we are helpless; and it begins again. First, we try to remember how to swap the mower blade and thatcher without loosing a finger. Then we try to remember what setting we had it on last year (was it three that made it too low? Or was it four?) and we putter off across a sea of brown grass.

It is then we remember what we hate about thatching which we forget from year to year.

The first is it always looks worse when we're done, which gives rise to the temptation to do it all again and set the mower a little bit lower. And second we forget that even a small lawn will cough up about twenty huge garbage bags full of dead grass.

Another problem is, after loading twenty garbage bags full of dead lawn, you can't walk upright. It just can't be done. Your back just won't straighten up.

And for what?

So you can have more grass to mow all summer? So you can get a hernia lifting all those bags of grass?

I don't know.

And then, as if to add insult to injury, when I'm done thatching and my lawn talks to me, it doesn't say "Thank you."

It says "Plug me!" And after that it says "Mow me!" and then it says "Trim me!"

"As soon as I can straighten up and walk like a human being, I'll get right on it," I reply.

Photo by Don Hamilton

Doug Hurd is a graduate of the University of Washington and Whitworth College. He is a writer and account executive for WhiteRunkle Associates, a Spokane advertising agency, and writes a column for The Edmonds Paper, in Edmonds, Washington. When not writing advertising for his clients or commentaries for KPBX he can usually be found playing or coaching volleyball. He splits his time between Spokane, Washington and Laclede, Idaho. He and his wife, Jeannie, have a daughter, Allyson.